LEGAL MOBILIZATION UNDER AUTHORITARIANISM

Legal mobilization is the process by which individuals invoke their legal rights and use litigation to defend or develop these rights against the government. In recent years, increasing attention has been paid to this phenomenon as it occurs under authoritarian regimes. It is often suggested that, in such situations, legal mobilization is caused by the strategic interests of the ruling elites. Using the case study of post-colonial Hong Kong, where legal mobilization has by no means unfolded as political authorities would wish, Waikeung Tam casts doubt on this contention. To do so, he examines in depth why and how legal mobilization arises under authoritarianism. Tam analyzes quantitative data of changes in the Hong Kong judiciary agendas over the last three decades, and uses detailed interviews with activists, politicians, cause lawyers, judges, and government officials to reveal the complex underlying socio-political forces at play.

WAIKEUNG TAM is Assistant Professor in the Department of Political Science at Lingnan University, Hong Kong.

CAMBRIDGE STUDIES IN LAW AND SOCIETY

Cambridge Studies in Law and Society aims to publish the best scholarly work on legal discourse and practice in its social and institutional contexts, combining theoretical insights and empirical research.

The fields that it covers are: studies of law in action; the sociology of law; the anthropology of law; cultural studies of law, including the role of legal discourses in social formations; law and economics; law and politics; and studies of governance. The books consider all forms of legal discourse across societies, rather than being limited to lawyers' discourses alone.

The series editors come from a range of disciplines: academic law; socio-legal studies; sociology; and anthropology. All have been actively involved in teaching and writing about law in context.

Books in the Series

Diseases of the Will
Mariana Valverde

The Politics of Truth and Reconciliation in South Africa: Legitimizing the Post-Apartheid State
Richard A. Wilson

Modernism and the Grounds of Law
Peter Fitzpatrick

Unemployment and Government: Genealogies of the Social
William Walters

Autonomy and Ethnicity: Negotiating Competing Claims in Multi-Ethnic States
Yash Ghai

Constituting Democracy: Law, Globalism and South Africa's Political Reconstruction
Heinz Klug

The Ritual of Rights in Japan: Law, Society, and Health Policy
Eric A. Feldman

The Invention of the Passport: Surveillance, Citizenship and the State
John Torpey

Governing Morals: A Social History of Moral Regulation
Alan Hunt

The Colonies of Law: Colonialism, Zionism and Law in Early Mandate Palestine
Ronen Shamir

Law and Nature
David Delaney

Social Citizenship and Workfare in the United States and Western Europe: The Paradox of Inclusion
Joel F. Handler

Law, Anthropology and the Constitution of the Social: Making Persons and Things
Edited by Alain Pottage and Martha Mundy

Judicial Review and Bureaucratic Impact: International and Interdisciplinary Perspectives
Edited by Marc Hertogh and Simon Halliday

Immigrants at the Margins: Law, Race, and Exclusion in Southern Europe
Kitty Calavita

Lawyers and Regulation: The Politics of the Administrative Process
Patrick Schmidt

Law and Globalization from Below: Toward a Cosmopolitan Legality
Edited by Boaventura de Sousa Santos and Cesar A. Rodriguez-Garavito

Public Accountability: Designs, Dilemmas and Experiences
Edited by Michael W. Dowdle

Law, Violence and Sovereignty among West Bank Palestinians
Tobias Kelly

Legal Reform and Administrative Detention Powers in China
Sarah Biddulph

The Practice of Human Rights: Tracking Law Between the Global and the Local
Edited by Mark Goodale and Sally Engle Merry

Judges Beyond Politics in Democracy and Dictatorship: Lessons from Chile
Lisa Hilbink

Paths to International Justice: Social and Legal Perspectives
Edited by Marie-Bénédicte Dembour and Tobias Kelly

Law and Society in Vietnam: The Transition from Socialism in Comparative Perspective
Mark Sidel

Constitutionalizing Economic Globalization: Investment Rules and Democracy's Promise
David Schneiderman

The New World Trade Organization Knowledge Agreements: 2nd Edition
Christopher Arup

Justice and Reconciliation in Post-Apartheid South Africa
Edited by François du Bois, Antje du Bois-Pedain

Militarization and Violence against Women in Conflict Zones in the Middle East: A Palestinian Case-Study
Nadera Shalhoub-Kevorkian

Child Pornography and Sexual Grooming: Legal and Societal Responses
Suzanne Ost

Darfur and the Crime of Genocide
John Hagan and Wenona Rymond-Richmond

Fictions of Justice: The International Criminal Court and the Challenge of Legal Pluralism in Sub-Saharan Africa
Kamari Maxine Clarke

Conducting Law and Society Research: Reflections on Methods and Practices
Simon Halliday and Patrick Schmidt

Planted Flags: Trees, Land, and Law in Israel/Palestine
Irus Braverman

Culture under Cross-Examination: International Justice and the Special Court for Sierra Leone
Tim Kelsall

Cultures of Legality: Judicialization and Political Activism in Latin America
Edited by Javier Couso, Alexandra Huneeus and Rachel Sieder

Courting Democracy in Bosnia and Herzegovina: The Hague Tribunal's Impact in a Postwar State
Lara J. Nettelfield

The Gacaca Courts and Post-Genocide Justice and Reconciliation in Rwanda: Justice without Lawyers
Phil Clark

Law, Society, and History: Themes in the Legal Sociology and Legal History of Lawrence M. Friedman
Robert W. Gordon and Morton J. Horwitz

After Abu Ghraib: Exploring Human Rights in America and the Middle East
Shadi Mokhtari

Adjudication in Religious Family Laws: Cultural Accommodation: Legal Pluralism, and Gender Equality in India
Gopika Solanki

Water On Tap: Rights and Regulation in the Transnational Governance of Urban Water Services
Bronwen Morgan

Elements of Moral Cognition: Rawls' Linguistic Analogy and the Cognitive Science of Moral and Legal Judgment
John Mikhail

A Sociology of Constitutions: Constitutions and State Legitimacy in Historical-Sociological Perspective
Chris Thornhill

Mitigation and Aggravation at Sentencing
Edited by Julian Roberts

Institutional Inequality and the Mobilization of the Family and Medical Leave Act: Rights on Leave
Catherine R. Albiston

Authoritarian Rule of Law: Legislation, Discourse, and Legitimacy in Singapore
Jothie Rajah

Law and Development and the Global Discourses of Legal Transfers
Edited by John Gillespie and Pip Nicholson

Ethnographic Forays into Law's Transformations
Edited by Julia Eckert, Zerrin Özlem Biner, Brian Donahoe and Christian Strümpell

Legal Mobilization under Authoritarianism: The Case of Post-Colonial Hong Kong
Waikeung Tam

LEGAL MOBILIZATION UNDER AUTHORITARIANISM

The Case of Post-Colonial Hong Kong

WAIKEUNG TAM

CAMBRIDGE
UNIVERSITY PRESS

CAMBRIDGE
UNIVERSITY PRESS

Shaftesbury Road, Cambridge CB2 8EA, United Kingdom

One Liberty Plaza, 20th Floor, New York, NY 10006, USA

477 Williamstown Road, Port Melbourne, VIC 3207, Australia

314–321, 3rd Floor, Plot 3, Splendor Forum, Jasola District Centre, New Delhi – 110025, India

103 Penang Road, #05–06/07, Visioncrest Commercial, Singapore 238467

Cambridge University Press is part of Cambridge University Press & Assessment, a department of the University of Cambridge.

We share the University's mission to contribute to society through the pursuit of education, learning and research at the highest international levels of excellence.

www.cambridge.org
Information on this title: www.cambridge.org/9781107031999

First published 2013

A catalogue record for this publication is available from the British Library

Library of Congress Cataloging-in-Publication data
Tam, Waikeung.
Legal mobilization under authoritarianism : the case of post-colonial Hong Kong / Waikeung Tam.
p. cm. – (Cambridge studies in law and society)
Originally presented as the author's thesis (Ph.D. University of Chicago, 2009)
Includes bibliographical references and index.
ISBN 978-1-107-03199-9 (Hardback)
1. Law reform – China – Hong Kong.
2. Law – Political aspects – China – Hong Kong. 3. Public interest law – China – Hong Kong. 4. Political questions and judicial power – China – Hong Kong.
5. Human rights – China – Hong Kong.
6. Hong Kong (China) – Politics and government 1997- I. Title.
KNQ9307.T36 2013
340′.3095125 dc23
2012025552

ISBN 978-1-107-03199-9 Hardback

To my Lord Jesus Christ
and
To my parents, Tam Yuk-bo and Yeung Sau-yung,
and
my wife, Wing Chee

CONTENTS

TABLES AND FIGURES

TABLES

FIGURE

ACKNOWLEDGMENTS

In writing this book and pursuing my graduate study, I received enormous intellectual guidance, support, and friendship from various individuals and institutions. I would like to take this opportunity to acknowledge them. This book began as a political science dissertation at the University of Chicago. I would like to express my sincere gratitude to the members of my dissertation committee: Professors Gerald N. Rosenberg (co-chair), Dali Yang (co-chair), and Dan Slater. Each contributed in unique ways to my dissertation and intellectual development. I thank Gerry for introducing me to the fascinating field of law and society and for his confidence in my project. I am indebted to Dali for suggestions on the importance of the China factor to legal mobilization in Hong Kong. I owe a very special thank you to Dan, who helped me to improve the theoretical dimensions of my work and provided excellent guidance and timely encouragement during a difficult time. For financial support I owe tremendous thanks to the Janco Travel Grant and the Center for East Asian Studies at the University of Chicago, which supported my fieldwork and dissertation writing through three generous grants.

While doing fieldwork in Hong Kong in 2007–2008, I was a student fellow in the Centre for Comparative and Public Law at the University of Hong Kong. I am enormously grateful to the then Centre Director, Professor Fu Hualing, who provided excellent guidance for my fieldwork – his contacts and advice were crucial to its success. In addition, Cheung Chor-yung, Ian Holliday, and Linda Li Che-lan kindly shared their contacts, which contributed much to my research. I would also like to extend my profound thanks to all my interviewees who generously shared their in-depth knowledge, insights, and time with me.

In revising my dissertation into the book manuscript, Gerald N. Rosenberg and Dan Slater gave me invaluable support and advice. I am particularly grateful to Professor Charles Epp, who read the entire manuscript and offered thoughtful, constructive, and detailed written comments. His comments greatly sharpened the arguments and the flow of my book. Tom Ginsburg, Ryon Lancaster, and Patrick Schmidt provided helpful comments on portions of my work as well.

I would also like to express my heartfelt gratitude to Professors Ian Holliday, Louie Kin-shuen, Jean Oi, and Andrew Walder, who offered strategic advice and critical support to me when I encountered the seemingly insurmountable difficulties in pursuing my goal of Ph.D. study in the United States. Their generosity and help is indispensable to my intellectual and professional development. I also thank Susan Stokes for her encouragement and guidance in my first years at the University of Chicago.

At Cambridge University Press, I am indebted to Finola O'Sullivan, Sarah Roberts, and Elizabeth Spicer, who provided me with invaluable guidance and suggestions throughout the process of book publication. I also wish to express my appreciation to Professor Sally Engle Merry, editor of Cambridge Studies in Law and Society, for her advice and confidence in my project. The incisive comments on my book manuscript from two anonymous reviewers for the press are much appreciated. An earlier version of Chapter 6 of this book appeared as "Political Transition and the Rise of Cause Lawyering: The Case of Hong Kong," *Law & Social Inquiry*, 35 (3): 663–687 (Summer 2010).

A group of brothers and sisters in Christ used prayer and various forms of support to sustain me over the years. They include: Lee Man-fai, Ng Man-fai, Dr. James Yu and Elizabeth Yu, Elise Kwok, Lee Wai, Becky Lai, Ben Chow, Lee Nuen-wing, Wallace Tsang, Isa and Brenda Cheung, Pastor Lawrence Yam, Law Kent-chung, and Rev. Choo Chee Wai.

My greatest thanks belong to my Lord Jesus Christ and my family. My Lord Jesus Christ, whose love, protection, and grace are indispensable to my long academic journey. My wife, Wing Chee, deserves very special thanks for all her love, kindness, and sacrifice. Last but not least, I sincerely thank my parents and siblings (especially Wai Kuen) for their unselfish support, love, and sacrifice. This book is dedicated to them and Wing Chee.

PART I

1

INTRODUCTION: EXPLAINING THE RISE OF LEGAL MOBILIZATION IN POST-COLONIAL HONG KONG

THE PUZZLE: RISE OF LEGAL MOBILIZATION IN POST-COLONIAL HONG KONG

> The range of areas covered by judicial review proceedings has broadened considerably in recent years . . . It is important for the public to understand the court's proper role. On judicial review, the courts do not assume the role of the maker of the challenged decision. The courts are concerned and only concerned with the legality of the decision in question . . . The courts could not possibly provide an answer to, let alone a panacea for, any of the various political, social and economic problems which confront society in modern times. Within the parameters of legality, the appropriate solution to any political, social or economic problem can only be properly explored through the political process . . . The responsibility for the proper functioning of the political process . . . rests with the administration and the legislature.[1]

> Some litigation that carried political objectives has caused great concern to the court. People are more ready to bring politically unresolved issues to the court . . . but the court is not legislature, judges are not legislators and cannot make policy decisions.[2]

[1] Speech delivered by the first Chief Justice of the Hong Kong Special Administrative Region (HKSAR), Andrew Li Kwok-nang, at the Ceremonial Opening of the Legal Year 2006, January 9, 2006. Andrew Li Kwok-nang became the first Chief Justice of the HKSAR in July 1997 and retired in September 2010. Justice Geoffrey Ma Tao-li succeeded Li and became the second Chief Justice of the HKSAR.

[2] Speech delivered by Patrick Chan, Permanent Judge of the Court of Final Appeal of the HKSAR. *Apple Daily*, September 4, 2005, p. A4 (in Chinese).

The foregoing excerpts of speeches by two judges of Hong Kong's highest court reflect an important political phenomenon in post-colonial Hong Kong, and more broadly around the globe, namely the rise of legal mobilization under authoritarianism. In this book, legal mobilization refers to the process by which individuals invoke their legal rights and use litigation to defend or develop these rights against the government (Zemans 1983, pp. 690–94; McCann 2008, pp. 527, 532). Using post-colonial Hong Kong as a case study, this book studies why and how legal mobilization arises in authoritarian regimes. Chan (2009) contends that democratic deficit is a primary factor behind the rise of legal mobilization in post-colonial Hong Kong. Legal mobilization, however, has not occurred in every political system with democratic deficit. For example, legal mobilization has failed to take place in Singapore, Myanmar, and Saudi Arabia. More importantly, the case of authoritarian Taiwan demonstrates that authoritarianism does not necessarily bring about legal mobilization. Indeed, authoritarianism wrought electoral mobilization in Taiwan during the 1970s–80s, as many liberal lawyers turned to oppositional politics (i.e., establishing an opposition political party) to pursue political liberalization and democratization (Winn and Yeh 1995, p. 565; Ginsburg 2007, p. 57).

Why did legal mobilization develop in Hong Kong during the process of the sovereignty transition from Britain to China and intensify after Beijing resumed its sovereignty over the city in July 1997?[3] My answer to this puzzle combines elements of "structure" and "agency." The key structural elements are the long-term institutionalization of the legal complex in Hong Kong, and the intervention of a critical juncture in the form of Beijing's military crackdown on the 1989 Tiananmen democratic movement and the process of the sovereignty transition. The key agentic elements are the growing strategic use of litigation in pursuit of human rights and more progressive public policies by Hong Kong's rights support structure (consisting of cause lawyers and rights advocacy organizations). In the next section, I discuss each of these factors in turn. Then I highlight the core contributions of my study to the literature on comparative courts and rights mobilization. Most importantly, the Hong Kong case suggests a path to judicial activism/rights-based legal mobilization under

[3] In July 1997, Britain ended its colonial rule over Hong Kong and transferred its sovereignty over the city to China.

authoritarianism that is quite different from the path identified by Moustafa (2007) and Ginsburg and Moustafa (2008) (i.e., facilitated by the interests of the authoritarian rulers). Legal mobilization in Hong Kong has by no means unfolded as political authorities would wish.

ARGUMENTS

Structural elements: the legal complex and a critical juncture

This book adopts historical institutionalism, particularly two of its building blocks, the concepts of critical antecedent and critical juncture, as the analytical framework to examine the structural factors of the rise of legal mobilization in post-colonial Hong Kong. I argue that Beijing's military crackdown on the 1989 Tiananmen democratic movement and the more gradual process of the sovereignty transition created a critical juncture during which a new legal opportunity structure was created and the legislature was weakened. On the one hand, the implementation of the Hong Kong Bill of Rights Ordinance and the Basic Law, together with the establishment of a new final appellate court in Hong Kong, created new legal opportunities for individuals to use the law to advance their interests. On the other hand, Beijing and its appointed Tung Chee-hwa administration[4] tightened the political opportunities available to pro-democracy politicians and civil society, by weakening the legislature and marginalizing their political influence in the legislature. These shifting political opportunities[5] from the legislature to the judicial branch, combined with the historical legacies of a legal complex (consisting of an independent and competent judiciary, an autonomous and

[4] Tung Chee-hwa, a pro-Beijing tycoon in Hong Kong, was selected as the first Chief Executive of the HKSAR.

[5] I adopt the concept of political opportunities from Tarrow's work on social movements (1998) and modify it to study the rise of legal mobilization in post-colonial Hong Kong. In this book, political opportunities include three important dimensions: (1) the opening of access to political participation; (2) the presence of influential allies within the ruling elites; and (3) changing power relationships among political institutions. Legal mobilization in post-colonial Hong Kong (and elsewhere) can be regarded as a social movement tactic. That is, the pursuit of the objectives of a social movement through institutionalized channels, as opposed to outsider tactics like demonstrations and strikes (Burstein 1991). However, my book focuses on legal mobilization, rather than other social movement tactics.

organized legal profession, and government-funded legal aid), constituted the structural factors behind the rise of legal mobilization in post-colonial Hong Kong. The following sections elaborate the logic through which the aforementioned processes and changes took place.

Historical institutionalism has two unifying themes.[6] First, this scholarship is institutionalist because it studies how the institutional arrangement of the polity and economy affects political behavior, strategies, and outcomes. By defining the incentives and constraints faced by political actors and structuring power relations among them, institutions heavily mediate political struggles. According to historical institutionalists, institutions are the formal or informal organizations and rules, procedures, routines, norms, and conventions that structure behavior. Examples include the rules of electoral competition and the relations among various branches of government. As will be discussed later in this book, changes in the relations between the legislature and the judiciary (i.e., a shift in the political opportunities from the legislature to the judiciary) during the process of the sovereignty transition in Hong Kong shaped the political strategies of pro-democracy politicians and civil society and prompted them to increasingly use the law to pursue their goals.

Second, historical institutionalism is historical because it argues that political development should be understood as a process that unfolds over time (Pierson 1996, p. 126). Viewing institutions largely as the legacy of concrete historical processes, historical institutionalists also contend that history and/or historical events play a major role in influencing political choices and outcomes. Relatively small or relatively early decisions affecting institutional design have large and long-term consequences. Explanation of political outcomes, therefore, requires a close analysis of events over long periods of time. Critical antecedents and critical junctures are two distinctive stages of the historical processes, which interact and cause the political outcomes. As subsequent chapters will demonstrate, legal mobilization in post-1997 Hong Kong is not a sudden political change. Indeed, its historical origins can be traced back to the mid nineteenth century when the British colonial authorities introduced the apparatus of English law like the rule of law and an independent judiciary to the newly

[6] The discussion on the analytical framework in this section is primarily based on Thelen and Steinmo (1992); Hall and Taylor (1996); Pierson (1996); Thelen (1999); Collier and Collier (1991); Slater and Simmons (2010).

acquired colony (see Chapter 3). Chapter 7 will examine how a group of transformative agents – cause lawyers[7] – have actively taken up the new legal opportunities and promoted legal mobilization since the 1990s. However, it should be noted that these cause lawyers had opportunistically and subversively wormed their way into the system over a long period, as many of them were admitted to practice in Hong Kong between the mid 1960s and the 1980s (see Chapter 6).

Critical antecedent – the legal complex

According to Slater and Simmons (2010, p. 889), critical antecedents are "factors or conditions preceding a critical juncture that combine with causal forces during a critical juncture to produce the outcome of interest." Unlike critical junctures which tend to unfold rapidly, critical antecedents are generally formed in slow-moving processes. More important, it takes considerable time and effort for a critical antecedent, like an independent and competent judiciary, to develop and mature. In their study of the role of the states in political and economic development, Skocpol (1985) and Rueschemeyer and Evans (1985) have argued convincingly that effective and capable state institutions like the civil service cannot be established overnight. The judiciary is no exception.

Institutions determine whether legal mobilization is feasible. Permissive and enabling institutions facilitate litigation and vice versa. Ginsburg and Hoetker (2006), for example, find that weaknesses of the Japanese legal system, like the relative scarcity of lawyers and judges per capita, have impeded the propensity of the Japanese to litigate. The incentive structures, like the payment system for legal representation (e.g., availability of legal aid) also influence whether aggrieved parties will take up the law to advance their claims (Kritzer 2001).

An autonomous and efficient legal complex[8] – composed of an independent and competent judiciary, an autonomous legal

[7] Cause lawyers are defined as lawyers who seek to use law-related means to achieve greater socio-political and economic justice both for individuals and for disadvantaged groups. Moral and/or political commitment is their defining attribute (Menkel-Meadow 1998, p. 37; Sarat and Scheingold 2005, p. 1).

[8] I borrow the concept of the legal complex from Halliday, Karpik, and Feeley (2007b, pp. 6–7), who define a legal complex as the system of relations among legally trained occupations which mobilize on a particular issue. At the core of the legal complex are lawyers and judges. By this definition, government-funded legal

profession[9] trained in common law systems, and government-funded legal aid – are the critical antecedents for legal mobilization in Hong Kong (see Figure 1.1). The legal complex was established by the British authorities during the centuries-long colonial rule. Some components of the legal complex, such as an independent judiciary staffed by professional judges and the common law system, were introduced to Hong Kong in the mid nineteenth century. Others, like the government-funded legal aid, were set up in the late 1960s.

Legal mobilization requires the (pre)existence of a legal complex for two important reasons. First, it takes considerable time and effort for an independent and efficient legal complex to develop and mature. Second, Beijing and its appointed post-colonial authorities would have had little if any incentive to create an autonomous legal complex. The following chapters will demonstrate how Beijing has paid great efforts to bringing different political institutions and social classes under its rein during and after the processes of the sovereignty transition.[10] In light of Beijing's determination to control Hong Kong's political development, it is hard to conceive why post-colonial authorities would have had the incentive to build up an autonomous judiciary and Bar Association that may challenge Beijing's interest. When Beijing regained its sovereignty over Hong Kong in July 1997, it inherited an autonomous and well-established legal complex from the British colonial government, and lacked the political will to eliminate this historical legacy. In sum, as only the British would have ever wanted to build up an independent legal complex, the latter was the critical antecedent for legal mobilization in post-colonial Hong Kong. Chapter 3 will elaborate how the legal complex in colonial Hong Kong has provided the necessary preconditions for legal mobilization in the post-colonial period. Here I discuss the importance of the legal complex in general.

aid is not part of the legal complex. Instead, government-funded legal aid is part of the rights support structure as Epp (1998) theorized that concept. In this book, I place government-funded legal aid in the legal complex because it is more "structural" than "agentic."

9 In this book, legal professions refer to practicing lawyers.

10 Xu Jiatun, a former director of the New China News Agency in Hong Kong (the *de facto* Chinese embassy in Hong Kong during the colonial period), discusses in his memoir how the Chinese government sought to bring various social classes in Hong Kong under its rein during the 1980s. See Xu (1993).

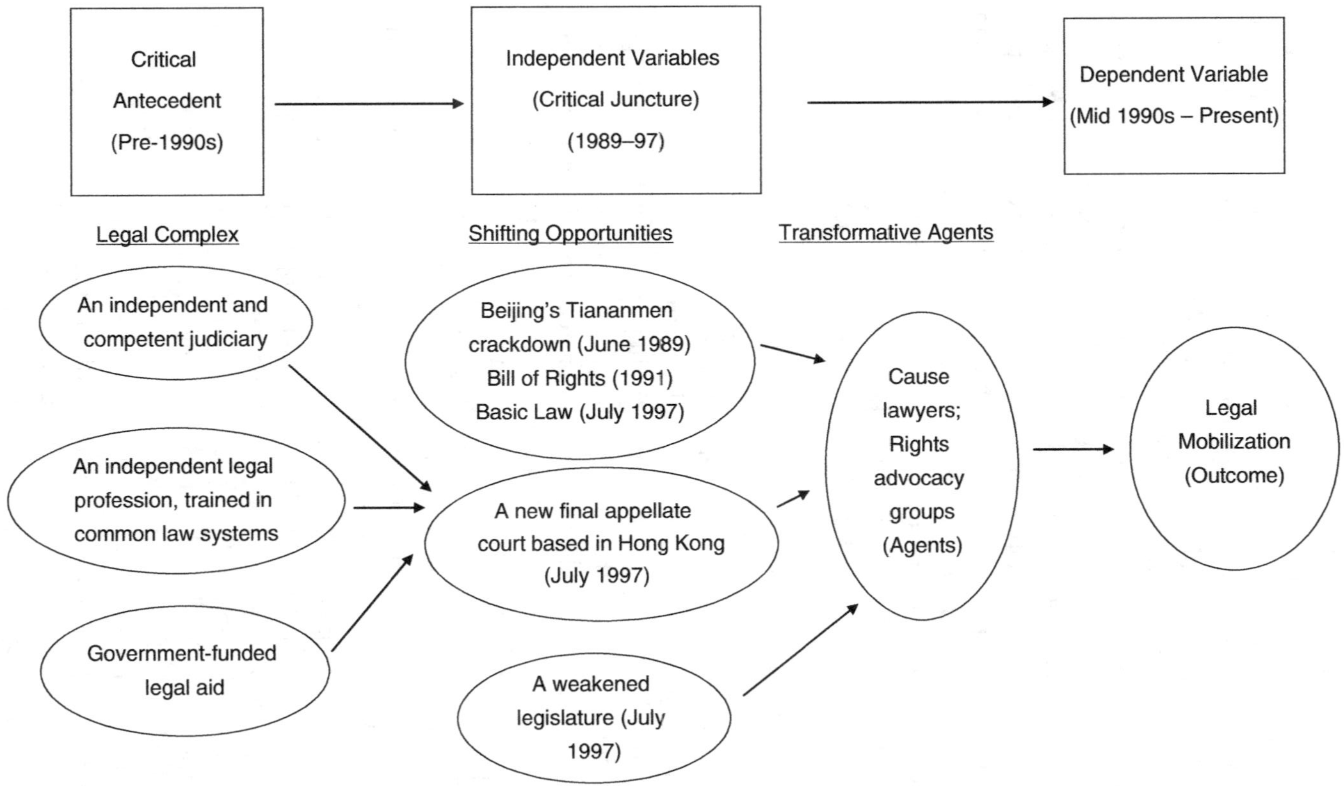

Figure 1.1: Flow of argument

An independent and competent judiciary is crucial because it is the arena where most activities of legal mobilization take place. Citizens' perception of the judiciary significantly affects their propensity to pursue their claims through the judicial branch. Citizens are more likely to litigate when they perceive that, compared to other political institutions, the courts are insulated from political pressure and exercise their duties impartially (Javeline and Baird 2007, p. 872). Courts are also the major platforms where cause lawyers exercise their expertise to promote the causes of the disadvantaged. Their political significance is heavily dependent on an independent and functioning judiciary. A corrupt and oppressive judiciary not only hinders cause lawyering work, but also puts cause lawyers in political danger. For example, post-war Indonesian judges, who are infamous for their corruption, incompetence, and abuse of power, have sought to silence activist lawyers (Lev 2007, p. 404). Absence of meaningful judicial independence has impeded cause lawyering in China (Michelson 2007; Fu and Cullen 2008, p. 126) and in Argentina and Brazil as well (Meili 1998, pp. 494–97).

An autonomous, well-trained, and organized legal profession is another component of the critical antecedent for successful legal mobilization. To be independent of state control, a bar must be capable of governing itself and hold disciplinary powers over its members. Human rights and public policy litigation frequently pits civil society against the government and/or powerful groups. An autonomous and unified bar can better protect cause lawyers who take up politically charged cases from state harassment and crackdown. If the state severely restricts the autonomy of the lawyer community, liberal lawyers are likely to replace litigation with other strategies in their pursuit of progressive socio-political changes. This happened in Taiwan during the 1970s–80s, when the authoritarian Kuomintang regime seriously undermined the autonomy of the legal profession. Encountering tremendous problems in exercising their influence in the legal arena, many liberal lawyers turned to oppositional politics to pursue political liberalization and democratization (Winn and Yeh 1995, p. 565; Ginsburg 2007, p. 57).

Further, a unified and autonomous legal profession can play a crucial role in defending judicial independence. It can mobilize public support, such as demonstrations to oppose any attempts by the state to dominate the judiciary. By contrast, a divided and weak legal profession erodes an important pillar of judicial independence (Halliday, Karpik and Feeley 2007b, p. 7; Lev 2007, pp. 410–11).

Legal aid, whether provided by the state or non-government organizations like trade unions, is critical to legal mobilization given that most prospective litigants in human rights cases are from the underprivileged class. The introduction of the federally financed Legal Services Program in the United States in 1965, for instance, greatly facilitated access of the poor to the courts (Lawrence 1990). Legal aid is especially important in legal systems which allow partial or full fee shifting (i.e., loser pays). Governments around the world have played a more active role in providing legal aid. Government-funded legal aid programs tend to ensure more stable sources of financing. These programs, however, may suffer from the autonomy problem. Epp (1998, p. 101), for example, notes that government legal aid programs in India have avoided cases that will have a deliberate impact on government policies. In China, state legal aid lawyers in criminal cases even claim that one of their responsibilities is to help their clients to acknowledge wrongdoing (Liebman 2007, pp. 345–46).

The legal complex alone does not enable citizens to actively take up the law to advance their interests, however. It must interact with the causal factors during the critical juncture to cause the rise of legal mobilization in Hong Kong since the mid 1990s. In the following section, I first study the events leading to the critical juncture from the late 1980s to 1997. Then I discuss how the critical juncture together with the legal complex caused legal mobilization.

Critical juncture

A critical juncture is characterized by significant changes. Collier and Collier (1991, p. 29) define a critical juncture as a period of significant changes which produce distinct legacies. Slater and Simmons (2010, p. 888) define it as "a period in history when the presence or absence of a specified causal force pushes multiple cases onto divergent long-term pathways, or pushes a single case onto a new political trajectory that diverges significantly from the old." Critical junctures can be analyzed from different perspectives. A critical juncture, for example, can be precipitated by either internal or external forces, or a combination of them. It can also range from a brief and rapidly unfolding moment to an extended period.

In Hong Kong, Beijing's military crackdown on the 1989 Tiananmen democratic movement and the process of the sovereignty transition created a critical juncture during 1989–97 – shifting political opportunities from the legislature to the judicial branch. The shift resulted from the establishment of a new legal opportunity structure and a weakened legislature (see Figure 1.1). The pro-democracy politicians and social activists whom I interviewed unanimously claimed that the shift of political opportunities from the legislature to the judiciary is *the* central motivation for them to mobilize the law (see Chapter 5).

New legal opportunity structure

The new legal opportunity structure consists of a bill of rights ordinance, a constitution, and a final appellate court with the power of judicial review. The new legal opportunity structure was caused by both an unexpected tragic event (Beijing's military crackdown on the democratic movement in 1989) and the more gradual process of the handover of Hong Kong's sovereignty from Britain to China. The Chinese authorities had long opposed the enactment of a bill of rights for post-colonial Hong Kong throughout the process of negotiating the future constitutional arrangements of Hong Kong. Indeed, neither Britain nor the Hong Kong government supported a bill of rights.

Beijing's military suppression of the democratic movement in June 1989 precipitated a confidence crisis in Hong Kong. At this critical juncture, London made an important choice. To restore public confidence and to provide an alternative to letting the people of Hong Kong emigrate to Britain, the British initiated the Hong Kong Bill of Rights Ordinance shortly after the crackdown, in spite of Beijing's stern opposition.[11] As Ghai (1997, p. 460) notes, "nothing would have been done [for enacting a bill of rights] but for the events of June 1989 in Beijing with the killing of student protesters . . . and the subsequent crackdown on dissent." The Hong Kong Bill of Rights Ordinance was passed by the legislature in 1991.[12] The Ordinance incorporates the International Covenant on Civil and Political Rights (ICCPR) into Hong Kong's law (with some reservations). It repeals all preexisting laws that contravene the ICCPR and prohibits the legislature from

[11] Beijing's intense dislike of the Hong Kong Bill of Rights Ordinance was reflected by its plan to repeal the Ordinance after taking back Hong Kong in July 1997. Beijing regarded the Ordinance as a violation of the Basic Law and a British conspiracy to undermine the dominance of the executive branch over the post-colonial political system. Even though Beijing finally did not repeal the entire Ordinance, four sections were abolished. See Ghai (2007a, p. 132).

[12] See the Hong Kong Bill of Rights Ordinance. www.hklii.hk/eng/hk/legis/ord/383/cur.html (accessed March 22, 2012).

making any laws that are inconsistent with provisions of the Covenant as applied to Hong Kong. The passage of the Ordinance has brought dramatic changes to subsequent political development in Hong Kong, in particular the emergence of legal mobilization.

Tables 1.1 and 1.2 illuminate the dramatic impact of the Hong Kong Bill of Rights Ordinance (HKBORO). Before the promulgation of the HKBORO, the Privy Council did not hear any human rights cases originating from the colony, except in 1983 (see column 3 in Table 1.1). Similarly, before 1991, the Court of Appeal (the intermediate appellate court) heard very few human rights cases. In 1981 and 1986, for example, human rights cases only accounted for 2 percent and 5 percent of the total number of cases involving the government as a litigating party (column 3 in Table 1.2).

The introduction of the HKBORO dramatically reversed the foregoing situation by providing the legal basis for both citizens and lawyers to litigate against the government. Thus, after the enactment of the HKBORO in 1991, human rights cases have appeared much more frequently on the agenda of the two appellate courts. Column 3 in Table 1.1 shows that the Privy Council heard seven human rights cases originated from Hong Kong between 1993 and 1997. On the agenda of the Court of Appeal, the percentage of human rights litigation in the total number of cases involving the government as a litigating party increased from 2 percent in 1981 to 23 percent in 1994 (see column 3 in Table 1.2).

Finally, the promulgation of the HKBORO six years before July 1997 provided judges with opportunities to acquire experience and knowledge in handling human rights cases so that they could be more competent in tackling the much more complicated constitutional issues arising from the Basic Law (the constitution of post-colonial Hong Kong).

China's resumption of sovereignty over Hong Kong in July 1997 produced two important causal factors during the critical juncture[13] – the promulgation of the Basic Law and the establishment of a new final appellate court (Court of Final Appeal). Britain and China signed the Joint Declaration in 1984, which stipulates that China would resume sovereignty over Hong Kong. Then the two countries began a decade-long negotiation and bargaining over the

[13] The handover was also the terminus of the critical juncture.

TABLE 1.1: Substantive appeals involving the government as a party heard by the Privy Council or the Court of Final Appeal (1981–2010)[1]

	Year	Total no. of cases that involved the government as a party	Human rights	Policy	Administrative decision/ Administrative power/ Administrative negligence	Compensation for land resumption by government	Criminal due process[2]	Criminal appeal[3]	Contract/ Agreement	Dispute over costs	Others
Privy Council	1981	4	0 [0%]	0	2 [50%]	0	1 [25%]	1 [25%]	0	0	0
	1982	2	0 [0%]	0	2 [100%]	0	0 [0%]	0 [0%]	0	0	0
	1983	5	2 [40%]	0	3 [60%]	0	0 [0%]	0 [0%]	0	0	0
	1984	6	0 [0%]	0	2 [33%]	0	3 [50%]	1 [17%]	0	0	0
	1985	2	0 [0%]	0	1 [50%]	0	1 [50%]	0 [0%]	0	0	0
	1986	7	0 [0%]	0	2 [29%]	0	0 [0%]	2 [29%]	2	0	1
	1987	8	0 [0%]	0	2 [25%]	0	3 [38%]	2 [25%]	1	0	0
	1988	6	0 [0%]	1	1 [17%]	0	3 [50%]	1 [17%]	0	0	0
	1989	3	0 [0%]	0	1 [33%]	0	2 [67%]	0 [0%]	0	0	0
	1990	6	0 [0%]	0	3 [50%]	0	1 [17%]	1 [17%]	0	0	1
	1991	5	0 [0%]	0	1 [20%]	0	3 [60%]	1 [20%]	0	0	0
	1992	5	0 [0%]	0	1 [20%]	0	4 [80%]	0 [0%]	0	0	0
	1993	7	3 [43%]	0	2 [29%]	0	0 [0%]	0 [0%]	1	0	1
	1994	5	0 [0%]	0	3 [60%]	0	1 [20%]	1 [20%]	0	0	0
	1995	5	1 [20%]	0	1 [20%]	1	1 [20%]	1 [20%]	0	0	0
	1996	9	3 [33%]	0	3 [33%]	0	0 [0%]	2 [22%]	1	0	0
	1997 (Jan–June)	9	0 [0%]	0	6 [67%]	0	3 [33%]	0 [0%]	0	0	0

Court of Final Appeal	1997 (July–Dec)	0	0 [0%]	0	0 [0%]	0	0 [0%]	0 [0%]	0	0	0
	1998	5	2 [40%]	0	1 [20%]	0	2 [40%]	0 [0%]	0	0	0
	1999	19	8 [42%]	0	3 [15%]	0	5 [26%]	2 [11%]	0	1	0
	2000	16	1 [6%]	0	3 [18%]	0	5 [31%]	4 [25%]	0	2	1
	2001	16	4 [25%]	0	3 [19%]	1	3 [19%]	2 [13%]	0	3	0
	2002	16	9 [56%]	0	2 [13%]	0	1 [6%]	2 [13%]	0	1	1
	2003	14	1 [7%]	0	4 [29%]	0	7 [50%]	1 [7%]	0	1	0
	2004	19	4 [21%]	1	2 [11%]	0	6 [32%]	3 [16%]	0	3	0
	2005	20	2 [10%]	3	3 [15%]	2	5 [25%]	2 [10%]	1	2	0
	2006	25	6 [24%]	2	2 [8%]	1	5 [20%]	1 [4%]	0	6	2
	2007	21	4 [19%]	1	7 [33%]	0	4 [19%]	2 [10%]	0	1	2
	2008	19	4 [21%]	0	7 [37%]	0	4 [21%]	1 [5%]	0	2	1
	2009	18	2 [11%]	1	5 [28%]	0	4 [22%]	4 [22%]	0	1	1
	2010	21	1 [5%]	0	1 [5%]	1	2 [10%]	10 [48%]	0	5	1

Notes:
[1] Exclude applications for leave to appeal.
[2] Criminal due process refers to the trial judge's direction to the jury, admissibility of evidence, trial procedure etc.
[3] Appeal not based on violation of criminal due process.

TABLE 1.2: Substantive appeals involving the government as a party heard by the Court of Appeal (Intermediate Appellate Court)[1]

Year	Total no. of cases that involved the government as a party	Human rights	Policy	Administrative decision/ Administrative power/ Administrative negligence	Compensation for land resumption by government	Criminal due process[2]	Criminal appeal[3]	Contract/ Agreement	Dispute over costs	Others
1981	121	2 [2%]	0	9 [7%]	0	25 [21%]	84 [69%]	1	0	0
1986	58	3 [5%]	0	4 [7%]	0	12 [21%]	32 [55%]	2	0	5
1991	42	5 [12%]	0	11 [26%]	0	8 [19%]	14 [33%]	2	0	2
1994	43	10 [23%]	0	6 [14%]	0	3 [7%]	17 [40%]	0	1	6
1995	47	8 [17%]	0	11 [23%]	0	4 [9%]	19 [40%]	1	1	3
1996	29	5 [17%]	1	7 [24%]	5	0 [0%]	10 [34%]	0	0	1
1998	44	12 [27%]	1	14 [32%]	0	0 [0%]	10 [23%]	2	2	3
2000	51	14 [27%]	1	13 [25%]	1	2 [4%]	13 [25%]	2	2	3
2002	35	2 [6%]	0	18 [51%]	3	0 [0%]	7 [20%]	0	2	3
2005	36	0 [0%]	2	10 [28%]	4	2 [6%]	12 [33%]	1	1	4
2006	46	3 [7%]	2	25 [54%]	2	3 [7%]	7 [15%]	0	1	3
2008	60	7 [12%]	2	25 [42%]	0	2 [3%]	14 [23%]	4	1	5

Notes:
[1] Exclude applications for leave to appeal.
[2] Criminal due process refers to the trial judge's direction to the jury, admissibility of evidence, trial procedure etc.
[3] Appeal not based on violation of criminal due process.

constitutional arrangements of post-colonial Hong Kong, which resulted in the promulgation of the Basic Law and the setting up of a new final appellate court.

Contrary to the colonial constitutional documents (the Letters Patent and the Royal Instructions), the Basic Law contains very detailed provisions on the protection of fundamental human rights and freedoms.[14] It has a whole chapter on the protection of political and civil rights, and the scope is much broader than those contained in the HKBORO. In addition to political and civil rights, the Basic Law provides extensive provisions of economic and social policies, ranging from civil servant remuneration, public finance, education, culture, and labor to social services. These comprehensive constitutional provisions of rights protection and socio-economic relationship open up numerous legal opportunities for citizens to pursue their interests through the courts.

Tables 1.1 and 1.2 and Appendix 1 illuminate the dramatic causal effects of the Basic Law on legal mobilization. Tables 1.1 and 1.2 show that the Court of Final Appeal (CFA) and the Court of Appeal have heard an increasing number of human rights and public policy cases (both in absolute and percentage terms) since the handover. Between 1998 and 2010, for instance, the CFA decided forty-eight human rights and eight public policy cases. In contrast, throughout the 1980s, the Privy Council only decided two human rights cases and one public policy case originating from Hong Kong (see columns 3 and 4 in Table 1.1). Appendix 1 (column 4) further illustrates that citizens have extensively invoked various provisions of the Basic Law to promote their causes in the judiciary.

The establishment of a new final appellate court based in Hong Kong is another important causal factor emerging during the critical juncture. Chapter 4 will elaborate how the new court has contributed to the rise of legal mobilization in the post-colonial period. Here I will focus on the importance of agency of the judges in building up a competent, trustworthy, and impartial final appellate court, in particular their efforts in creating a distinguished panel of overseas judges to join the bench.

[14] See the Basic Law of the Hong Kong Special Administrative Region. www.basiclaw.gov.hk/en/basiclawtext/images/basiclaw_full_text.pdf (accessed March 22, 2012).

Recognizing the danger of an assertive judiciary to its rule over Hong Kong, the Chinese government took great measures to ensure that the post-1997 highest court would be under its control. Indeed, one of the most contentious issues in designing the CFA concerned the number of foreign judges to be allowed to sit on the final appellate court. China insisted that only one foreign judge would be allowed to sit in each substantive hearing, whereas the Bar, civil society, and pro-democracy forces argued that more than one should be allowed (Lo 2000).

Beijing's view eventually prevailed. Although the Chinese authorities set a broad constraint on the CFA, judges still had much room to maneuver and exercise their agency role when the Court was in the phase of institutional fluidity and important operational rules remained to be established. Chan (2009) notes that the replacement of the well-respected Privy Council by the CFA had highlighted the need for the latter to build up its reputation. Seeking to enhance the international standing of the Court, the first Chief Justice of the Hong Kong Special Administrative Region (HKSAR), Andrew Li Kwok-nang, took great efforts to set up a distinguished panel of overseas non-permanent judges (see also Jones 2007, p. 135). Additionally, the first Chief Justice adopted a practice that an overseas non-permanent judge will sit in almost every substantive hearing before the CFA. These overseas judges come from other common law jurisdictions and hold or have held prestigious positions in their home countries, such as judges of the Supreme Court. A number of them, notably Sir Anthony Mason and Lord Woolf of Barnes, have been longtime activist judges and famous for their liberal stance in safeguarding rights of the disadvantaged. As will be explained in Chapter 4, the presence of these prestigious and activist overseas judges makes it more difficult for the Chinese authorities to manipulate the CFA, and boosts the confidence of civil society in using the court to pursue its goals.

Shifting political opportunities

Beijing's tightening up of political opportunities in the legislature and other major decision-making bodies (except the judiciary) immediately after the end of the colonial era was another causal factor during the critical juncture. From the beginning of the 1980s, the colonial authorities implemented limited democratic reforms in Hong Kong, focusing on expanding the franchise in the legislative elections. Direct elections of about one-third of the legislative seats were introduced in 1991. Although the Basic Law has laid down the schedule of democratic development like the composition of the legislature until 2007, there is still much room for political entrepreneurs to enact substantial reforms. This happened when Christopher Patten became the last colonial governor in 1992.

Taking advantage of the grey areas in the Basic Law, Patten introduced more progressive democratic reforms to Hong Kong. Chapter 5 will elaborate how Patten's reforms substantially expanded political opportunities for pro-democracy and grassroots forces. Here I will highlight that the reforms enabled them to capture half of the legislative seats in 1995 so that they could use the legislature to enact progressive socio-political policies. If Patten's reforms had been maintained, pro-democracy and grassroots groups could have continued using the legislature as a primary avenue to advance their causes. However, Patten's reforms and the subsequent political opening were short-lived because of Beijing's opposition.

Arguing that Patten's reforms contravened the Sino-British agreement on the political development in Hong Kong, the Chinese government completely dismantled all reform measures after the handover. Instead, Beijing and the Tung Chee-hwa administration implemented various policies like a new electoral system to reassert their control over the legislature and to marginalize pro-democracy political influence. Chan (2002, pp. 10–11) has noted that pro-democracy forces have been marginalized from the legislature and important power centers during the post-colonial era.

The foregoing discussion shows that during the 1990s there was a shift in political opportunities from the legislature to the judicial branch in Hong Kong. The entrenchment of a wide variety of rights in the HKBORO and the Basic Law and the setting up of a new final appellate court marked the beginning of a new legal opportunity structure. The judicial branch has become a viable institution through which citizens can pursue their causes. As will be argued later in this book, the judiciary, especially the CFA, has signaled to society that it is ready to safeguard the civil and political rights of the disadvantaged through various important decisions. In my interviews, many litigants and rights advocacy groups indicated that a particular court judgment(s) has significantly inspired them to mobilize the law to advance their interests. Contrary to the judicial branch, the legislature and other major decision-making bodies have become less accessible to pro-democracy groups and civil society. Having been marginalized from the political arena and dissatisfied with the failure of major political institutions to adequately promote their interests, pro-democracy groups and civil society turn to the last resort – the courts.

Interdependence of critical antecedents and critical junctures and legal mobilization

Critical antecedents must interact and combine with the causal factors during critical junctures in order to produce the outcome of interest (Slater and Simmons 2010). The rise of legal mobilization in post-colonial Hong Kong results from the interaction between the legal complex, the new legal opportunity structure, and shifting political opportunities. Let us consider first a rival hypothesis – the legal complex itself was responsible for legal mobilization.

If the hypothesis is established, legal mobilization would have happened by the time the legal complex had taken root. The legal complex has had a long history in Hong Kong. However, as I will show in Chapter 2, before the first causal factor during the critical juncture (i.e., the confidence crisis after June 1989 and the subsequent enactment of the HKBORO), human rights cases appeared rarely on the judiciary's agenda. An independent and common law-trained legal profession had also existed in Hong Kong decades before the rise of legal mobilization. Indeed, the majority of cause lawyers were admitted to practice in Hong Kong between the late 1960s and 1980s. Nevertheless, they rarely engaged in cause lawyering during that period. As will be discussed in Chapter 6, it was not until the promulgation of the HKBORO and the Basic Law in the 1990s that they began actively to use their legal expertise to fight for the disadvantaged in the courts. Thus, we can argue that the legal complex itself did not directly cause legal mobilization.[15] Instead, its impact must be mediated by and combined with the critical juncture in producing legal mobilization.

Though not directly responsible for the rise of legal mobilization, the legal complex has provided the critical and necessary conditions. In their study of the role of the states in political and economic development, Skocpol (1985), and Rueschemeyer and Evans (1985) have argued convincingly that effective and capable state institutions

[15] One can also argue that the legal complex was incomplete prior to the promulgation of the HKBORO and the Basic Law. As legal tools such as human rights laws were not available before the 1990s, cause lawyers and social activists had to use other forms of activism rather than litigation to pursue their objectives.

like the civil service cannot be established overnight. Instead, it takes considerable time and effort for state institutions to develop and mature. The judiciary is no exception. Although the HKBORO and the Basic Law provide a broader and solid legal basis for society to litigate against the government, particularly on human rights and constitutional issues, the judiciary itself must be competent and independent enough to take up the new and complicated tasks. Commenting on the rise of legal mobilization in Hong Kong since the early 1990s, a judge specializing in human rights and constitutional cases said that:

> Apart from having the best lawyers, sustained litigation against the government requires competent courts and judges. Judges must have sufficient caliber to deal with the complexity and subtlety of constitutional and human rights issues. Hong Kong has reasonably neutral and competent courts. Judges are well-paid, highly respected and honest.[16]

A cause lawyer also pointed out that his cause lawyering has benefited from a well-established independent and impartial judiciary.[17]

Contrary to Hong Kong, the case of China illustrates how the lack of an independent and competent judiciary can impede legal mobilization. Liebman (2007, p. 346) notes that, although the Chinese government has sought to steer the increasing socio-economic disputes into the court system since the 1990s, the courts are not capable of handling many cases because of widespread corruption and poor quality of judges.

Similarly, government-funded legal aid, established in the late 1960s, has provided the necessary condition for social actors to take up the new legal opportunities created by the critical juncture. The last column in Appendix 1 demonstrates that an overwhelming majority of human rights cases were financed by government legal aid. Given the prohibitive litigation cost and the underprivileged background of most litigants, legal mobilization would not have occurred without government-funded legal aid.

Agentic elements: the rights support structure

Epp (1998, 1999) contends that successful legal mobilization requires a support structure – consisting of activist lawyers and rights advocacy

[16] Author's interview with Justice Michael Hartmann, March 5, 2008.
[17] Author's interview with Hectar Pun, February 13, 2008.

organizations – to bring rights cases into the judiciary's agenda.[18] Taking cues from Epp, this book also argues that agency by cause lawyers and rights advocacy groups is required to seize upon and transform the shifting political opportunities into legal mobilization in post-colonial Hong Kong (see Figure 1.1). This book goes one step further than Epp, however. It explores why these agents, especially cause lawyers, have emerged and actively engaged in promoting legal mobilization.

The importance of the rights support structure to the rise of legal mobilization in post-colonial Hong Kong can be illustrated by the failure of an environmental protection group, Green Sense, to litigate against the government's town planning policy in 2007. In that year, Green Sense sought to sue the government over the designation of a parcel of land near the waterfront. Green Sense, however, failed to find lawyers to represent them. Although a few lawyers were sympathetic with Green Sense's cause, they refused to represent the environmental protection group in court. These lawyers feared that their legal representation for Green Sense would offend the property developers and undermine their business prospects. Without any legal assistance, Green Sense produced a poorly written and unclear notice of application for *certiorari*, which prompted the judge to dismiss their application.[19]

Columns 2 and 7 in Appendices 1 and 2 highlight the fact that the majority of human rights and public policy litigation was launched and represented by rights advocacy organizations and cause lawyers. For example, the Society for Community Organization and a group of cause lawyers (Denis Chang, Mark Daly, Kwok Sui-hay, Gladys Li, Margaret Ng, and Pamela Baker) launched the decade-long right-of-abode litigation on behalf of mainland-born children of Hong Kong permanent residents. Between 2002 and 2007, the Neighborhood and Workers' Service Center organized three lawsuits against the government's public housing rental policy, the privatization of shopping and car park facilities within public housing estates, and minimum wages policy.

[18] According to Epp, a support structure includes government-supported legal aid as well. In this book, I place government-funded legal aid in the legal complex because it is more "structural" than "agentic."

[19] Author's interviews with Roy Tam (Chairman of the Green Sense), December 16, 2007 and Lam Ho-yeung (Democratic Party's district councillor), January 10, 2008.

Chapters 6 through 8 will address how rights advocacy organizations and cause lawyers – two transformative agents – have contributed to legal mobilization.[20] In particular, I will highlight how rights advocacy organizations have used their status as repeat players in litigation to strategically use law to promote progressive social reforms.

COMPETING EXPLANATIONS

Before moving on, I assess two competing explanations for the rise of legal mobilization in Hong Kong and highlight their weaknesses. The first explanation is: the economic downturn associated with the Asian Financial Crisis in 1997–98. Some socio-legal studies argue that economic change may affect the level of litigation. Ginsburg and Hoetker (2006, pp. 51–6), for instance, claim that the prolonged economic downturn in Japan in the 1990s contributed to a rapid growth of civil litigation by disrupting established socio-economic relationships. The Asian Financial Crisis brought economic recession to post-1997 Hong Kong. Economic difficulties played a role in causing legal mobilization, especially public policy litigation. The litigation over the reduction of civil service salaries was triggered by the need to contain the ballooning budget deficits. The lawsuit against public housing rental policy was partially caused by the unprecedented deflation in Hong Kong between late 1997 and mid 2004.[21] The decision of the Hong Kong Housing Authority to divest itself of shopping and parking facilities within public housing estates was indirectly caused by economic downturn as well.[22]

[20] Transformative agents are the actual actors who change institutions. See Mahoney and Thelen (2010).

[21] The 1997 Housing (Amendment) Ordinance stipulated that public housing rent shall not exceed 10 percent of tenants' median household income. The decline of household income in Hong Kong since late 1997 made public housing rent exceed the 10 percent limit in 2000. Instead of reducing public housing rent, the government only froze it. The decision was challenged by housing rights activists.

[22] To support the plummeting property market in Hong Kong after the Asian Financial Crisis, in late 2002 the government requested the Housing Authority to temporarily stop the Home Ownership Scheme (HOS) through which the Housing Authority built and sold subsidized apartments to the public. As the HOS had long been a lucrative revenue source, the Housing Authority experienced severe financial stress. In response, the government advised the Housing Authority to privatize its retail and parking facilities within public housing estates in order to generate sufficient revenue.

Economic recession, however, cannot adequately explain the growing trend of legal mobilization against the post-colonial government. For one thing, a majority of human rights cases have little if any relationship to economic downturn. For example, litigation on the right of abode, the right of non-indigenous villagers to participate in village elections, and the right of peaceful demonstration by Falun Gong practitioners had nothing to do with economic conditions. For another thing, Hong Kong had experienced economic recession in the 1970s and 1980s. Nevertheless, legal mobilization did not emerge during those periods.[23]

The second competing explanation for the rise of legal mobilization is that the post-colonial Hong Kong government has become increasingly incompetent, and thus produces more issues that can be brought to the courts by pro-democracy politicians and social activists. Scott (2000), for example, argues that Hong Kong's post-colonial political system has become disarticulated. The relationships between the executive, the legislature, and bureaucracy are uncoordinated, poorly developed, and dysfunctional, which in turn adversely affect the coherence and implementation of government policy.

Legal mobilization, however, has not happened to every incompetent government. For instance, in spite of its long-standing incompetent governance, the Myanmar government has not faced the challenge of legal mobilization. The case of Myanmar shows that government incompetence alone cannot adequately explain the rise of legal mobilization. Indeed, successful legal mobilization requires other favorable conditions, such as a judiciary that is receptive to human rights arguments and a rights support structure that brings rights cases into the judiciary's agenda.

[23] It should be noted that although the economic recession associated with the Asian Financial Crisis cannot adequately explain the growing trend of legal mobilization against the post-colonial government, the economic downturn had increased the Hong Kong government's reliance on Beijing for economic support, as Beijing provided Hong Kong with various preferential deals. The increasing economic dependence on China made it much harder for the Hong Kong government to defend the territory's political autonomy, thus affecting its *response* to legal mobilization, like turning to the Chinese legislature to overturn an unfavorable ruling on the right of abode in 1999. See the discussion of *Ng Ka Ling and Another* v. *The Director of Immigration* in Chapter 4 of this book.

THEORETICAL AND COMPARATIVE IMPLICATIONS

Using post-colonial Hong Kong as a case study, my book examines how legal mobilization can arise in authoritarian regimes. Specifically, my book makes four contributions to the literature on comparative courts and rights mobilization. First, it engages and contributes to the emerging literature on judicial politics under authoritarianism by arguing that historical legacies play an important role in the rise of legal mobilization and that legal mobilization in authoritarian regimes by no means unfolds as political authorities would wish. While largely concurring with Moustafa (2007) and Ginsburg and Moustafa (2008) that judicial politics can happen in authoritarian polities, I argue that these studies are too *ahistorical*. The case of Hong Kong demonstrates the important role of historical legacies to sustained legal mobilization. Additionally, unlike Moustafa (2007) and Ginsburg and Moustafa (2008), who suggest that authoritarian regimes empower the judiciary for strategic reasons (e.g., enhancing bureaucratic compliance), which in turn contributed to legal mobilization, my study presents a different story. As will be discussed throughout the remainder of this book, legal mobilization in Hong Kong has by no means unfolded as political authorities would wish. Beijing, for example, inherited an autonomous and efficient legal complex (the judiciary and the Bar Association) from British colonial rule. Although the legal complex has played a crucial role in facilitating legal mobilization, Beijing has found it politically costly to overturn it and decided to live with it.

Second, the Hong Kong case shows that legal mobilization under authoritarianism requires *both* the legal complex and the rights support structure. Thus, in their research on legal mobilization, Halliday, Karpik, and Feeley (2007a) underestimate the contribution of the rights support structure, and Epp (1998) underestimates the contribution of the legal complex as an institutional actor. Halliday, Karpik, and Feeley (2007a) focus on how the legal complex (encompassing lawyers and judges, collectively organized by the organized bar) fights for political liberalism. But they overlook the important roles played by rights advocacy groups and government-funded legal aid. Epp (1998) studies how the rights support structure facilitates legal mobilization. But he underestimates the significant contribution made by an independent and competent judiciary and an organized bar.

Third, my book highlights the impact of different forms of authoritarianism on the modes of opposition mobilization. The contrasting experience of Taiwan and Hong Kong is a case in point. During the 1970s and 1980s, the authoritarian Kuomintang regime seriously undermined the autonomy of the legal profession. Facing tremendous problems in exercising their influence in the legal arena and a partial opening of electoral competition, many liberal lawyers turned to oppositional politics and actively engaged in local elections to promote political liberalization and democratization (Winn and Yeh 1995, p. 565; Ginsburg 2007, p. 57). By contrast, the presence of a well-established and autonomous Bar Association and the tightening of political opportunities in the post-colonial legislature prompted many liberal lawyers in Hong Kong to use the law to pursue democratic changes. In the concluding chapter, I will address the implications of this Hong Kong–Taiwan divergence for the likely modes of opposition mobilization in future China.

Finally, through studying how cause lawyers in Hong Kong have used their expertise and networks to promote democratic changes and the difficulty they have encountered, my book informs the literature on economic modernization and democratization, especially the role of the middle class. Students of political development, such as Lipset (1959), Moore (1966), Cheng (1989), and Diamond (1992) claim that economic modernization is an important requisite for democratic development. A crucial reason is that economic modernization is likely to create a middle class, which can stand up against an authoritarian state. However, this claim may be too one-sided. As will be elaborated in Chapters 6 and 7, although cause lawyers (an important component of the middle class) in Hong Kong have actively pursued gradual democratic changes through cause lawyering, the strength of capitalism (especially economic pressure from Beijing and large corporations in Hong Kong) has also posed substantial difficulty to their cause lawyering work. Economic modernization can hinder the efforts of cause lawyers to pursue democracy when large corporations side with an authoritarian regime to exert economic pressure on them. In short, economic modernization does not necessarily foster democratic development. The relationship between economic modernization and democratization is more dynamic and complex, which requires more nuanced analysis.

ORGANIZATION OF THE BOOK

This book is organized into four parts. Part I includes this introductory chapter and Chapters 2 and 3. Chapter 2 presents and discusses the data concerning changes in the judiciary's dockets and agendas between 1981 and 2010, with a view to highlighting the growth of legal mobilization in the post-colonial period. Chapter 3 traces the development of the critical antecedent – the legal complex – and examines how it serves as the foundation for post-1997 legal mobilization. In this chapter, I will also present a Shanghai–Hong Kong comparison in order to highlight the importance of an efficient legal complex to legal mobilization. The law and society literature finds that societies which experienced dramatic socio-economic and political transitions were linked to increases in legal mobilization (e.g., Giles and Lancaster 1989). One might expect that Shanghai, which has undergone profound socio-economic transformation since the late 1980s, would have witnessed a substantial increase in legal mobilization as well. As will be discussed later, however, lack of an autonomous and efficient legal complex has impeded legal mobilization in China's most economically and legally developed city and in China more broadly.

Part II studies how the critical juncture associated with Beijing's military crackdown on the 1989 Tiananmen democratic movement and the process of the sovereignty transition brought a shifting of political opportunities. Chapter 4 analyzes how the promulgation of the Hong Kong Bill of Rights Ordinance and the Basic Law and the setting up of the Court of Final Appeal created a new legal opportunity structure. The new structure has significantly enhanced the judicial branch as a viable institution for citizens to pursue their goals in the post-colonial era. Chapter 5 discusses how Beijing and the post-colonial Hong Kong government dismantled the democratic reforms introduced by the last governor Christopher Patten, and marginalized pro-democracy and grassroots forces from major decision-making bodies, particularly the legislature. My discussion will focus on Beijing's efforts to undermine the legislature as an effective countervailing force to the executive branch. The opposite development of the power of the judiciary and the legislature produced shifting political opportunities in the post-colonial era, which in turn motivated politically disadvantaged actors to go to the courts to advance their claims.

Part III analyzes two transformative agents – cause lawyers and rights advocacy organizations – who have actively seized upon the legacies of the legal complex and the new legal opportunity structure to drive legal mobilization. Chapter 6 analyzes the political origin of the rise of cause lawyering in Hong Kong, and the interplay of opportunities and constraints of cause lawyering. Chapter 7 discusses how a group of cause lawyers have taken up the shifting political opportunities associated with the process of the sovereignty transition and promoted legal mobilization in Hong Kong. Chapter 8 studies rights advocacy organizations and emphasizes how their status as repeat players in litigation has facilitated their use of law to promote progressive social reforms.

Part IV concludes. Chapter 9 examines three important impacts of the judicialization of politics in post-colonial Hong Kong. Finally, Chapter 10 discusses the theoretical and comparative implications of this study, including different paths to legal mobilization under authoritarianism, the indispensable role played by *both* the legal complex and the rights support structure, the likely mode of opposition mobilization in future China, and the relationships between economic modernization and democratization (specifically the role of the middle class).

METHODOLOGY

This book adopts both quantitative and qualitative approaches. To document the patterns and trends of legal mobilization, I conducted quantitative analysis of changes in the judiciary's agenda during the period 1981–2010. The quantitative analysis provides an overview of the actors involved, the claims they contended for, and the results in the courts.

In addition to quantitative studies, I undertook semi-structured and in-depth interviews with sixteen cause lawyers,[24] twenty-five rights advocates, and two pro-democracy politicians. I also interviewed

[24] Except for Denis Chang, Paul Harris, and Pamela Baker, I interviewed all the cause lawyers whose names appear in Table 6.1 in Chapter 6. (Chang and Harris declined my invitation to be interviewed; Baker passed away in 2002). In addition, I interviewed cause lawyer A (a barrister) and B (a solicitor). To protect their anonymity, their information does not appear in Table 6.1.

three barristers, five senior government officials, and three judges. All interviews were conducted in Hong Kong during the period 2006–2008 and 2011, lasted between half an hour to two hours, and took place in person. All named interviewees gave permission for their identities to be revealed. Appendix 3 lists the details of my interviewees. I chose my interviewees from four sources. First, I read court judgments and identified the lawyers who represented the non-government parties. Second, I searched local newspapers with a view to finding the background of the litigants, especially whether any rights advocacy groups had been actively involved in a particular case. Third, I was a student fellow at the Centre for Comparative and Public Law, the University of Hong Kong between July 2007 and March 2008. During my visit, Professor Hualing Fu, the then Director of the Centre, kindly introduced me to some interested parties for interviews. Finally, during my interviews, some interviewees suggested the names of other interested parties to whom I should talk. After identifying the potential interviewees, I either sent letters inviting them for interviews or asked my former professors in Hong Kong to introduce me to these potential interviewees.

The objective of the interviews was to understand the entire processes of legal mobilization, including the litigants' motivations and strategies, government responses, the role of the judiciary, and the operation of the legal system in Hong Kong. To supplement the quantitative and qualitative data, I collected materials from local newspapers, magazines and journals, and books and articles by cause lawyers and judges.

2

THE GROWTH OF LEGAL MOBILIZATION IN POST-COLONIAL HONG KONG

CHANGING COURT DOCKETS AND AGENDAS

The dramatic changes in the judiciary's agenda illuminate the growth of legal mobilization in Hong Kong since the early 1990s and particularly after China resumed sovereignty over Hong Kong in July 1997. This book focuses on three courts: the Judicial Committee of the Privy Council (the highest court in the colonial era); the Court of Final Appeal (which replaces the Privy Council after the sovereignty handover); and the Court of Appeal (the intermediate appellate court). I focus on these courts because only crucial cases can reach their agendas and therefore their decisions often have far-reaching socio-political implications. However, I will also discuss important cases heard at the lower court (the Court of First Instance).

The number of human rights and policy-oriented cases on the judiciary's agenda has increased substantially since the early 1990s and particularly after July 1997. To capture such changes, I analyzed all lawsuits involving the government as a litigating party that the Judicial Committee of the Privy Council, the Court of Final Appeal (CFA), and the Court of Appeal heard during 1981–2010.[1] The data

[1] Unlike some research which only focuses on judicial review (e.g., Cheung and Wong 2006; Chan 2009), my book studies *all* substantive appeals involving the government as a litigating party that the appellate courts heard. An exclusive focus on judicial review will overlook criminal cases which contain significant human rights elements. Prominent examples include *HKSAR* v. *Ng Kung Siu and Another* [Court of Final Appeal 1999] (freedom of expression, national flag desecration);

come from three sources. First, for the Privy Council cases, I searched the "Westlaw International – All Cases from Hong Kong" database and generated 94 substantive cases. Second, for the CFA and Court of Appeal cases, apart from using the already mentioned "Westlaw" database, I searched the "Hong Kong Legal Information Institute" database.[2] For the CFA and the Court of Appeal, 229 and 612 substantive cases were retrieved respectively.[3] Third, I examined the collections at the High Court Library in Hong Kong in order to confirm whether any cases have been omitted in the foregoing electronic databases. Tables 1.1 and 1.2 in Chapter 1 present the results of the analysis.

Table 1.1 demonstrates the number and distribution of substantive appeals involving the government as a litigating party that the Privy Council and the CFA heard. The figures reveal several salient trends. First, the CFA heard twice as many cases annually than the Privy Council. From 1981 to June 1997, each year the Privy Council decided on average five to six cases that originated from Hong Kong. Since July 1997, there has been a substantial increase in the number of cases that the CFA has heard. The CFA decided on average seventeen cases a year. Some lawyers suggest that the increase was primarily caused by the right-of-abode litigation movement launched by mainland-born children of Hong Kong permanent residents.[4] This claim, however, is not persuasive. If we deduct the nineteen right-of-abode cases that the CFA heard between 1999 and 2008 (see Table 2.1), the CFA each year still heard about sixteen substantive appeals that involved the government as a litigating party.

Second, we observe an enormous growth of human rights and public policy cases since the early 1990s and particularly after the sovereignty handover. Human rights cases are defined as cases in which the

Yeung May Wan and Others v. *HKSAR* [Court of Final Appeal 2005] (right to peaceful assembly and demonstration by the anti-Beijing religious sect Falun Gong); and *Leung Kwok Hung and Others* v. *HKSAR* [Court of Final Appeal 2005] (right to procession).

2 Available at www.hklii.hk/eng. Hong Kong Legal Information Institute is a free access legal information system developed and operated by the Faculty of Law and the Department of Computer Science at the University of Hong Kong. It covers judgments of the Court of Final Appeal, the Court of Appeal, the Court of First Instance, the District Court, the Family Court, and the Lands Tribunal.

3 For the Court of Appeal cases, I have analyzed twelve years. See Table 1.2.

4 Author's interview with barrister A, September 19, 2007.

TABLE 2.1: Right-of-abode litigation brought by mainland-born children/adopted children of Hong Kong permanent residents, Court of Final Appeal (1999–2008)

1999	*Chan Kam Nga* v. *Director of Immigration*
	Lau Kong Yung and Others v. *The Director of Immigration*
	Ng Ka Ling and Another v. *The Director of Immigration*
	The Director of Immigration v. *Cheung Lai Wah*
	Tsui Kuen Nang v. *The Director of Immigration*
2000	Nil
2001	*Tam Nga Yin and Others* v. *Director of Immigration*
	Xie Xiaoyi v. *Director of Immigration*
	Director of Immigration v. *Chong Fung-Yuen*
2002	*Li Shuk Fan* v. *Director of Immigration*
	Ng Siu Tung and Others v. *Director of Immigration* (10/1/2002)
	Ng Siu Tung and Others v. *Director of Immigration* (25/2/2002)
	Ng Siu Tung and Others v. *Director of Immigration* (30/7/2002)
	Sin Hoi Chu and Others v. *Director of Immigration*
2003	Nil
2004	*Ng Siu Tung and Others* v. *Director of Immigration* (9/1/2004)
	Ng Siu Tung and Others v. *Director of Immigration* (26/3/2004)
2005	Nil
2006	*Ng Siu Tung and Others* v. *Director of Immigration* (5/1/2006)
	Ng Siu Tung and Others v. *Director of Immigration* (13/11/2006)
2007	*Ng Siu Tung and Others* v. *Director of Immigration*
2008	*Ng Siu Tung and Others* v. *Director of Immigration*

litigants mainly argue about fundamental human rights principles, such as freedom of expression and association, right of peaceful assembly and demonstrations, right not to be subject to torture or unlawful detention, and right of abode. Appendix 1 describes in detail all the human rights cases that the Privy Council and the CFA heard between 1981 and 2010. It should be noted that there was some ambiguity in the process of coding several cases.[5] These cases (all criminal cases) could be coded either as human rights cases or as criminal appeals. In deciding how to categorize these ambiguous cases, I examined whether the litigants had invoked the Hong Kong Bill of Rights Ordinance (HKBORO) and/or the Basic Law (especially Chapter III on the protection of fundamental political and civil rights) or not. If the HKBORO and/or the Basic Law had been invoked

[5] These Court of Final Appeal cases include: *Li Defan and Another* v. *HKSAR* 2002; *So Wai Lun* v. *HKSAR* 2006; *Mo Yuk Ping* v. *HKSAR* 2007.

(see column 4 in Appendix 1), I would categorize that ambiguous case as a human rights case. No matter how these few cases are categorized, however, it does not affect the finding that there has been an enormous growth of human rights cases since the early 1990s.

Public policy cases refer to cases in which the litigants primarily dispute the policy in question *per se*. An example of a public policy case is *Lo Siu Lan* v. *Hong Kong Housing Authority*.[6] The appellant challenged the government policy of privatizing the retail and parking facilities within public housing estates. Public policy litigation differs from administrative litigation in the sense that the latter does not challenge the policy *per se*, but challenges the way the government implements or interprets the policy. For example, in most administrative lawsuits against profits tax assessment, the challenges are not directed at the profits tax policy *per se*, but at the way the government assesses the tax burden.

Throughout the 1980s, the Privy Council only decided two human rights cases that originated from Hong Kong. The number rose to seven between 1993 and 1997. In contrast, the CFA had decided forty-eight human rights cases between1998 and 2010, and they had taken up an increasing proportion of the total caseload (see column 3 in Table 1.1). More important, Appendix 1 (column 5) demonstrates that, compared to the colonial era, post-colonial human rights litigation has addressed broader concerns. New concerns such as the right to participate in public affairs (village elections),[7] gay rights,[8] peaceful assembly and demonstration,[9] freedom and privacy of communication,[10] freedom from torture,[11] and non-permanent residents' right to travel and enter into Hong Kong[12] have been advocated before the CFA.

Apart from issue diversity, many human rights cases are politically charged. In *HKSAR* v. *Ng Kung Siu and Another*,[13] two social activists argued that their act of desecrating the national flag was justified by freedom of expression. In *Leung Kwok Hung and Others* v. *HKSAR*,[14]

[6] *Lo Siu Lan* v. *Hong Kong Housing Authority* [Court of Final Appeal 2005].
[7] *Secretary for Justice and Others* v. *Chan Wah and Others* [Court of Final Appeal 2000].
[8] *Secretary for Justice* v. *Yau Yuk Lung Zigo and Another* [Court of Final Appeal 2007].
[9] *Leung Kwok Hung and Others* v. *HKSAR* [Court of Final Appeal 2005].
[10] *Koo Sze Yiu and Another* v. *Chief Executive of the HKSAR* [Court of Final Appeal 2006].
[11] *Secretary for Security* v. *Sakthevel Prabakar* [Court of Final Appeal 2004].
[12] *Gurung Kesh Bahadur* v. *Director of Immigration* [Court of Final Appeal 2002].
[13] *HKSAR* v. *Ng Kung Siu and Another* [Court of Final Appeal 1999].
[14] *Leung Kwok Hung and Others* v. *HKSAR* [Court of Final Appeal 2005].

the appellants challenged the Public Order (Amendment) Ordinance, which had severely restricted public procession and peaceful assembly since the late 1960s. In *Ng Ka Ling and Another* v. *The Director of Immigration*, the appellants indirectly challenged the immigration policy of the Chinese government.[15]

Besides human rights cases, public policy litigation has become more prominent on the agenda of the CFA. Between 1981 and 1997, the Privy Council merely decided one public policy case – *Elvira Vergara and Another* v. *Attorney General*,[16] in which two Filipino domestic helpers challenged a new immigration policy concerning foreign domestic helpers. By contrast, between 1998 and 2010, the CFA heard eight public policy cases that carried far-reaching socio-political impacts (see column 4 in Table 1.1). In *Town Planning Board* v. *Society for the Protection of the Harbour Ltd*, the Society successfully challenged a crucial harbor reclamation plan and more broadly the government harbor reclamation policy.[17] Given that the Hong Kong government has long heavily relied on reclamation for acquiring usable land, this environmental litigation will continue to affect the development of large infrastructure projects.[18] In *Ho Choi Wan* v. *Hong Kong Housing Authority*,[19] the appellant contested the public housing rental policy. In *Lo Siu Lan* v. *Hong Kong Housing Authority*,[20] the appellant opposed the government's policy of privatizing the retail and parking facilities within public housing estates, which involved the world's largest

[15] *Ng Ka Ling and Another* v. *The Director of Immigration* [Court of Final Appeal 1999]. The appellants contended that paragraph 2(c) of Section 1 of the Immigration (Amendment) (No. 3) Ordinance was invalid, because it required Hong Kong permanent residents residing in China to hold a one-way permit (approved and issued by the Chinese government) before they can enjoy the constitutional right of abode in Hong Kong.

[16] *Elvira Vergara and Another* v. *Attorney General* [Privy Council 1988].

[17] In its judgment, the CFA declared that in future the government has to demonstrate an overriding public need before it can start any harbor reclamation project. See *Town Planning Board* v. *Society for the Protection of the Harbour Ltd* [Court of Final Appeal 2004].

[18] In 2008, the Society for the Protection of the Harbour adopted the argument of overriding public need and successfully defeated a substantial reclamation plan in the Court of First Instance. See *Society for Protection of the Harbour* v. *Secretary for Justice* [Court of First Instance 2008].

[19] *Ho Choi Wan* v. *Hong Kong Housing Authority* [Court of Final Appeal 2005].

[20] *Lo Siu Lan* v. *Hong Kong Housing Authority* [Court of Final Appeal 2005].

property trust listing (the Link REIT case). The two lawsuits not only deeply influenced the livelihoods of 630,000 households but also the policy of privatizing other crucial public assets. Finally, in *Secretary for Justice* v. *Michael Reid Scott* 2005, two senior government officials challenged the government policy to cut civil servant salaries after the Asian Financial Crisis.

Data from the Court of Appeal (the intermediate appellate court) show similar trends as discussed earlier and provide further evidence of the rise of legal mobilization in post-colonial Hong Kong. Table 1.2 reports a substantial growth of human rights litigation since the passage of the Hong Kong Bill of Rights Ordinance in 1991. The percentage of human rights litigation in the total number of cases involving the government as a litigating party increased from 2 percent in 1981 to 23 percent in 1994 (see column 3 in Table 1.2). Further, a number of them were politically charged. In *Lau San Ching* v. *Appollonia Liu*,[21] political activists contested unreasonable restrictions on the right to stand for district council elections. In *Lee Miu Ling and Another* v. *The Attorney General*,[22] social activists challenged the undemocratic electoral system in the legislature. In *Lau Wong Fat* v. *Attorney General*,[23] pro-Beijing Heung Yee Kuk (an organization representing the interests of indigenous inhabitants) mobilized the law to *counteract* a liberal legislation which granted women the right to inherit land in rural villages. Like the CFA, the Court of Appeal has heard more public policy litigation as well. Before the sovereignty handover, civil service localization policy was challenged in *The Association of Expatriate Civil Servants of Hong Kong* v. *The Secretary for the Civil Service and Another*.[24] In 2006 the government policy to levy a tax on foreign domestic helpers was litigated.[25]

Finally, interviews with a veteran cause lawyer and a judge also confirm that legal mobilization did not take place until the last years of the colonial rule. Cause lawyer A, who has frequently represented

[21] *Lau San Ching* v. *Appollonia Liu* [Court of Appeal 1994].

[22] *Lee Miu Ling and Another* v. *The Attorney General* [Court of Appeal 1995].

[23] *Lau Wong Fat* v. *Attorney General* [Court of Final Appeal 1997].

[24] *The Association of Expatriate Civil Servants of Hong Kong* v. *The Secretary for the Civil Service and Another* [Court of Appeal 1996].

[25] *Julita F. Raza and Others* v. *Chief Executive in Council and Others* [Court of Appeal 2006].

either government or citizens in judicial reviews, noted that, "Before the mid 1990s, there were very few judicial reviews challenging the government. Aggrieved citizens rarely thought to sue the government."[26] Justice Michael Hartmann also mentioned a noticeable change in his work after July 1997. As he put it, "Since the implementation of the Basic Law, a great deal of my work has focused on the interpretation of the meaning and intent of the Basic Law, particularly human rights litigation and cases concerning the power relationships among the executive, legislative, and judicial branches."[27]

It should be noted that the foregoing data do not provide a complete picture of legal mobilization in post-colonial Hong Kong. The data only cover substantive appeals that the Privy Council, the CFA, and the Court of Appeal had decided. But they miss some crucial human rights and politically charged litigation that had either been settled out of the court or aborted. The litigation includes: the right to public housing[28] and social security[29] for Chinese migrant families;

26 Author's interview with cause lawyer A, September 19, 2007.

27 Author's interview with Justice Michael Hartmann, March 5, 2008. Upon joining the judiciary in 1991, Hartmann has specialized in handling constitutional and administrative law cases.

28 In 1999, the Evangelical Lutheran Church of Hong Kong initiated a lawsuit on behalf of immigrants from mainland China, who claimed that the government's public housing allocation policy discriminated against them. The policy stated that for a family to be eligible to apply for a government apartment, more than half of family members must have lived in Hong Kong for at least seven years. Before the court heard the litigation, the Tung Chee-hwa administration changed the residency rule in favor of Chinese immigrant families. Author's interview with Wong Kwok-kei (Supervisor of Social Service Head Office) and Wong Chui-shan (social worker) of the Evangelic Lutheran Church of Hong Kong, December 19, 2007. See also Alex Ho, "Legal aid row over migrants' bid for flats," *South China Morning Post*, October 27, 1999, p. 6; Felix Chan, "Family set for new life off rooftop," *South China Morning Post*, November 5, 1999, p. 4.

29 In the early 2000s, the Society for Community Organization (SoCO) planned to file a lawsuit on behalf of a newly arrived Chinese immigrant whose application for social security was denied. The government regulation stipulates that applicants for social security must have lived in Hong Kong for at least seven years. SoCO argued that the seven-year residency rule violated the Basic Law. Before SoCO submitted the application for leave to appeal to the court, the government made concessions and approved the social security application of that Chinese immigrant. Author's interview with Wong Chi-yuen, community organizer of SoCO, December 19, 2007.

the right to social welfare and work for a stateless person;[30] and the tenure of a Chief Executive of the Hong Kong Special Administrative Region (HKSAR) who is elected to fill a vacancy arising from resignation.[31] In the first three cases, the government made concessions to the litigants before the courts formally heard the litigation. These cases show that the threat of legal mobilization can sometimes achieve policy changes.

CONCLUSION

In this chapter, I documented the dramatic changes in the judiciary's agenda since the early 1990s, particularly after the sovereignty transition in July 1997. Human rights and public policy cases have appeared much more frequently on the judiciary's agenda. Throughout the remainder of this book, I explain the rise of legal mobilization in post-colonial Hong Kong.

[30] In 2007, Salimuchai Todd, a stateless person in Hong Kong, filed a judicial review against the government's inhumane treatment of him. Salimuchai came from a remote opium-farming region in the Golden Triangle and in 1999 he smuggled into Hong Kong for a debt collection. He was arrested by the immigration authorities and imprisoned. After his release, the government neither provided welfare to Salimuchai nor repatriated him to his home country. Salimuchai argued that the Hong Kong government violated the United Nations 1954 Convention relating to the Status of Stateless Persons. The court had agreed to hear his case. Before the legal proceedings commenced, the government settled with Salimuchai and allowed him to work in Hong Kong. Nick Gentle, "Stranded migrant's case to be reopened," *South China Morning Post*, November 30, 2007, p. 5; and *Ming Pao*, April 13, 2008.

[31] In March 2005, Tung Chee-hwa resigned from the position of the Chief Executive of the HKSAR in the middle of his second term. Tung's resignation aroused a debate over the term of office of his successor. Beijing contended that Tung's successor should serve the remainder of the outgoing Chief Executive's second term. Accordingly, the SAR government amended the Chief Executive Election Ordinance to reflect Beijing's policy. By contrast, pro-democracy parties and the legal professions held that Tung's successor should serve a new term of five years. Chan Wai-yip, a pro-democracy legislator, filed an application for judicial review challenging that the amendment to the Ordinance violated the Basic Law. The court had accepted Chan's application and scheduled to hear the litigation. Chan was forced to drop his judicial review, however, after the Chinese legislature offered its interpretation of the relevant provisions of the Basic Law. See Chen (2005) and *Hong Kong Economic Journal*, April 14, 2005, p. 7. On the power of the Chinese legislature to interpret the Basic Law and its impact on the constitutional interpretation power of the Hong Kong courts, see Chapter 4 of this book.

3

CRITICAL ANTECEDENT – LEGAL COMPLEX

HISTORICAL ORIGINS OF LEGAL MOBILIZATION

Legal mobilization in post-1997 Hong Kong has its historical origins in the mid nineteenth century when the British colonial authorities introduced the apparatus of English law like the rule of law and an independent judiciary to the newly acquired colony. In this chapter, I discuss how the British-built legal complex – an independent and competent judiciary; an autonomous legal profession trained in common law systems; and government-funded legal aid – serves as the critical antecedent for post-colonial legal mobilization. The legal complex has three significant causal impacts on the rise of legal mobilization. First, a well-established and independent judiciary provides the necessary foundation like a reservoir of experienced judges for a new final appellate court, and boosts the confidence of citizens in using the courts to advance their interests. Second, an autonomous body of legal profession can provide better protection and support for cause lawyers against arbitrary state intervention. Third, a government-funded legal aid scheme provides the necessary financial resources for citizens and social actors to use the law to promote their causes.

The legal complex could not arise during the critical juncture alone because of two factors. First, it takes considerable time and effort for an independent and competent judiciary and legal profession to develop and mature (Skocpol 1985; Rueschemeyer and Evans 1985). Second, Beijing would have had little if any incentive to create an autonomous legal complex in post-colonial Hong Kong from scratch.

This chapter is divided into two main parts. In the first, I study individual components of the legal complex and highlight their importance to legal mobilization in general. The second part discusses how the British colonial authorities set up a legal complex in Hong Kong, and analyzes how this has contributed to the rise of legal mobilization in post-colonial Hong Kong.

THE SIGNIFICANCE OF LEGAL COMPLEX TO LEGAL MOBILIZATION

Sustained legal mobilization does not occur in a vacuum. An efficient legal complex, consisting of an independent and competent judiciary, an autonomous and organized legal profession, and government-funded legal aid, provides an indispensable foundation for legal mobilization.

An independent and competent judiciary

Judicial independence is defined as the autonomy of judges – collectively and individually – from other individuals and institutions. It is a relational term describing the relationship the judiciary should have with other political institutions.[1] Russell (2001) has identified three key dimensions of an independent judiciary: structural, personnel, and administration.

Structural independence means whether and to what extent the executive and legislature have the power to create and modify and even dismantle the structure of judicial institutions. Judicial independence is undermined when the government uses or threatens to use its control over judicial structure to influence court judgments. Franklin Roosevelt's infamous 'court packing plan' in 1937 was an example. Apart from court packing, governments can remove the court's jurisdiction over important and sensitive matters and transfer it to other institutions.

Personnel independence refers to the methods of appointing, promoting, transferring, removing, disciplining, and remunerating judges. Security of tenure is a crucial safeguard of judicial independence under which judges can only be removed on reasonable grounds, such as incapacity of discharging their responsibilities, or

[1] The discussion of judicial independence in this section is primarily based on Russell (2001).

misbehavior. Moreover, the removal processes must be transparent and fair. Regarding appointment, the three major systems – popular election, appointment by elected politicians, and appointment into a professional career judiciary – are all subject to varying degrees of undue external influence and therefore compromise judicial independence. To guard against a politically unbalanced judiciary, legal scholars have recently suggested that a carefully structured judicial service commission can be a viable mechanism for judicial appointment (Russell 2001, p. 17). South Africa, for example, established a Judicial Service Commission in 1994 for judicial selection and appointment. The Commission is composed of the chief justice, the president of the Constitutional Court, four practicing barristers and solicitors, a law professor, members of the National Assembly and the National Council of Provinces, and persons designated by the president. Corder (2001) argues that the Commission has brought marked positive effects on the demographic composition and legitimacy of the judiciary and helped to maintain judicial independence.

Remuneration for judges is crucial to judicial independence as well. When judges receive meager salary and benefits, they are more vulnerable to bribery and are more likely to be influenced by special interests. As a result, judicial independence will be undermined. Further, judges' remuneration should be determined in a regularized and objective way, and not subject to the whims of politicians (Russell 2001, p. 18).

Finally, judicial administration – the management of courts and judges' work – is significant to judicial independence. Judicial independence requires the judiciary to control the assignment of judges to cases and courtrooms, the sitting of the courts, and court lists (Russell 2001, p. 20).

Judicial competence is also important for the development of an efficient legal complex. Judges must be of sufficient caliber to handle increasingly complicated cases arising from a globalized and fast-changing environment. In addition, judges must maintain a high level of integrity and impartiality in order to be competent for their work. Corruption in particular will undermine judges' competence for adjudicating cases in accordance with the law.

An independent and competent judiciary is crucial because it is the arena where most activities of legal mobilization take place. Citizens' perception of the judiciary significantly affects their propensity to pursue their claims through the judicial branch. Citizens are more likely to litigate when they perceive that, compared to other political institutions, the courts are insulated from political pressure and exercise their duties impartially (Javeline and Baird 2007, p. 872). By contrast, citizens will turn away from court when they perceive it as arbitrary. For example, as noted by Abel (1988, p. 27), the public's lack of confidence in the judicial system (perceiving it as arbitrary) has been a major reason for the relatively low civil litigation rates in many civil law countries. Courts are also the major platforms where cause lawyers exercise their expertise to promote the causes of the disadvantaged and press for progressive social changes. Their political influence is heavily dependent on an independent and functioning judiciary. A corrupt and oppressive judiciary not only hinders cause lawyering work, but also puts cause lawyers in political danger. For example, post-war Indonesian judges, who are infamous for their corruption, incompetence, and abuse of power, have sought to silence activist lawyers (Lev 2007, p. 404). Absence of meaningful judicial independence has impeded cause lawyering in China (Michelson 2007) and Argentina and Brazil as well (Meili 1998, pp. 494–7).

The foregoing discussion of judicial independence focuses on freedom from dismissal, freedom from arbitrary reduction of remuneration, and freedom from undue political pressure from other state institutions. As Simpson (1989, pp. 147–8) points out, however, there is more to the concept of judicial independence than the negative elements mentioned earlier. Simpson distinguishes between negative elements of judicial independence from positive elements. The latter mean that the judiciary serves as a check or restraint on the executive and support the ideal of the rule of law. This implies a more proactive role of the judiciary. Effective realization of these positive elements of judicial independence requires other kinds of institutional support including an autonomous and organized legal profession.

An autonomous and organized legal profession

An autonomous, well-trained, and organized legal profession is another component of the legal complex. To be independent from state control, the bar must have the authority to determine matters important to professional independence, including: the size of the profession, admission and education requirements, modes of organization, fee schedules, and disciplinary powers over its members. Most importantly, the bar leadership is selected by the professionals themselves instead of being controlled by the state.

Human rights and public policy litigation frequently pits civil society against the government and/or powerful groups. An autonomous and unified bar can offer stronger protection to cause lawyers from state harassment and crackdown. If the state severely restricts the autonomy of the legal profession, liberal lawyers are likely to replace litigation with other strategies in their pursuit of progressive socio-political changes. This happened in Taiwan during the 1970s–80s when the authoritarian Kuomintang regime seriously undermined the autonomy of the legal profession. Facing great difficulty in exerting their influence in the legal arena, many liberal lawyers turned to oppositional politics to promote political liberalization and democratization (Winn and Yeh 1995, p. 565; Ginsburg 2007, p. 57).

Further, a unified and autonomous legal profession can play a vital role in defending judicial independence from state control. It can mobilize public support like demonstrations to oppose any attempts by the state to dominate the judiciary. In the 1960s, the Korean Bar Association was an important force in defending the judiciary against encroachment by the military dictatorship (Kim 2007, pp. 60–1). By contrast, a divided and weak legal profession erodes an important pillar of judicial independence (Halliday, Karpik, and Feeley 2007b, p. 7; Lev 2007, pp. 410–1).

State-financed legal aid

Legal aid is a crucial part of the legal complex and central to legal mobilization because most prospective litigants in human rights cases are from the underprivileged class. Government-funded legal aid is indispensable in legal systems which allow partial or full fee shifting (i.e., loser pays). Voluntary legal aid (e.g., pro bono legal representation offered by trade unions or political parties) cannot sustain legal mobilization under the loser-pays system, because a losing non-state litigant has to pay the government legal fee. Given the power of the purse, governments can expend enormous economic resources on litigation, like retaining the best and most experienced lawyers. If it loses, the non-state litigating party will incur exorbitant financial costs.

Government-financed legal aid can compensate for this problem by paying the non-legal-aided winning party. Furthermore, government-funded legal aid programs tend to ensure more stable sources of financing. However, these programs may also suffer from the autonomy problem when states want to retain tight fiscal and political control (Abel 1988, p. 28).

THE LEGAL COMPLEX IN HONG KONG

The British established an efficient legal complex during their colonial governance in Hong Kong. This legal complex consists of an independent and competent judiciary, an autonomous legal profession trained in common law systems, and a state-financed legal aid system. This section will elaborate how these permissive and enabling institutions have served as the critical antecedents for post-colonial legal mobilization.

An independent and competent judiciary

Britain began the construction of a legal complex in colonial Hong Kong in the mid nineteenth century when it introduced an apparatus of English common law.[2] The English doctrine of the rule of law with justice administered by an independent and competent judiciary was a central ingredient of the apparatus. Despite its shortcomings, the rule of law set the standards and procedures of the colony's legal system. A Supreme Court was set up in the 1840s, where the Chief Justice and a jury tried serious criminal cases. Judges were well aware of the importance of judicial independence, and some of them used the court to promote progressive social reforms. For instance, Chief Justice Sir John Smale used the bench as a platform for a campaign against slavery and trafficking of human beings between 1866 and 1881 (Munn 2001, p. 20). In the administration of criminal law, the accused were protected by the remedy of *habeas corpus*, the presumption of innocence, the right to a fair and open trial, trial by jury, and the right to silence.

As documented by Munn, the procedures and values inherited in English common law enabled judges and jurors to pursue justice in the face of considerable opposition. For example, a jury acquitted the men

[2] The discussion in this and following paragraphs is mainly based on Munn (2001).

charged with the attempted poisoning of the European community in 1857, when many colonists and some officials demanded their summary execution. In light of the track record of the Supreme Court in championing the rule of law, a historian had lauded the Court as "the one and probably only monument of integrity and uprightness during the darkest days of the colony's early history." Indeed, its stature increased as time progressed (quoted in Munn 2001, p. 21).

The British colonial authorities adopted various institutional measures to protect judicial independence in Hong Kong and these measures have continued in the post-1997 period. My discussion here focuses on the appointment and removal of judges, their financial security, and judicial administration – three major pillars of judicial independence.[3] The Basic Law provides that judges are appointed by the Chief Executive in accordance with the advice of the Judicial Officers Recommendation Commission (JORC).[4] JORC's choices are based on the candidates' proven competence, integrity, and professional qualities. The Basic Law requires the Chief Executive to implement JORC's recommendations. As pointed out by Wesley-Smith (2001, p. 109), because the Chief Executive is constitutionally prohibited from exercising discretion in judicial appointment, judicial independence is considerably enhanced. The Basic Law also sets up institutional mechanisms to protect the security of tenure of judges. A judge may only be removed by the Chief Executive for inability to discharge her duties or for misbehavior. Before the Chief Executive can dismiss a judge, he has to get the recommendation from a judicial tribunal appointed by the Chief Justice and obtain the legislature's endorsement.

Financial security of judges and the judiciary is also well protected. The Basic Law stipulates that judges that were serving in Hong Kong before the handover can retain their seniority with pay, benefits, and conditions of service no less favorable than before. The Chief Justice directs the budgetary and expenditure processes of the judiciary.

Finally, the Chief Justice is responsible for the administration of the judiciary. Court leaders control the assignment of judges, sittings

[3] The discussion is primarily based on Wesley-Smith (2001).

[4] JORC consists of nine members: the Chief Justice and two local judges, the Secretary for Justice, representatives from the two legal professional bodies (the Bar Association and the Law Society), and eminent persons from other sectors. It is supposed to be an independent body and all members are appointed by the Chief Executive.

of the courts, and court lists. Further, they are in charge of monitoring, appraising the performance of judges, and disciplinary matters.

Given the aforementioned institutional safeguards, a constitutional expert claims that, "Judicial independence . . . seems largely secure . . . regular judges are in general well protected from outside while exercising their judicial functions" (Wesley-Smith 2001, p. 125).

The foregoing discussion highlights that the negative elements of judicial independence have been well established since the colonial period. Nevertheless, the positive elements of judicial independence were not fully developed. During most of the colonial era, the courts did not actively restrain the executive because the colonial constitution granted extensive powers to the Governor to rule Hong Kong on behalf of the Queen (Miners 1998, p. 69). As a constitutional judge remarked, "Before July 1997, the prerogative of the Queen did not leave much room to challenge the executive."[5] It was not until the promulgation of the Hong Kong Bill of Rights Ordinance (HKBORO) and the Basic Law that the courts were empowered to actively restrain the executive. The following chapter will address how judicial empowerment has contributed to legal mobilization.

In conclusion, the British established an independent and competent judiciary during their centuries-long colonial rule. As a veteran scholar of Hong Kong politics notes, "A foremost British legacy for colonial Hong Kong is the rule of law, which includes the British style common law legal system with an independent and impartial judiciary" (Chan 1997, pp. 567–70). This important legacy has been taken up by civil society to advance their causes when political opportunities shifted to the judiciary during the process of the sovereignty transition in the 1990s.

An autonomous and organized legal profession

Following the British legal system, the legal profession in Hong Kong is divided into two separate branches: barristers and solicitors.[6] As of May 2008, there were about 800 practicing barristers and 4,900 practicing solicitors in Hong Kong. All barristers are sole practitioners and are prohibited from forming partnerships with one another. They are, however, generally associated through offices that enable them to share overhead costs such as rent and secretarial services. Barristers

[5] Author's interview with Justice Michael Hartmann, March 5, 2008.

[6] The discussion in this section is primarily based on Wesley-Smith (1998, pp. 100–5).

are not allowed to act directly for clients; a client must first consult a solicitor, who will then contact a barrister. Barristers have the exclusive rights of audience before the higher courts and belong to the Bar Association, the professional organization of barristers. Solicitors can join law firms either as salaried personnel or as partners. Their rights of audience are typically confined to the lower courts (the district and magistrates' courts).[7] The Law Society represents the professional interests of solicitors.

Barristers and solicitors have different professional and political ideologies. Since the 1960s, the Bar Association has adopted a more proactive and progressive stance in promoting democracy and human rights, and frequently led opposition against the government's illiberal policies. By contrast, the Law Society has taken a more conservative and detached attitude, and has often distanced itself from the Bar's endeavors.[8] The relatively conservative stance of the Law Society may explain why cause lawyers in Hong Kong are mainly barristers.[9]

By adopting a liberal approach to regulating the legal profession, the British colonial authorities helped to cultivate an autonomous and organized legal profession in Hong Kong. Like other common law jurisdictions, the British colonial government took a non-intrusive approach to regulating the legal profession.[10] Since the colonial era, the Bar Association and the Law Society have been the governing bodies for barristers and solicitors respectively. They resemble

[7] In January 2010, Hong Kong's legislature passed a law that allows experienced solicitors to apply for the right to advocate in the higher courts. An assessment board, comprising three judges, three barristers, three solicitors, an official from the Department of Justice, and an ordinary citizen, is responsible for scrutinizing and approving all the applications.

[8] Jones (2007, p. 128) attributes the different political ideologies between the Bar and the Law Society to the fact that the Bar has a greater proportion of expatriates and many of its members were educated in prestigious British universities where they had been imbued with both the values of a liberal education and the *noblesse oblige* ethos of the UK Bar. I argue that an equally important reason lies in the fact that Hong Kong's solicitor firms have had much more business transactions with the Chinese authorities.

[9] Among the cause lawyers that I interviewed, Ho Chun-yan, Michael Vidler, Mark Daly, John Clancey, and cause lawyer B are solicitors. All others are barristers. See Table 6.1 in Chapter 6.

[10] Compared to the civil law world, governments in the common law world generally adopt a more liberal approach to regulating the legal profession. Governments are less worried about challenge from the legal profession and therefore do not closely monitor them. See Abel (1988, p. 6).

closely the American model of self-regulatory bars and have effective control over matters crucial to professional independence, including: the size of the profession, fee schedules, admission and educational requirements,[11] modes of organization, and disciplinary powers over their members.

Unlike their counterparts in China, legal professional bodies in Hong Kong are not subordinate to the state.[12] Instead, the judiciary, especially the Chief Justice, is responsible for managing the legal profession. For example, the rules and membership of the disciplinary tribunals of the two professional bodies are set by the Chief Justice.[13] The professional bodies are not required to submit their bylaws to the government for approval. More importantly, the leadership of the Bar Association and the Law Society are elected by their members and government officials do not hold any leadership positions.

An autonomous and organized legal profession in Hong Kong can offer better support to cause lawyers who help the disadvantaged to challenge the government in the courts. The experience of China is illuminating. Liu and Halliday (2008) show that the dependence of Chinese criminal defense lawyers on the state has significantly constrained their capacity to mobilize for the protection of basic legal freedoms of citizens. Although Hong Kong lawyers have not faced such a risky practicing environment as their Chinese counterparts did, an autonomous Bar has played a crucial role in supporting cause lawyering and legal mobilization. This is evident in the right-of-abode litigation that occurred shortly after the sovereignty handover. The Bar actively mobilized its members to offer pro bono legal services to the litigants who failed to get government-funded legal aid (see Chapter 6). The move by the Bar, however, was criticized by some pro-China figures as a confrontation against the Hong Kong government. Then Bar chairwoman Audrey Eu openly defended the Bar against the criticism.[14] If the Bar Association was as highly dependent

[11] The Hong Kong Legal Practitioners Ordinance has given the right to the legal profession to devise rules governing admissions to the profession, and the educational and licensing requirements of their members. See Nathanson (1999, pp. 649–52).

[12] Chinese legal professions have been subject to tighter control by the state (Ministry of Justice) and the Communist Party. See Alford (2007, p. 294), Halliday and Liu (2007, p. 69).

[13] Sections 9 and 72 of the Hong Kong Legal Practitioners Ordinance.

[14] Linda Choy, "Rita Fan lands in 'II' legal aid row," *South China Morning Post*, July 15, 1997, p. 1.

on the government as lawyers in China, it might not have adopted a firm stand in helping the litigants. A former Bar chairman-cum-cause lawyer, Philip Dykes, also stressed the importance of an autonomous Bar, as he remarked, "the Bar Association should not have a close relationship with the government."[15]

Government-financed legal aid

Established by the colonial government in 1966, a government-financed legal aid system constitutes the last component of the legal complex.[16] In 1958 the colonial authorities conducted the first feasibility study of a legal aid scheme for the poor in both civil and criminal cases. And it was not until 1966 that the legislature passed the Legal Aid Bill and the legal aid scheme came into operation in 1967. The Legal Aid Department (LAD), a government agency set up in 1970, is responsible for administering the legal aid scheme. The scheme is primarily financed by the government and covers both civil and criminal cases. All legal aid applicants have to pass the means and merit tests. The means test requires an applicant's financial resources to not exceed the limit determined by the government. It is waived for applications which involve the HKBORO. The merit test is more controversial (see Chapter 7) and an applicant has to demonstrate that his claim in the court has a reasonable prospect of success (Legal Aid Services Council 2006, p. 117).

The government-funded legal aid scheme has a number of features which are favorable to legal mobilization. First, once granted, legal aid not only covers the legal costs of the recipient, but also pays for the non-legally aided opposing party who wins the litigation. This is crucial in view of the loser-pays system in Hong Kong.[17] It also effectively reduces the cost of legal mobilization relative to alternative means. As two labor union activists put it, "Legal aid made judicial review an economical means to challenge government inaction on labor rights."[18] Second, there is no predetermined

[15] Author's interview with Philip Dykes, November 29, 2007.

[16] The discussion of this section is mainly based on Legal Aid Services Council (2006).

[17] Depending on his financial condition, a legal aid litigant may be required to make a certain contribution to the legal costs as well. However, the Director of the Legal Aid Department will notify the maximum amount of the litigant's contribution before the commencement of the litigation. Legal Aid Services Council (2006, p. 122).

[18] Author's interview with Walker Fung Kai-yuen and Huang Ngai-fung of the Hong Kong Confederation of Trade Unions, December 21, 2007.

funding limit for the total legal aid costs. Supplementary appropriation can be sought when the expenses of legally aided cases in the year exceed the original amount of appropriation. Third, there is no predetermined funding cap for each *individual* case (Legal Aid Services Council 2006, p. 53). Thus, lawyers in legal aid cases have more room to mobilize and deploy resources to fight for their clients. Chapter 6 will elaborate how this unique funding method contributes to cause lawyering.

Furthermore, for the sake of enhancing the independence of the legal aid scheme from undue government influence, the following types of cases are outsourced to lawyers in private practice. These include applications for writ of habeas corpus, judicial review, cases involving the government or a public agency as a defendant, and cases where a human rights or Basic Law issue is involved.[19] By assigning private practitioners rather than in-house LAD counsel to handle the foregoing politically charged cases, the practice not only minimizes undue government interference in the operation of the legal aid scheme, but also promotes the development of cause lawyering (see Chapter 6).

Finally, the Legal Aid Ordinance establishes varying mechanisms which enable society to appeal to the judiciary against LAD's refusal of legal aid applications. The Registrar and Masters of the High Court hear and determine appeals against the decision of the LAD to refuse, discharge, or revoke civil legal aid. In the case of criminal legal aid, judges can grant legal aid in certain circumstances despite refusal by the LAD (Legal Aid Services Council 2006, p. 91). Starting from April 2002, applicants who fail to get legal aid for a proposed appeal to the Court of Final Appeal will be funded by the government to obtain lawyer's certificates as to whether the proposed appeal has reasonable prospects of success.

Despite other shortcomings, which will be discussed later, the foregoing features have enhanced the independence of the legal aid scheme and provided an indispensable financial

[19] The Legal Aid Department has a Litigation Division, which consists of Civil Litigation Sections and the Crime Section. The former handles litigation on civil legal aid cases assigned in-house, focusing on personal injuries, family matters, insolvency, and general civil matters. The latter is responsible for the majority of legal aid committal proceedings of indictable offences assigned in-house. See Legal Aid Services Council (2006, pp. 66–7).

resource for legal mobilization. The last column in Appendix 1 demonstrates that the government legal aid scheme has financed the majority of human rights and public policy litigation since the 1990s.

SHANGHAI–HONG KONG COMPARISON

In the previous discussion, I argued that the British-established legal complex is important to sustained legal mobilization in post-colonial Hong Kong. In this section I will present a Shanghai–Hong Kong comparison, with a view to highlighting that in authoritarian settings, legal mobilization requires the *inheritance* of an autonomous and efficient legal complex because authoritarian regimes have no incentive to build it. The law and society literature found that societies which experienced dramatic socio-economic and political transition were linked to substantial increases in legal mobilization (e.g., Giles and Lancaster 1989). In 1989 China enacted the Administrative Litigation Law, which provides for lawsuits challenging government actions. The former Supreme People's Court President Xiao Yang praised Shanghai for its outstanding achievement in the nationwide five-year judicial reform plan (1999–2003).[20] Leading the country in the judicial and economic reforms, one might expect that Shanghai would have witnessed substantial increases in legal mobilization. A lack of an autonomous and efficient legal complex, however, has impeded legal mobilization in Shanghai and more broadly in China.

A dependent judiciary in Shanghai

A politically dependent judiciary has impeded legal mobilization in Shanghai. Despite measures to reduce the interference of the Communist Party and the government in the court system, the judiciary in Shanghai is still subject to considerable political interference, particularly in politically sensitive cases.[21] Party and government officials, especially those at lower ranks, have frequently pressured judges not to take administrative lawsuits filed by aggrieved citizens.

20 The five-year judicial reform plan aimed to establish a fair, open, highly effective, honest, and well-functioning judicial system. Judicial fairness was the central theme of the reform. See Gechlik (2005, pp. 98–9).

21 Unless specified otherwise, the discussion in this section is primarily based on Gechlik (2005).

Judges have in many instances bowed to the pressure, because Party and government leaders dominate the financial and personnel arrangement of the courts. The small proportion of administrative cases in the courts' agenda illustrates the impact of intense political interference on legal mobilization. Between 1991 and 2004, administrative cases accounted for about 0.9 percent of all first-instance cases that courts in Shanghai heard, and the nationwide figure was 1.4 percent. In short, a lack of judicial independence has deprived many aggrieved individuals in Shanghai of the opportunity to use the law to pursue their causes.

Even if a judge has accepted an administrative lawsuit, the Communist Party and government can still exert enormous pressure on the outcome of the case. In deciding politically sensitive cases against government agencies, judges have to consult the Communist Party's political-legal committees, which are comprised of senior party members and leaders of government agencies. This consultation procedure has enabled the Party and the government to control the results of these important cases. Eviction-related litigation, which has become increasingly common during rapid urbanization, can demonstrate the Party's control over important cases. Government agencies in Shanghai (and in other provinces) have seldom lost in eviction lawsuits, given that rapid urbanization and economic development is a top priority of the city government. The difficulty of winning lawsuits has discouraged aggrieved citizens from going to the courts to settle their disputes with the government. Instead, many of them took to the streets to redress their grievances (Gechlik 2005, p. 117).

A dependent legal profession in Shanghai

The Communist Party has had little if any intention to establish an autonomous legal profession in China since taking power in China in 1949. The subordination of the Chinese legal profession to the party-state has hampered legal mobilization in Shanghai and more broadly in China. If a legal profession is well established historically, lawyers will feel less reluctant to challenge the state. However, this is not the case in China. The Ministry of Justice tightly controls the All China Lawyers Association on matters crucial to professional independence, including: the bar leadership, the size of the profession, fee schedules, admission and educational requirements, modes of organization, and disciplinary powers over lawyers.

A politically subordinate bar association increases the vulnerability of cause lawyers to state sanction, particularly in authoritarian states like China. The substantial vulnerability to state sanction and the notorious record of the state for imprisoning cause lawyers have indeed deterred many Chinese lawyers from taking cases that challenge the government, especially administrative litigation and criminal defense. Gechlik (2005, p. 137) notes that fear for party-state retaliation has often put off lawyers in Shanghai from taking administrative lawsuits.[22] The reluctance of lawyers to accept cases that challenge the party-state has weakened citizens' ability to use the courts to further their interests.[23]

It should be noted that a lack of an independent and efficient legal complex has also diverted aggrieved citizens away from the courts in other parts of China. Cai (2007, pp. 181–3) reports that the lack of an autonomous judiciary has prompted homeowners to use other modes of resistance, instead of legal mobilization, to defend their rights. Liebman (1998, p. 1533) also highlights that limited competence of the courts, like rampant corruption, has weakened the government's efforts to enhance the role of the courts in resolving the rising socio-political disputes in China, especially in class action litigation.

22 In their survey of 268 lawyers in Changsha city of Hunan Province in 2002, Cai and Yang (2006, p. 166) also found that about 90 percent of the respondents were reluctant to take administrative and criminal cases for fear of party-state retaliation.

23 Critics may argue that the major difference between Shanghai and Hong Kong is the level of state repression against lawyers (i.e., compared with Shanghai, Hong Kong has a relatively non-repressive state), not historical legacies of an autonomous legal complex. However, the case of post-war Japan shows that Hong Kong's legal mobilization is a function of historical legacies of an autonomous legal complex, and not just a relatively non-repressive state. In 2001, a Japanese government-sponsored report acknowledged that the historical underdevelopment of the legal complex has significantly stymied citizen efforts to use the law to hold government officials accountable for their actions. Since the late nineteenth century, Japan has had a low number of lawyers and judges per capita compared to most other industrialized countries. Worse still, the figure has declined markedly since the 1930s. See Feeley and Miyazawa (2007, pp. 152, 160, 181). Thus, the case of post-war Japan (where state repression against lawyers is not great) illustrates that legal mobilization is a function of historical legacies of an autonomous and efficient legal complex, and not merely a relatively non-repressive regime.

Active participation of foreigners in Hong Kong's legal complex

Compared to Shanghai, Hong Kong possesses a more independent and capable legal complex, which facilitates legal mobilization. The earlier part of this chapter documented the British-built legal complex and its significance to legal mobilization. Chapter 4 will further analyze how an autonomous and capable judiciary has actively protected rights and freedoms in post-colonial Hong Kong. Here I would like to emphasize one important feature of Hong Kong's legal complex, which not only distinguishes it from that in China but also enhances its independence under an authoritarian regime. That feature concerns the active participation of foreign legal practitioners in the judiciary and the legal profession.[24]

Unlike the executive and legislature, Hong Kong's judiciary is highly open to foreign participation, even after China assumed its sovereignty over the city. During the colonial rule, judges in Hong Kong were mostly foreigners. Localization of the judiciary was implemented after the British decided to return Hong Kong to China. Despite the sovereignty handover, foreigners still have a large presence in the judiciary.[25] This is because the Basic Law allows all judges who served in Hong Kong before the handover to continue in office after July 1997. There is no nationality restriction for judges except for two positions – the Chief Justice and the Chief Judge of the High Court. The presence of a large number of foreign judges, who have a strong belief in the rule of law and/or linkage with prestigious judicial institutions in liberal democracies, has made it more difficult for Beijing to control the judiciary.

[24] Active participation of foreign legal practitioners in Hong Kong's legal complex not only distinguishes it from that in China, but also from legal complexes in Singapore, Malaysia, and Myanmar – three authoritarian Asian states which were former British colonies. The Singapore government allowed foreign lawyers to set up law offices in Singapore in 1980, more than a decade after the city-state's independence from Britain. However, foreign lawyers have faced substantial restriction on practicing Singaporean law. They are prohibited from practicing constitutional and administrative law, criminal law, and appearing or pleading in any courts in Singapore. See Part I of the Singapore Legal Profession (International Services) Rules 2008. In Malaysia, admission to become a legal practitioner is restricted to Malaysians or permanent residents of Malaysia. See section 11 of the Malaysia Legal Profession Act 1976.

[25] As of June 2008, the Court of Appeal and the Court of First Instance together have thirty-six judges and twenty of them are non-Chinese.

The legal profession in Hong Kong has also been highly open to overseas lawyers since colonial rule. This openness remains unchanged after the sovereignty transition. Apart from possessing at least three years of practicing experience in his jurisdiction of admission, an overseas lawyer can practice in Hong Kong after passing the bar examination.[26] The continued presence of foreign lawyers makes it more politically costly for Beijing to control and sanction lawyers who litigate for politically charged cases. Indeed, a number of cause lawyers in Hong Kong are expatriates. Some of them, like Paul Harris and Mark Daly, moved their practice to Hong Kong in the early 1990s with a view to defending civil liberties and rule of law in post-colonial Hong Kong. As we will see in Chapter 6, the arrival of these foreign human rights lawyers helped to jumpstart the process of human rights litigation.

In contrast to Hong Kong, China's judiciary is wholly staffed by Chinese citizens. Foreign legal professionals also encounter numerous restrictions on practicing in China. Foreign law firms are not allowed to interpret and advise on Chinese law, or engage in litigation. Moreover, foreign lawyers are prohibited from sitting for the bar examination. As reported by Peerenboom (2002, pp. 358, 370), the Ministry of Justice imposes these restrictions because it fears that foreign lawyers will take an aggressive stance in political cases. The prohibition of foreign lawyers from participating in litigation deprives many aggrieved individuals of legal representation in political cases. The lack of legal representation in turn makes it easier for the Chinese government to hinder legal mobilization by aggrieved individuals.

To summarize, the marked contrast between Hong Kong and Shanghai/China in terms of the independence and capability of their legal complex and the openness to foreign participation has significantly influenced the trajectories of legal mobilization in the two places.

CONCLUSION

In this chapter, I have traced the historical origins of post-1997 legal mobilization to the legal complex established during the centuries-long British colonial rule. Consisting of an independent and competent

[26] Section 27 (1) of the Hong Kong Legal Practitioners Ordinance.

judiciary, an autonomous and organized legal profession, and a government-funded legal aid scheme, the legal complex has provided the necessary basis – an institutional arena, agents, and financing – for legal mobilization. An independent and competent judiciary serves as a viable institutional arena through which society can advance their interests. An autonomous and organized legal profession offers stronger protection for cause lawyers who transformed the changing political opportunities during the sovereignty transition into legal mobilization. Finally, a government-funded legal aid scheme provides a relatively sustainable financing for legal mobilization.

However, it should be noted that the legal complex *by itself* cannot cause legal mobilization. This is illustrated by the fact that legal mobilization did not occur until the mid 1990s – long after the establishment of the legal complex. Instead, the legal complex causes legal mobilization *in combination* with the changing political opportunities during the sovereignty transition. The next two chapters examine how the process of the sovereignty transition opened up a critical juncture, which significantly reshaped the political opportunities in post-colonial Hong Kong. Specifically, on the one hand, the process of the sovereignty transition opened up new legal opportunities. On the other, it tightened political opportunities in the legislature.

PART II

4

THE OPENING OF NEW LEGAL OPPORTUNITIES

THE IMPORTANCE OF LEGAL OPPORTUNITIES

This chapter studies how the process of the sovereignty transition in Hong Kong during the 1980s and 1990s opened up three important legal opportunities for legal mobilization. In particular, as will be argued later, Beijing's crackdown of the 1989 Tiananmen democratic movement had a galvanizing role in making the process of the sovereignty transition look as it did. In this book, legal opportunities are defined as the opportunities to use the judicial branch to pursue one's interests (Andersen, 2004, pp. 1–16). The establishment or empowerment of courts with the power of judicial review and the enactment of a Bill of Rights are two typical examples of the opening up of new legal opportunities (Wilson and Rodriguez Cordero, 2006). A favorable legal framework (particularly a Bill of Rights) and courts with the power of judicial review are two basic requirements for legal mobilization.[1] Citizens and social groups who want to pursue their interests through litigation have to present their claims in legal terms and convince the judges that the government's policies or actions have contravened the law. This is because judges reach decisions within a legal framework. Effective enforcement of rights by courts

[1] It should be noted that a court, which lacks the power of judicial review but has broad power of statutory interpretation, may also be a potential site of legal mobilization.

generally requires the entrenchment of these rights in the constitution and/or a Bill of Rights.

Courts must be readily accessible if citizens want to mobilize the law to pursue their interests. However, citizens may face tremendous difficulty in accessing the courts. For example, authoritarian governments can suspend the operation of the courts. Courts may also be geographically far away from the potential litigants. For instance, colonial Hong Kong's final appellate court – the Privy Council – was located in London. Under these circumstances, litigation may not be a viable avenue for citizens to advance their interests. Accordingly, the promulgation of law, especially constitutions and a bill of rights, and the establishment of courts that are accessible to society laid down the necessary foundations for the public to use the law to pursue their objectives.

In Hong Kong, the process of the sovereignty transition from Britain to China in July 1997 brought three new legal opportunities for legal mobilization, namely: (i) the enactment of the Hong Kong Bill of Rights Ordinance in June 1991; (ii) the promulgation of the Basic Law; and (iii) the establishment of a final appellate court within Hong Kong – the Court of Final Appeal (CFA). These new legal opportunities provide a more solid and broader legal basis for society to challenge the government in the courts.

THE HONG KONG BILL OF RIGHTS ORDINANCE

The Hong Kong Bill of Rights Ordinance (HKBORO) was passed by Hong Kong's legislature and came into effect in June 1991. Beijing's military suppression of the 1989 Tiananmen democratic movement was the primary factor leading to the introduction of the HKBORO. The crackdown caused a serious confidence crisis in Hong Kong, as society and investors feared the loss of rights and freedoms after China resumed sovereignty over Hong Kong in July 1997. Indeed, a group of business and community elites proposed to pay the Chinese government HK$10 billion to exchange for self-rule in Hong Kong for ten years after the handover. The proposal was rejected by Beijing.[2] At this critical juncture, the British government made an important decision: the promulgation of a bill of rights. A month after the

[2] Chris Yeung, "Tycoons' plan for self-rule treasonous," *South China Morning Post*, July 4, 2007, p. A1.

military suppression, Britain announced a number of measures that sought to restore confidence in Hong Kong, among which was the enactment of a bill of rights, in spite of Beijing's opposition (Miners, 1998, pp. 27–28; Chan and Ghai, 1993, p. 2).

The HKBORO incorporates the International Covenant on Civil and Political Rights (ICCPR) into Hong Kong's law (with some reservations). It repeals all preexisting laws that contravene the ICCPR and prohibits the legislature from making any laws which are inconsistent with provisions of the Covenant as applied to Hong Kong. The courts are responsible for enforcing the HKBORO. For the first time, Hong Kong society was provided with legal protection of fundamental civil rights. The colonial constitution – the Letters Patent and the Royal Instructions – did not have any provision safeguarding fundamental civil rights. Although Britain extended the ICCPR to Hong Kong in 1976, it did not incorporate the Covenant into Hong Kong's law, arguing that the Covenant had been effectively implemented through various laws in Hong Kong (Chan and Ghai, 1993, p.1).

The HKBORO opened up a new legal opportunity for the public to challenge the government through the judiciary. Before the implementation of the HKBORO, the public lacked a sound legal framework to sue the government. The Letters Patent delegated wide powers to the Governor and the legislature to make laws for peace, order, and good government. As Justice Kemal Bokhary remarked, "[before the HKBORO] it was very difficult for the public to argue before the courts that the government violated the law, since the definition of 'peace, order and good government' was too broad."[3] An experienced cause lawyer also said that:

> Before the promulgation of the HKBORO, citizens could challenge the government in the courts only under the following two conditions: either the government's decision was so unreasonable that it was *Wednesbury* unreasonableness or the decision contravened the legislation. Nevertheless, as political powers were concentrated in the executive branch (Governor) during much of the colonial period, it was very difficult for citizens to persuade judges that the government had made very unreasonable decisions or violated the legislation.[4]

[3] Author's interview with Justice Kemal Bokhary, February 28, 2008.
[4] Author's interview with Gladys Li, February 21, 2008.

By guaranteeing the rights and freedoms contained in the ICCPR, the HKBORO provides a solid and broad legal basis for the public to litigate against the government. This is illustrated by the rapid growth of the human rights cases on the judiciary's agenda after 1991. Appendix 1 shows that between 1981 and 1992 the Privy Council only decided two human rights cases originating from Hong Kong. In 1983, two illegal Chinese immigrants challenged the colonial government's removal order in the Privy Council. In *Attorney General of Hong Kong* v. *Ng Yuen Shiu*,[5] the respondent argued that he was entitled to a fair hearing by the immigration authorities before being deported. In *Mak Yui Ming and Others* v. *The Attorney General*,[6] the appellants claimed that they had the right of abode in Hong Kong. The passage of the HKBORO, however, made human rights cases from Hong Kong appear more frequently on the Privy Council's agenda (Appendix 1). In 1993, the Privy Council heard two human rights cases on the rights of criminal defendants. In *Attorney General of Hong Kong* v. *Lee Kwong-kut*[7] and *Attorney General of Hong Kong* v. *Lo Chak-man and Another*,[8] the defendants used article 11 of the HKBORO to contest their charges (possessing revenue from drug trafficking), arguing that parts of the Summary Offences Ordinance and of the Drug Trafficking (Recovery of Proceeds) Ordinance were inconsistent with the presumption of innocence of everyone charged with a criminal offence. In 1995 and 1996, a criminal defendant and a liberal-oriented newspaper also used the HKBORO to challenge the government on the right to benefit from a lesser penalty and freedom of expression respectively.[9]

Political activists also took up the new legal opportunity afforded by the HKBORO to pursue their cause, and this is reflected by the changing agenda of the Court of Appeal. Like the Privy Council, the Court of Appeal heard a very small number of human rights cases before the enactment of the HKBORO. In 1981 and 1986, for example, human rights cases only accounted for 2 percent and 5 percent of the total number of cases involving the government as

5 *Attorney General of Hong Kong* v. *Ng Yuen Shiu* [Privy Council 1983].
6 *Mak Yui Ming and Others* v. *The Attorney General* [Privy Council 1983].
7 *Attorney General of Hong Kong* v. *Lee Kwong-kut* [Privy Council 1993].
8 *Attorney General of Hong Kong* v. *Lo Chak-man and Another* [Privy Council 1993].
9 *Chan Chi Hung* v. *The Queen* [Privy Council 1995]. *Ming Pao Newspapers Limited and Others* v. *The Attorney General of Hong Kong* [Privy Council 1996].

a litigating party that the Court of Appeal heard (see column 3 in Table 1.2). The promulgation of the HKBORO, however, changes this situation. Human rights cases have increased significantly, and in 1994 they took up 23 percent of the total number of cases involving the government as a litigating party, much higher than the corresponding figure a decade ago (see column 3 in Table 1.2). More importantly, political activists used the HKBORO to launch politically salient litigation against the government. In 1994, veteran activist Lau San Ching challenged the government's decision to refuse his candidacy in the District Board elections, contending that the decision contravened the HKBORO.[10]

In 1995, another political group – United Ants – challenged the undemocratic political system through the HKBORO.[11] United Ants argued that by providing some voters with two votes in the legislative elections, the functional constituency arrangement in the legislature, violated article 21 of the HKBORO which guarantees universal and equal suffrage.[12] This case represented the first attempt by political activists in Hong Kong to democratize the political system through legal mobilization. The litigation outcome had a potentially far-reaching and destabilizing impact on political development, given that the Basic Law stipulates that functional constituency arrangement will be continued after the sovereignty transition.[13]

[10] Lau, a member of the Marxist, radical April 5th Action Group, has been a political activist since he was a college student in the early 1970s. In 1981, Lau was arrested for a counter-revolutionary offence while visiting the relatives of democratic activists in China. He was imprisoned in China until 1991. He was rejected by the election officer for standing as a candidate in the 1994 District Board elections because he had not resided in Hong Kong for the ten years immediately preceding the date of his nomination. Lau argued that this qualification was contrary to the Bill of Rights (article 21), which stipulates that there shall be no unreasonable restrictions on the right of a candidate to stand for election. See *Lau San Ching* v. *Appollonia Liu* [Court of Appeal 1994].

[11] United Ants, formed by a dozen political activists in the early 1990s, advocated universal and equal suffrage. Its members mainly came from the election campaign teams of pro-democracy legislator Emily Lau and Amnesty International Hong Kong. Law Yuk-kai, who is also the Director of the Hong Kong Human Rights Monitor, was its spokesperson. Author's interview with Law Yuk-kai, February 15, 2008.

[12] *Lee Miu Ling and Another* v. *The Attorney General* [Court of Appeal 1995].

[13] Recognizing the potentially destabilizing effect of the litigation on the political system and the sovereignty transition, in hearing the United Ants' application for leave to appeal, some judges of the Judicial Committee of the Privy Council asked

To summarize, by creating a broader legal framework for society to challenge the government through the judiciary, the HKBORO provided a favorable condition for legal mobilization in Hong Kong in the late colonial period. Apart from the HKBORO, the sovereignty transition also opened up another important legal opportunity – the implementation of the Basic Law.

THE BASIC LAW

After China resumed sovereignty over Hong Kong in July 1997, the Basic Law became Hong Kong's constitution. Compared to the Letters Patent and the Royal Instructions, the Basic Law has more comprehensive provisions of civil and political rights and socio-economic relationships. Article 39 stipulates that the provisions of the ICCPR and the International Covenant on Economic, Social and Cultural Rights as applied to Hong Kong will remain in effect after the sovereignty handover. It also has a whole chapter on the protection of fundamental political and civil rights, and the scope of protection is much broader than those contained in the HKBORO.[14] In addition to political and civil rights, the Basic Law provides extensive provisions of economic and social policies, ranging from public finance, trade, education, culture, labor to social services. These comprehensive constitutional provisions open up numerous legal opportunities for citizens to pursue their interests through the courts, because, as Ghai notes, "questions of fiscal policies, education ... just to give a few examples can be constitutional questions" (Ghai, 1999, p. 306).

Together with the HKBORO, the numerous rights elaborated in the Basic Law open up more legal opportunities for the public to use the law to challenge the government in three ways. First, these two constitutional documents give more power to the courts, as judges are responsible for interpreting and enforcing the newly expanded rights and freedoms. Second, the new constitution guarantees citizens with a variety of rights which they did not enjoy before. These

the United Ants' lawyers what would happen to the legislature and future political development in Hong Kong if the appeal succeeded. Author's interview with Law Yuk-kai, February 15, 2008.

[14] For example, Articles 24, 31, and 33 stipulate the right of abode, the right to travel, and freedom of choice of occupation respectively. See The Basic Law of the Hong Kong Special Administrative Region of the People's Republic of China.

constitutional rights in turn establish the legal basis for the public to sue the government. The right of abode of mainland-born children of Hong Kong permanent residents and the housing rights lawsuits illuminate the importance of the new legal opportunities provided by the Basic Law.

In the right of abode cases, a non-governmental organization (NGO) activist who organized the litigation remarked that:

> Many parents of these mainland-born children sought our assistance to help their children to get the right of abode in Hong Kong several years before the sovereignty handover. However, we could not take legal action against the government at that time because we had no legal basis. The Basic Law, which granted these mainland-born children the right of abode here, took effect only after July 1, 1997. Before that date, mainland-born children of Hong Kong permanent residents did not have the right of abode here. Therefore what we could do before July 1997 was preparation for the litigation if the SAR government refused to grant the right of abode to mainland-born children of Hong Kong permanent residents.[15]

In the litigation for the right to public housing for Chinese migrant families in 1999, a social worker who organized the lawsuit also claimed that, "Without the Basic Law, we would not have the legal basis to challenge the government's discriminatory housing policy through the court. Instead, we could only apply political and social pressure to push the government to change its policy."[16]

Finally, the HKBORO and the Basic Law have created crucial opportunities for cause lawyers to use their expertise to represent individuals and social groups in the courts. Chapter 7 will examine the roles cause lawyers played in legal mobilization in post-colonial Hong Kong. Here a comment by Martin Lee, a prominent cause lawyer, partly illuminates how the HKBORO and the Basic Law have provided favorable conditions for cause lawyering. Lee noted that:

> Without the HKBORO and the Basic Law that guarantee important rights and freedoms, it would have been extremely difficult for me to defend citizens whose rights have been infringed by the government.

[15] Author's interview with Sze Lai-shan, community organizer of the Society for Community Organization, December 19, 2007.

[16] Author's interview with Wong Kwok-kei, Supervisor of Social Service Head Office, Evangelical Lutheran Church of Hong Kong. December 19, 2007.

> What would have been the legal basis for suing the government? In an undemocratic state like Hong Kong, the government has numerous powers to pass a draconian law which violates civil rights.[17]

A NEW FINAL APPELLATE COURT

The sovereignty transition also brought important institutional changes in the judicial branch by the setting up of a new final appellate court in Hong Kong – the Court of Final Appeal (CFA). Since July 1997, the Judicial Committee of the Privy Council (JCPC) no longer hears any appeal from Hong Kong. The following sections systematically assess the role of courts in generating the conditions of legal mobilization. First, we examine how two salient institutional features of the CFA – geographical proximity and the practice of inviting one overseas non-permanent judge to sit on every case – have promoted legal mobilization.

Geographical proximity

Socio-legal scholars like Black (1973, p. 140) noted that physical proximity to legal institutions is an important determinant for citizens' ability to mobilize the law. Throughout the colonial period, the JCPC in London served as the final appellate court of Hong Kong. The geographical remoteness of the JCPC to Hong Kong had significantly weakened the viability of using it to challenge the government for two major reasons. First, compared to the CFA, it was much more costly to litigate before the JCPC. When litigants from Hong Kong wanted to bring a case to the JCPC, they had to first hire a local law firm. The local law firm then instructed lawyers in Britain to conduct the litigation. Hong Kong law firms usually did not handle the litigation themselves because the majority of them had no branch in Britain.[18] More important, it was more convenient for lawyers in Britain to carry out the work. As Justice Bokhary pointed out, "Counsel in Britain could simply take the subway to the JCPC, whereas counsel in Hong Kong had to take a long and expensive flight to London to conduct litigation."[19] The practice of hiring lawyers in Britain to bring

17 Author's interview with Martin Lee, February 20, 2008.
18 Author's interview with barrister B in Hong Kong, February 19, 2008.
19 Author's interview with Justice Kemal Bokhary, February 28, 2008.

litigation to the JCPC deterred legal mobilization in colonial Hong Kong in a number of ways.

First, the litigation expense was duplicated, as litigants had to pay for both Hong Kong and London's lawyers. By contrast, it is less costly to bring a case to the CFA because litigants only need to pay for local lawyers. According to an experienced barrister, "after the sovereignty handover, the litigation expense at the CFA is only a fraction of that before July 1997."[20] Moreover, given that lawyers in Britain were often assigned to arguing before the JCPC, Hong Kong's lawyers were less likely to develop expertise in constitutional litigation. This made it more difficult to build up a competent team of local cause lawyers.[21] However, with the setting up of the CFA, local lawyers have taken up most of the litigation work before the final appellate court, especially in human rights and public policy cases. The expanded opportunities to practice help to nurture an experienced team of cause lawyers for legal mobilization.

Second, the geographical remoteness of the JCPC from Hong Kong undermined legal mobilization in the colonial era by making it more difficult for social groups to use the court to pursue their cause. Due to the enormous traveling and accommodation costs, social activists could not afford to attend the JCPC proceedings in person. This in turn deprived them of the opportunity of working closely with their English legal team to make informed choices about the preparation and strategy of their litigation. The experience of the United Ants' endeavor to challenge the functional electoral system in the legislature through the JCPC is a case in point. After losing in the Hong Kong Court of Appeal, the United Ants applied to the JCPC for leave to appeal. However, they did not send any members to attend the application proceeding in London because of the tremendous cost involved. Thus, the social activists had few opportunities to work closely with their English counsel and make informed choices throughout the litigation process. For example, they could not work together with counsel to develop an appropriate strategy in response to their opponents during the hearing. These activists even did not know that the JCPC had finished hearing their

20 Author's interview with barrister B in Hong Kong, February 19, 2008.
21 Author's interview with Justice Kemal Bokhary, February 28, 2008.

application.[22] This undermined the effectiveness of mobilizing the law to challenge the government.

By expanding access for social activists and more broadly for the public, the establishment of the CFA in Hong Kong after the sovereignty transition has generated favorable conditions for legal mobilization. It becomes much easier for the public to use the final appellate court to pursue their goals. For one thing, they no longer need to travel to London to appeal, hear the judicial proceedings, and discuss the litigation strategy with English lawyers. A senior official in the Department of Justice (DoJ) noted that:

> Hong Kong has its own final appellate court after July 1997. Geographical proximity of the CFA has made it more convenient for citizens to use the court to promote their cause. The CFA is just one station away from the Department of Legal Aid. After going to the Department of Legal Aid to apply for legal aid to sue the government, citizens then simply take the train to the CFA to lodge their application for leave to appeal.[23]

Additionally, geographical proximity has enabled social activists to use the CFA more effectively to advance their goals. The experience of a veteran activist-cum-legislator, Leung Kwok-hung, can illustrate this point. Since the sovereignty handover, Leung has filed important human rights and public policy litigation against the government in the CFA[24] and the lower courts. Instead of hiring lawyers to represent himself, Leung usually argued on his own. Through self-defense Leung wanted to use court hearings to advocate his cause and highlight the inadequacy of the political and social systems. Leung remarked that lawyers would only analyze and argue from the legal perspective. Through self-defense in the court and media coverage of the hearings, Leung would like to remind both judges and society of important macro issues like social justice and democracy. As highlighted by Leung:

> In my challenge to the Public Order Ordinance which granted the police the power to reject applications for demonstrations out of the

[22] Author's interview with Law Yuk-kai, February 15, 2008.

[23] Author's interview with a senior official in the Department of Justice (official B), February 2008.

[24] See, for example, *Leung Kwok Hung and Others* v. *HKSAR* [Court of Final Appeal 2005]; *Koo Sze Yiu and Another* v. *Chief Executive of the HKSAR* [Court of Final Appeal 2006].

> need to preserve public order, during the court hearings I asked the judges the definition of national security. The judges failed to give a clear answer. As the judges who are well educated in law could not even answer this question adequately, I challenged the government on what basis they let the police decide whether a particular demonstration would threaten public order. I hoped that through media coverage of the court proceedings, my arguments in the court could raise public awareness of political and social justice.[25]

Situated in Hong Kong, the establishment of a final appellate court in the post-colonial period provides favorable conditions for Leung to use court hearings to promote his cause. If the JCPC still served as the final appellate court of Hong Kong, it would have been enormously difficult for Leung and other social activists to fly there frequently to argue their cases.[26]

Overseas non-permanent judges

The practice of inviting one overseas non-permanent judge to sit on every case in the CFA has encouraged legal mobilization by boosting public confidence in the independence and credibility of the CFA. In setting up the CFA, the number of overseas judges that can be allowed in each substantive hearing was a contentious issue. Like its policy towards the executive and legislative branches, Beijing sought to restrict foreign influence in the judiciary, especially in the CFA. Although the British government, the Bar Association, and civil society in Hong Kong argued that more than one overseas judge could sit in each hearing, Beijing finally only allowed one overseas judge (Lo 2000).

Chan (2009) notes that the replacement of the well-respected JCPC by the CFA had highlighted the need for the latter to build up its reputation. Seeking to enhance the Court's credibility and competency, the Chief Justice Andrew Li Kwok-nang has taken great efforts to set up a distinguished panel of overseas non-permanent

[25] Author's interview with Leung Kwok-hung, January 3, 2008.

[26] It should be noted that the cost of using the courts only constitutes a necessary but insufficient condition for legal mobilization under authoritarianism. Legal mobilization fails to happen in many authoritarian countries, where citizens can file lawsuits against the government *locally*. Accordingly, we have to study other factors like the support structure and the receptivity of the judiciary to human rights arguments.

judges.[27] The Chief Justice also adopted a practice that an overseas non-permanent judge will sit in almost every substantive hearing before the CFA. These overseas judges come from other common law jurisdictions and are holding or had held prestigious positions in their home countries like judges of the Supreme Court of the United Kingdom. A number of them, notably Sir Anthony Mason and Lord Woolf of Barnes, were famous for their liberal stance in safeguarding the rights of the disadvantaged.[28]

The setting up of a distinguished panel of foreign judges to hear appeals before the CFA has enhanced public confidence in the impartiality and credibility of the new final appellate court. This public confidence is critical to successful legal mobilization. If citizens perceive that the courts are not fair in arbitrating their disputes with the government, this perception of unfairness is likely to undermine their incentive to use the judicial branch to pursue their cause.[29] The comment by the former chairman of the Society for Protection of the Harbour demonstrates how important public confidence in the court is to legal mobilization. Chu remarked that:

[27] For example, shortly after the sovereignty handover, the Chief Justice sought the approval of the Lord Chancellor of Britain to invite serving judges of the Privy Council to be CFA overseas non-permanent judges. Angela Li, "Stage set for final court's debut," *South China Morning Post*, July 26, 1997, p. 1; Charlotte Parsons, "British Law Lords to sit in top court," *South China Morning Post*, September 9, 1997, p. 4.

[28] Sir Anthony Mason was the Chief Justice of the High Court of Australia from 1987 to 1995 and was appointed as an overseas non-permanent judge of the CFA in 1997. Under his leadership, the High Court of Australia made varying liberal decisions. In *Australian Capital Television Pty Ltd* v. *Commonwealth* (1992), for example, the Mason court asserted the right to freedom of political communication. Lord Woolf served as the Chief Justice of England and Wales between 2000 and 2005 and was appointed as an overseas non-permanent judge of the CFA in 2003. In his judicial career, Woolf had stood up to both Labor and Tory home secretaries on important human rights issues. For example, in 2004 he opposed the government's Clause 11 of the Asylum and Immigration (Treatment of Claimants) Bill, which attempts to prevent the courts from hearing a legal challenge to a decision of an immigration tribunal, even if there is an error of law, unfair procedure, or human rights violation. See David Pannick, "Asylum: an abuse of power that would embarrass even Mugabe," *The Times*, February 24, 2004, p. 4; "The accused profile: Lord Woolf our highest ranking judge finds himself pilloried in the press for his stand on civil rights," *The Sunday Telegraph*, March 7, 2004, p. 25.

[29] However, citizens may still use litigation to pursue their interests if they perceive other institutions as more unfair than the courts.

> When we considered suing the government over the reclamation of the Victoria Harbor in 2003, we were worried that local judges might be biased towards the government. However, as we expected that the litigation would be ultimately brought to the CFA, we were confident that the overseas non-permanent judge would play a very critical role in monitoring whether other local CFA judges had biased towards the government.[30]

AN INDEPENDENT AND ASSERTIVE JUDICIARY

The previous discussion identified two components of the new legal opportunity structure: the HKBORO and the Basic Law. However, neither of them is purely institutional – the new tools have to be used actively by judges in response to cases brought by aggrieved parties. The remaining parts of this chapter examine how the independence of the judiciary and its demonstrated records in using the new legal opportunities to protect civil and political rights have made it a viable and credible institution through which pro-democracy and progressive social forces pursue their interests. First, I examine why and how the judiciary enjoys a higher level of independence from Beijing, when compared with the executive and the legislature. Second, I discuss role conceptions among judges in Hong Kong. Third, I analyze the judiciary's performance in safeguarding civil and political rights and its liberal policies, which in turn have facilitated legal mobilization.

Judicial independence

The Chinese government has retained tight control over both the executive and legislative branches in post-colonial Hong Kong. Like the colonial governor who was a loyal agent to London, the Chief Executive also owes his loyalty to Beijing. An 800-member Election Committee, which is constituted primarily by the business sector and pro-China figures, is responsible for choosing the Chief Executive. Beijing wields the power to appoint and dismiss the Chief Executive, which ensures that only the candidate who is favored and trusted by Beijing can become and hold the position.[31] The Chief Executive

[30] Author's interview with Winston Chu, former chairman of the Society for Protection of the Harbour, November 6, 2007.

[31] In March 2005, Beijing forced the former Chief Executive Tung Chee-hwa to resign, because Tung failed to govern Hong Kong effectively.

forms his cabinet by nominating senior government officials and prominent public figures for Beijing's approval. The Chinese authorities have also exerted significant influence over the legislature through their agents and allies in Hong Kong. The largest political party in post-colonial legislature, the Democratic Alliance for the Betterment and Progress of Hong Kong (DAB), is Beijing's flagship party. Furthermore, the functional constituency seats in the legislature, which are elected by a small number of electors and represent mainly the richest and most privileged economic sectors, have enabled the Chinese government and its conservative business alliance in Hong Kong to dominate the legislature.

Compared with the executive and legislative branches, the judiciary is more insulated from the influence of the Chinese authorities for three reasons. First, Beijing has little influence over the appointment of judges. As mentioned previously, judges are appointed by the Chief Executive in accordance with the advice of the Judicial Officers Recommendation Commission (JORC). JORC's choices are based on the candidates' proven competence, integrity and professional qualities.

Second, the Basic Law sets up institutional mechanisms to protect the security of tenure of judges. A judge may only be removed by the Chief Executive for inability to discharge his or her duties or for misbehavior. Before the Chief Executive can dismiss a judge, he has to get the recommendation from a judicial tribunal appointed by the Chief Justice and obtain the legislature's endorsement. Secure tenure prevents Beijing and its agent in Hong Kong (the Chief Executive) from removing unsubmissive judges. Thus, even though both Beijing and the Tung Chee-hwa administration thought that the CFA rulings in various politically charged cases significantly undermined their interests (see below), they could not remove any CFA judges.

Third, the post-1997 judiciary, especially the upper courts, are still staffed primarily by expatriates. It is more difficult for Beijing to co-opt foreign judges, who have a strong belief in the rule of law and/or links with prestigious judicial institutions in liberal democracies.[32] The Basic Law (Article 93) allows all judges who served in Hong Kong before the handover to continue in office after July 1997. There is no

[32] For example, Justice Kemal Bokhary (a CFA permanent judge) is an honorary bencher of the Honorable Society of the Middle Temple, one of the four Inns of Court in London.

nationality restriction for judges except for two positions – the Chief Justice and the Chief Judge of the High Court. As of June 2008, two out of three permanent judges of the CFA are foreign nationals and over half of the High Court judges are non-Chinese.[33]

Summing up, the Basic Law has established various institutional measures to protect the judiciary from undue interference of Beijing and the Chief Executive. The protection provides the necessary basis for the judiciary, especially the CFA, to serve as a committed defender of political and civil rights. The following sections discuss how the judiciary has actively exercised the powers provided by the HKBORO and the Basic Law to advance political and civil rights.

Role conceptions of the Hong Kong judiciary

In his comparative study of the impact of the bills of rights on judicial behavior in Canada and Israel, Dotan (2005) maintains that the content of a bill of rights is not a sufficient condition for a shift in judicial behavior. A bill of rights only empowers courts to safeguard certain rights, but courts may not actively exercise the new constitutional power. Instead, Dotan finds that judicial ideology is an equal, if not more important, determinant of judicial behavior. An ideologically supportive judiciary, for example, greatly facilitated women's rights litigation in Israel, despite the exclusion of such rights in the Israeli bill of rights.

In her research on the persistent failure of the Chilean judges to defend civil rights and rule of law principles, Hilbink (2007) also argues that the way judges define their role has critically influenced their behavior. As Hilbink notes:

> the ideal of apoliticism furnished judges with understandings and incentives that discouraged assertive behavior in defense of rights and rule of law principles ... Chilean judges were trained to be 'slaves of the law' ... in which law, particularly public law, was understood as the will of the executive. Judges were expected to defer to the other branches of government.

Indeed, the foregoing judicial thinking had also rendered judges in various civil law and common law countries (e.g., post-war Japan and

[33] As of June 2008, the Court of Appeal and the Court of First Instance together have thirty-six judges and twenty of them are non-Chinese.

South Africa) unwilling and unable to assertively safeguard human rights (Hilbink 2007, pp. 225–6, 232).

Given the importance of judicial ideology to judicial behavior, we should examine how judges in Hong Kong interpret their role. Analysis of court judgments, judges' public speeches, and my interviews with two senior judges indicate that judges (especially the CFA judges) generally interpret their role as guardians of fundamental rights and freedoms and the rule of law. In *Ng Ka Ling and Another* v. *The Director of Immigration*, the CFA declared that the judiciary has the constitutional jurisdiction to review the legality of legislation and executive acts and to invalidate those inconsistent with the constitution.[34] In short, the judiciary serves as a constitutional check on the executive and legislative branches (*Ng Ka Ling*, paragraphs 59–62).[35] This role conception contravenes Beijing's long-held view that Hong Kong should not adopt a checks-and-balances political system. A series of liberal judgments (see next section) have further worried Beijing that the judiciary may undermine the executive-led political system in Hong Kong. Accordingly, since July 1997, the Chinese government has reiterated that Hong Kong cannot establish the separation of powers principle and that the judicial branch should have a cooperative working relationship with the executive. Some mainland legal scholars have even claimed that Hong Kong's courts do not have the power of constitutional review.[36]

The judiciary has not yielded to the pressure, however. The first Chief Justice, Andrew Li Kwok-nang, argues that the courts' power of

[34] *Ng Ka Ling and Another* v. *The Director of Immigration* [Court of Final Appeal 1999].

[35] The CFA's emphasis of the judiciary's checks-and-balances function was also indicated by the Chief Justice's invitation of Lord Irvine of Lairg (Lord Chancellor of Britain) to deliver a speech in Hong Kong in 1998. In his speech, Lord Irvine discussed the importance of the separation of powers and the role of the judiciary in advancing human rights and democracy in Britain. See *Ta Kung Pao*, September 19, 1998, p. A7.

[36] In June 2007, Wu Bangguo, head of the Chinese legislature, stated that the Chief Executive must play a dominant role in Hong Kong's political system, and that Hong Kong should not establish the separation of powers system. Denise Hung, "NPC warns on HK autonomy," *South China Morning Post*, June 7, 2007, p. A1. A year later, China's vice-president, Xi Jinping, asserted that the executive, legislative, and judicial branches should have mutual understanding and support each other in order to maintain Hong Kong's stability. Ambrose Leung, "Xi tells Tsang to govern sensibly," *South China Morning Post*, July 8, 2008, p. A1.

constitutional review has been entrenched and that the Basic Law has fully guaranteed judicial independence and its separation from other branches of government.[37] The Chief Justice's responses reflect his widely recognized liberal ideology and independent mind.[38] The Chief Justice's conception of the judicial role is shared by many of his colleagues. Justice Kemal Bokhary, a CFA permanent judge, contends that a judiciary's highest duty is constitutional stewardship (Bokhary 2007, p. 126) and that the real danger to the common law is judicial inactivism (Bokhary 2004, p. 136). As Justice Bokhary remarked, "Courts have the constitutional role to review whether the government's actions and legislation are consistent with the constitution, and to adjudicate disputes over power relationships among different branches of government."[39]

What is more, Justice Bokhary believes that courts have a positive role to play in an undemocratic political system. As he mentioned:

> Democracy in Hong Kong has a long way to go. This shortfall in democracy may prompt citizens to come to the courts to address their concerns, which may in turn put additional burden on the courts. The CFA is willing to accept that heavier burden.[40]

Finally, Justice Michael Hartmann highlights the judiciary's checks-and-balances function as well, asserting that:

> It is not necessarily a bad thing for citizens and social groups increasingly going to courts to challenge the government. Because under the

[37] See Andrew Li Kwok-nang's interviews with *Ming Pao*, June 15, 2007, p. A2 and *South China Morning Post*, June 15, 2007, p. A1.

[38] The first Chief Justice, Andrew Li Kwok-nang, was admitted to practice in Hong Kong in 1973 and designated as a Queen's Counsel in 1988. He had served as a deputy High Court judge and as a member of the Executive Council during the late colonial era. Li's liberal ideology has been recognized within the legal community. As pointed out by Denis Chang, a cause lawyer and a former chairman of the Hong Kong Bar Association, Li appreciates that judges have to learn human rights culture. Li's colleague in the Executive Council, Felice Lieh Mak, commented that Li is liberal on issues concerning civil liberties and rights, but more conservative on economic matters. Christopher Chan Cheuk (a former Law Society president) and Yash Ghai (an emeritus law professor at the University of Hong Kong) also agreed that the first Chief Justice has a liberal and independent mind. See "Ability to administer crucial warns top solicitor," *South China Morning Post*, May 21, 1997, p. 6; Ghai (2007b, p. 10).

[39] Author's interview with Justice Kemal Bokhary, February 28, 2008.

[40] Author's interview with Justice Kemal Bokhary, February 28, 2008.

> constitution, courts have an obligation to safeguard fundamental human rights and to check whether the government has acted according to law.[41]

The foregoing conception of the judicial role is not confined to individual judges. The CFA and the lower courts have actively relied on international human rights treaties, international human rights judgments, and commentaries by international treaty monitoring bodies in hearing and deciding civil and political rights cases. As pointed out by Petersen (2007, pp. 34–9), this active embrace of a universal standard of civil liberties has often put the government on the losing side of litigation.[42] Indeed, Hong Kong's courts are more progressive than their British counterparts in using several international human rights treaties (e.g., the Convention on the Elimination of All Forms of Discrimination against Women) in constitutional interpretation. More important, the courts have rejected government arguments that would discourage judges from adopting emerging international jurisprudence (Petersen 2007, pp. 38, 43).

It should be noted that the receptivity of the judiciary to human rights arguments varies by the category of rights. Although the judiciary is assertive in defending civil and political rights, it is relatively reluctant to assume an active role with respect to social and economic rights. The judiciary's conservative stance toward social and economic rights is illustrated by its judgments of the following cases: minimum wage,[43] public housing rental policy,[44] privatization of retail and parking facilities within public housing estates,[45] and

[41] Author's interview with Justice Michael Hartmann, March 5, 2008.

[42] Prominent examples include: *Leung TC William Roy* v. *Secretary for Justice* [Court of First Instance 2005] (gay rights); *HKSAR* v. *Hung Chan Wa and Another* [Court of Final Appeal 2006] (presumption of innocence); and *Yeung May Wan and Others* v. *HKSAR* [Court of Final Appeal 2005] (right to public assembly).

[43] In *Chan Noi Heung and Others* v. *The Chief Executive in Council* [Court of First Instance 2007], the Court of First Instance rejected the plaintiffs' demand for enactment of a minimum wage law.

[44] In *Ho Choi Wan* v. *Hong Kong Housing Authority* [Court of Final Appeal 2005], the Court of Final Appeal upheld the government's policy of refusing to reduce rents for public housing in times of deflation.

[45] In *Lo Siu Lan* v. *Hong Kong Housing Authority* [Court of Final Appeal 2005], the Court of Final Appeal upheld the government's policy of privatizing the retail and parking facilities within public housing estates.

the right of mainland spouses of Hong Kong residents to subsidized public hospital services.[46]

To sum up, judges in Hong Kong generally define their role as guardians of civil and political rights and the rule of law. The following section discusses how this role definition has prompted them to actively and assertively defend civil and political rights and the rule of law principles in the courts.

Judicial assertiveness in safeguarding civil and political rights

After reviewing the judiciary's role conception, I examine whether judges have lived up to their role conception in exercising their power. I argue that the judiciary, led by the CFA, has assertively defended individual rights and freedoms since July 1997. The track record of the judiciary as a rights protector has encouraged the public to mobilize the law.

When Hong Kong became a Special Administrative Region of China in July 1997, the CFA was a new institution and it was uncertain how an independent judiciary would function under a non-democratic regime. In the right-of-abode litigation, the CFA positioned itself as a guardian of the rights of the disadvantaged, the rule of law, and Hong Kong's high degree of autonomy (Tai 2002, p. 190; Chen 2006, pp. 634–5). The CFA showed that it was neither a Beijing nor a Tung Chee-hwa court. In *Ng Ka Ling and Another* v. *The Director of Immigration*, mainland-born children of Hong Kong permanent residents claimed that they had the right of abode in Hong Kong under the Basic Law.[47] They challenged the legality of the Provisional Legislative Council (PLC)[48] to amend the Immigration Ordinance restricting their right of abode. They contended that the Basic Law had not mentioned the establishment of a PLC and therefore the latter was not legally constituted. As the PLC was established in

46 In *Fok Chun Wa and Another* v. *The Hospital Authority and Another* [Court of First Instance 2008], the Court of First Instance upheld the government's policy of charging the market rate for mainland spouses of Hong Kong residents who use public hospital services.

47 *Ng Ka Ling and Another* v. *The Director of Immigration* [Court of Final Appeal 1999].

48 Protesting against Governor Patten's unilateral introduction of democratic reforms to Hong Kong in 1994, the Chinese government abolished the legislature and set up a Provisional Legislative Council (PLC) after July 1997. I will elaborate on the PLC in Chapter 5.

accordance with the decision of the Standing Committee of the National People's Congress (NPCSC, Chinese legislature), the CFA had to decide whether such legislative act of the NPCSC was consistent with the Basic Law.

The CFA ruled in favor of the appellants. What is more, the CFA made two decisions which signaled that it was an institution through which the disadvantaged might effectively pursue their goals. First, the CFA struck down the section of the Immigration Ordinance which denied the right of abode to mainland-born illegitimate children whose fathers were Hong Kong permanent residents.[49] Thus, even though they are not the majority in the legislature, pro-democracy forces and the disadvantaged in future may use the courts to contest laws or policies they oppose. Second, the CFA declared that the Hong Kong courts have jurisdiction to examine whether any legislative acts of the National People's Congress (NPC) are consistent with the Basic Law and to invalidate those found to be inconsistent.[50] This decision directly challenged Beijing's political authority because the Chinese Constitution states that all political powers are vested in the NPC (at least on paper).

The CFA's second decision provoked Beijing, however. Beijing criticized the CFA for putting itself above the national government by asserting its power to review the legislative acts of the NPC. A few months after *Ng Ka Ling*, the Tung Chee-hwa administration asked the Chinese government to refer the relevant Basic Law provisions to the NPCSC for interpretation. In June 1999, the NPCSC issued its interpretation, which overturned the CFA's ruling of *Ng Ka Ling* and reiterated that under Article 158 of the Basic Law, Hong Kong's courts are required to seek an interpretation from the NPCSC when the

[49] The CFA's liberal decision was beyond the expectations of the litigants. There were three categories of litigants: (i) those who were born *before* their parents became Hong Kong permanent residents; (ii) those who were born *after* at least one of their parents became such residents; (iii) illegitimate children. The Society for Community Organization (SoCO), the rights advocacy group which organized the litigation, initially anticipated that the first and third groups had a slim chance of winning. Accordingly, before the CFA announced its judgment, SoCO contacted the Director of Immigration to plan the deportation arrangements for the first and third groups of litigants. See *Hong Kong Economic Journal*, February 4, 1999, p. 13.

[50] During the colonial period, the courts in Hong Kong could not question the acts of the British government under the doctrine of British sovereignty. See Cottrell and Ghai (2001, pp. 219–21).

litigation involves Basic Law provisions concerning the national government's responsibility or Beijing–HKSAR relationship.

The NPCSC interpretation illustrates the limit of Hong Kong's courts in safeguarding rights or advancing democracy. When the litigation involves Beijing's vital interests, the NPCSC rather than the CFA has the final say. After the NPCSC interpretation, the CFA retreated strategically from its bold assertion of judicial power over the Chinese authorities. As Yap (2007) notes, after the NPCSC interpretation, the CFA would always defer to Beijing when the litigation involves the validity of mainland Chinese law or NPCSC decisions.

The foregoing retreat, however, is the only major concession the CFA made to Beijing and the Tung Chee-hwa administration. After the NPCSC interpretation, the Hong Kong government had again requested the CFA to refer to the NPCSC for an interpretation of provisions of the Basic Law in four important cases.[51] Nevertheless, the CFA had skillfully resisted all requests with a view to preserving its freedom for constitutional interpretation and judicial independence (Lo 2007). The CFA's reluctance to cede its power of constitutional interpretation to Beijing is also reflected by the statements of two judges. Justice Bokhary mentioned that he hoped there would never be another reinterpretation of the Basic Law by Beijing. Justice Anthony Mason (an overseas non-permanent judge of the CFA) even wrote that, "There were no checks and balances on the powers of the NPCSC, an arrangement that was fraught with questions."[52]

The judiciary – led by the CFA – has continued to actively safeguard civil liberties and check against arbitrary government decisions. Table 4.1 reports how the Privy Council and the CFA disposed of cases that involved the government as a litigating party and particularly human rights litigation. In the period 1981–June 1997, the overall success rate of the government was 63 percent. However, the government's advantage has been eroded since July 1997. The CFA ruled in favor of the government in less than half (48 percent) of all cases (see column 2 in Table 4.1). Regarding human rights litigation,

[51] *HKSAR* v. *Ng Kung Siu and Another* [Court of Final Appeal 1999]; *Lau Kong Yung and Others* v. *The Director of Immigration* [Court of Final Appeal 1999]; *The Director of Immigration* v. *Chong Fung Yuen* [Court of Final Appeal 2001]; *Ng Siu Tung and Others* v. *The Director of Immigration* [Court of Final Appeal 2002].

[52] Ravina Shamdasani, "Judge hopes for no more Basic Law reinterpretations," *South China Morning Post*, February 18, 2002, p. 2.

citizens won 67 percent of cases during the colonial era (column 6 in Table 4.1). However, the absolute number of human rights cases (N=9) was too small to reach a robust conclusion. Between July 1997 and 2010, the CFA heard forty-eight human rights cases, and the larger size may allow us to draw a stronger conclusion concerning the CFA position toward civil liberties.

The CFA has served as a strong guardian of human rights. Regarding human rights litigation, the government won 42 percent and citizens 44 percent (see columns 5 and 6 in Table 4.1).[53] In other words, citizens have approximately a 50 percent chance of defeating the government in human rights litigation before the final appellate court. This is a very impressive record for an East Asian court, as the studies below show that the majority of the supreme or constitutional courts in East and Southeast Asian countries have a much less satisfactory performance in safeguarding human rights.

In Chapter 3 the poor record of China's courts in protecting human rights was discussed. In Japan, the Supreme Court has adopted a deferential stance toward the government in deciding human rights cases. The Court had struck down laws that violated human rights only four times from the late 1940s to the mid 2000s (Matsui 2006). In Singapore, the courts only play a limited role in human rights protection due to the narrow range of constitutional rights and the collectivist judicial ethos (Thio 2006). The Malaysian courts have also not served as effective guardians of human rights, as they have taken a submissive attitude toward the executive and the legislature (Lee 2006). In the post-Suharto Indonesia, varying structural limitations have made it difficult for the new Indonesian Constitutional Court to protect citizens' constitutional rights (Hendrianto 2010). Finally, from its establishment in 1998 to its overthrow by the 2006 military coup,

[53] The remaining 15 percent of human rights cases have partial results. Partial results refer to either of the following two situations. First, when there is more than one appellant, the court allows some appellants' appeals and dismisses others'. For example, in *Ng Siu Tung and Others* v. *The Director of Immigration* [Court of Final Appeal 2002], the CFA allowed the appeals of three appellants and rejected the other thirteen appellants'. Second, an appellant presents multiple claims and the court only allows some of them. In *Chau Ching Kay, Nauthum* v. *HKSAR* [Court of Final Appeal 2002], the appellant made two claims: his confessions to the police were not voluntary and the Court of Appeal's order for loss of time deprived his right to appeal. The CFA only accepted the appellant's second claim.

TABLE 4.1: Disposition of all types of cases and human rights cases by the Privy Council and the Court of Final Appeal (1981–2010)

Privy Council						
	All types of cases (81–Jul 1997) N=94			Human rights cases N=9		
	Government won	Government lost	Partial result	Government won	Government lost	Partial result
1981	2	2	0	0	0	0
1982	2	0	0	0	0	0
1983	3	2	0	1	1	0
1984	4	2	0	0	0	0
1985	1	1	0	0	0	0
1986	3	4	0	0	0	0
1987	7	1	0	0	0	0
1988	2	4	0	0	0	0
1989	2	1	0	0	0	0
1990	4	2	0	0	0	0
1991	3	2	0	0	0	0
1992	4	1	0	0	0	0
1993	5	2	0	1	2	0
1994	5	0	0	0	0	0
1995	3	1	1	1	0	0
1996	4	5	0	0	3	0
Jan–Jul 97	5	4	0	0	0	0
Total	**59** (63%)	**34** (36%)	**1** (1%)	**3** (33%)	**6** (67%)	**0** (0%)

Court of Final Appeal						
	All types of cases (Jul 97–2010) N=229			Human rights cases N=48		
	Government won	Government lost	Partial result	Government won	Government lost	Partial result
Jul–Dec 97	0	0	0	0	0	0
1998	2	2	1	1	0	1
1999	9	8	2	4	4	0
2000	7	9	0	0	1	0
2001	10	6	0	3	1	0
2002	8	5	3	3	3	3
2003	7	6	1	0	1	0
2004	6	12	1	1	2	1
2005	9	11	0	1	1	0
2006	12	9	4	3	2	1
2007	11	10	0	2	2	0
2008	12	6	1	2	1	1
2009	10	7	1	0	2	0
2010	7	11	3	0	1	0
Total	**110** (48%)	**102** (45%)	**17** (7%)	**20** (42%)	**21** (44%)	**7** (15%)

the Constitutional Court of Thailand failed to vigorously defend and enforce human rights (Harding 2010).

In East and Southeast Asia, perhaps only Taiwan's Council of Grand Justices and the Korean Constitutional Court may be measured up to Hong Kong's CFA regarding human rights protection.[54] The Council of Grand Justices and the Korean Constitutional Court have played an important role in promoting democratic development by striking down laws and government actions that violated human rights and democratic norms (Ginsburg 2003, 2010; Cooney 1999).

Indeed the CFA and the lower courts have made a series of important judgments protecting and expanding the following civil rights: the right to public participation; the right to equality; and freedom of assembly and procession. In *Secretary for Justice and Others* v. *Chan Wah and Others*, two non-indigenous villagers challenged the village representative electoral systems for denying them the right to vote and to stand as candidates.[55] The electoral arrangements only permitted indigenous villagers (i.e., those descended through the male line of an ancestor who was a resident of an established village in Hong Kong in 1898) to participate in village representative elections. The CFA declared that the electoral arrangements deprived non-indigenous villagers of the right to participate in public affairs through freely chosen representatives. The CFA's ruling caused the government to reform village representative elections by introducing legislation enabling indigenous and non-indigenous villagers to elect their own representatives.

The judiciary has also expanded rights protection to homosexuals and female students. In *Secretary for Justice* v. *Yau Yuk Lung Zigo and Another*, two homosexuals were charged with committing buggery in public.[56] The CFA held that the penal code which criminalized the defendants was unconstitutional because it discriminated against homosexuals. In *Leung TC William Roy* v. *Secretary for Justice*, the Court of Appeal held that a section of the Crimes Ordinance infringed homosexual rights to equality and privacy, because it set the minimum age for buggery at 21, whereas the minimum age for heterosexual

[54] Existing studies on the constitutional courts in Taiwan and Korea do not have comparative data on how often the governments lost human rights cases.

[55] *Secretary for Justice and Others* v. *Chan Wah and Others* [Court of Final Appeal 2000].

[56] *Secretary for Justice* v. *Yau Yuk Lung Zigo and Another* [Court of Final Appeal 2007].

intercourse was 16.[57] Finally, the Court of First Instance declared that the Broadcasting Authority had made a discriminatory ruling against a television program on homosexual marriage.[58]

The judiciary also struck down gender discrimination in the government's policy regarding the allocation of secondary school places to students completing primary school education. Under the policy, boys had a better chance of admission to a preferred secondary school than girls, even though they had equal academic achievements. The court held that the government's policy was discriminatory against female students and declared it unlawful.[59] What is more, the court demonstrated its receptivity to international human rights treaties by using the Convention on the Elimination of All Forms of Discrimination Against Women (CEDAW) as a guide in rejecting the government's defense, whereas judges in some foreign jurisdictions like Britain have been reluctant to adopt CEDAW as a guide to interpreting domestic gender discrimination (Petersen 2007, pp. 42–4).

The CFA has questioned the government's interpretation concerning public order in two politically charged cases and helped to safeguard freedom of assembly, demonstration, and communication. In *Yeung May Wan and Others* v. *HKSAR*, in 2002, a group of Falun Gong activists were convicted of obstructing a public place and assaulting police officers while holding a peaceful demonstration outside Beijing's highest representative office in Hong Kong.[60] The CFA quashed the activists' convictions and held that their right to peaceful assembly and demonstration should be given due protection.[61] The judgment is politically significant because it shows that the judiciary is willing to rigorously protect the civil rights of Beijing's enemies, even though the Tung Chee-hwa administration and pro-Beijing politicians had severely criticized the religious sect.[62]

[57] *Leung TC William Roy* v. *Secretary for Justice* [Court of Appeal 2006].

[58] *Cho Man Kit* v. *Broadcasting Authority* [Court of First Instance 2008]. See also Yvonne Tsui, "TV watchdog curbed free speech," *South China Morning Post*, May 9, 2008, p. A1.

[59] *Equal Opportunities Commission* v. *Director of Education* [Court of First Instance 2001].

[60] Falun Gong is an outlawed religious sect in China. In 1999, more than 10,000 Falun Gong members demonstrated peacefully outside the Chinese Communist Party's headquarters. Since then the Chinese government has severely persecuted the sect.

[61] *Yeung May Wan and Others* v. *HKSAR* [Court of Final Appeal 2005].

[62] In February 2001, Tung Chee-hwa declared Falun Gong as an evil cult.

TABLE 4.2: Citizens' confidence in various government institutions and political parties (%)

Number of interviewees who expressed "very confident" or "confident" (%)

	Mar 2001	Sep 2001	Feb 2002	Oct 2002	Mar 2003
Courts	337 (64.1)	417 (68.7)	427 (70.6)	462 (71.1)	438 (71.4)
Civil Service	322 (61.2)	282 (46.5)	325 (53.7)	311 (47.9)	284 (46.4)
Legislature	283 (53.8)	283 (46.7)	310 (51.2)	283 (43.5)	281 (45.8)
Executive	292 (55.5)	272 (44.8)	296 (48.9)	261 (40.2)	256 (41.8)
Political parties	158 (30.0)	172 (28.4)	169 (27.9)	193 (29.7)	183 (29.8)

Lingnan University of Hong Kong conducted the longitudinal telephone surveys.
Source: www.ln.edu.hk/pgp/pdf/RP03C1(3).pdf

In *Koo Sze Yiu and Another* v. *Chief Executive of the HKSAR*, two political activists challenged covert surveillance (wire-tapping) conducted by law enforcement agencies and the Chief Executive's order to authorize covert surveillance when public interests required.[63] The CFA held that the law and the executive order authorizing covert surveillance violated the constitutional freedom and privacy of communication. The judgment contributed to a comprehensive reform of the existing law on covert surveillance.

Public confidence in the judiciary and legal mobilization

The foregoing overview of important human rights judgments demonstrates that the judiciary, led by the CFA, has served as a guardian of the rule of law and human rights in post-colonial Hong Kong.[64] The courts' track record has made them the most trustworthy political institutions since the sovereignty handover. Tables 4.2 and 4.3 present

[63] *Koo Sze Yiu and Another* v. *Chief Executive of the HKSAR* [Court of Final Appeal 2006].

[64] Chen (2006, pp. 629–30) describes the courts' decisions in human rights litigation as moderately liberal – neither radically liberal nor conservative.

data on two longitudinal telephone surveys of the public evaluation of the performance of major political institutions in the first decade of the HKSAR. Both studies show that the public has generally given the judiciary the highest ratings. Moreover, the ratings of the judiciary have often been substantially higher than those of other institutions. In October 2006, for example, almost 60 percent of the respondents were satisfied with the performance of the judiciary, whereas the corresponding figures for civil service, the chief executive, and the legislature were 41 percent, 38 percent, and 21 percent respectively (see Table 4.3).

The high level of confidence in the courts has encouraged aggrieved citizens to mobilize the law to pursue their interests. The twenty-seven rights advocates and pro-democracy politicians that I interviewed (see Appendix 3) unanimously believe that, compared with other political institutions, the courts are more trustworthy and will handle their claims impartially and competently. As one social activist described:

> People in Hong Kong generally perceive social movements as radical. Given the high rating and legitimacy of the judiciary, however, social movements can minimize their radical images and legitimize their claims through using judicial review. If the government does not abide by the courts' rulings, it has to face the accusation of violation of the rule of law.[65]

The judiciary's liberal decisions also send signals to the minorities that the courts can be viable avenues for them to attain their objectives. Roddy Shaw, chairperson of Civil Rights for Sexual Diversities (CRSD), noted that the CFA's stance in the *Ng Ka Ling* case

[65] Author's interview with Andrew Shum, December 22, 2007. Shum is a core member of the Civil Human Rights Front and the Hong Kong Christian Student Movement. Indeed, legal mobilization not only enables social movement organizers to minimize their radical images but it also reduces their personal dangers and the risk of prosecution, especially in a semi-authoritarian regime like Hong Kong. Many social activists have argued that, compared to the colonial era, the post-colonial Hong Kong government is far more hostile to street protests and demonstrations. For example, they point out that the colonial government rarely prosecuted the arrested protestors, whereas the post-colonial government has increasingly prosecuted protestors. The validity of this claim requires verification. The point, however, is that the judiciary is a relatively safe channel through which social activists can pursue their goals in non-democracies. On the increasing frequency of the post-colonial government to prosecute protestors, see the environmental protection activist Chu Hoi-dick's column in *Ming Pao*, August 3, 2008.

TABLE 4.3: Citizens' satisfaction with the performance of government institutions (%) 1998–2006

Percentage of interviewees who said that they were satisfied with the performance of a government institution

	Judiciary	Civil service	Legislature	Chief Executive	Executive Council
Apr 1998	53.3	38.9	21	31.9	21.8
Oct 1998	59.1	35.4	26.4	25	19.7
Apr 1999	47.4	34.9	27.7	27.7	27.2
Nov 1999	43.7	28	21.1	22.5	19.2
Apr 2000	45.6	33.9	21.7	19.9	17.9
Oct 2000	39.4	32.3	19.4	18.3	12.4
Apr 2001	38.2	40.3	21.9	19.3	18
Nov 2001	43.3	36.2	21.6	12.6	14.5
Apr 2002	48.5	42.9	19.5	20.2	15
Oct 2002	46.1	37.3	19.7	13.4	14.2
Apr 2003	43.7	35.2	21.4	8.4	14.2
Oct 2003	40.4	33.3	15.8	8.5	12.8
Apr 2004	43.7	35.9	15.5	8.9	11
Oct 2004	52.3	42.4	18.7	15.8	13.9
Apr 2005	51.3	40.9	14.8	57.8	17.6
Oct 2005	50.7	42.8	19.7	61.8	21.5
Apr 2006	58.5	43.8	19.1	58.6	19.4
Oct 2006	59.7	41.4	21.2	38.6	17.5

The Hong Kong Institute of Asia-Pacific Studies of the Chinese University of Hong Kong conducted the longitudinal telephone surveys.
Source: Adapted from Wong and Wan (2007, p. 90).

significantly strengthened his confidence in going to the courts to pursue their cause.[66] The courts' favorable rulings on homosexual rights have also encouraged gay rights activists to keep using the law as their weapon. Joseph Cho Man-kit mentioned that Justice Michael Hartmann's liberal decision in *Leung TC William Roy* v. *Secretary for Justice*[67] significantly bolstered his confidence in the judiciary's sympathy with gay rights and therefore emboldened him to sue the Broadcasting Authority for discriminating against a gay marriage TV program.[68]

66 Author's interview with Roddy Shaw, December 21, 2007.
67 *Leung TC William Roy* v. *Secretary for Justice* [Court of First Instance 2005].
68 Author's interview with Joseph Cho Man-kit, November 20, 2007. Cho is a vice-president of the Hong Kong Ten Percent Club.

CONCLUSION

The promulgation of the HKBORO and the Basic Law which guarantee numerous rights and freedoms opened up important legal opportunities for citizens to mobilize the law after the sovereignty handover in July 1997. The actual impact of the two constitutional documents, however, depends heavily on the way judges interpret and apply them. The judiciary, led by the CFA, has actively used the HKBORO and the Basic Law to safeguard civil liberties and the rule of law in response to cases brought by aggrieved parties. The responsive judiciary has presented opportunities for legal mobilization.

However, legal mobilization is a costly and lengthy process and it often cannot bring the progressive socio-political change sought by activists (Rosenberg 1991). Before taking up the new legal opportunities, social actors may consider the opportunities and constraints of other institutions. If they find that it is feasible for them to advance their causes through other institutions (e.g., legislature or protests) or if they feel hopeless (Gaventa 1980), they may not use the legal opportunities. While opening up new legal opportunities, Hong Kong's reversion to Chinese sovereignty also significantly narrowed political opportunities in the post-colonial period. Chapter 5 studies how Beijing and the Tung Chee-hwa government dismantled the democratization programs introduced by the last governor, Christopher Patten, and restricted the political opportunities available to pro-democracy forces and civil society. I argue that these changes in the opportunities and constraints in the legal and political arenas have been a crucial factor in legal mobilization in post-1997 Hong Kong.

5

THE REVERSAL OF POLITICAL OPPORTUNITIES

This chapter examines how the sovereignty handover shifted political opportunities from the legislature to the judicial branch in post-1997 Hong Kong, as Beijing and the Tung Chee-hwa administration weakened the legislature and politically marginalized pro-democracy and grassroots forces. The last colonial governor, Christopher Patten, introduced faster democratization reforms to Hong Kong, which significantly expanded political opportunities. However, these new political opportunities were short-lived, because they were completely closed down by Beijing and the Tung Chee-hwa administration. Having been marginalized from the political arena, pro-democracy politicians and grassroots groups are increasingly turning to the more accessible legal arena and mobilizing the law to advance their goals. The pro-democracy politicians and social activists whom I interviewed unanimously claimed that a shift of political opportunities from the legislature to the judiciary in the post-handover era is *the* central motivation for them to mobilize the law.

This chapter proceeds as follows. First, it discusses the concept of political opportunities. Second, it studies how Patten's democratization reforms created new political opportunities for pro-democracy and grassroots forces in the final colonial years. The third part examines how Beijing and the Tung Chee-hwa government shut down political openings by weakening the legislature and marginalizing pro-democracy politicians from important power centers. The chapter concludes by highlighting how shifting political opportunities have prompted aggrieved parties, especially pro-democracy and grassroots groups, to advance their claims through the courts.

THE CONCEPT OF POLITICAL OPPORTUNITIES

In this book, political opportunities include three important dimensions: (1) the opening of access to political participation; (2) the presence of influential allies within the ruling elite; and (3) changing power relationships among political institutions (Tarrow 1998). Changes in political opportunities condition individuals' political calculations and strategies, specifically the institutions through which they choose to promote their cause.

The first dimension of political opportunities concerns the expansion of access to political participation for new actors. In democracies, this is typically expressed through elections. In non-democracies, the opening of access to participation is often associated with top-down, gradual political liberalization, such as the toleration of non-state organizations. The second aspect of political opportunities refers to the presence of influential allies among the governing elite. Civil society groups with important political allies within the governing elite generally enjoy greater protection of their interests. Thus, they are less likely to mobilize law or use non-institutionalized means like protests to pursue their cause. However, when their allies are weakened or lose power and no longer able to offer effective protection, these civil society groups may be forced to use other viable institutions to support their endeavors.

Changing power relationships among political institutions constitutes the last dimension of political opportunities. In post-colonial Hong Kong, a weakening of the power of the semi-democratically elected legislature vis-à-vis the executive has made it more difficult for pro-democracy groups and civil society to promote their cause through the legislature. Instead, they need to find alternative avenues, among which are courts, to advance their cause.

Hong Kong experienced abrupt changes in the development of political opportunities in the 1990s. In the last years of the colonial period, Governor Patten introduced democratic reforms which created more political opportunities for pro-democracy forces and civil society. These new opportunities, however, were entirely dismantled by Beijing and the Tung Chee-hwa government after the sovereignty handover. The next two sections examine these abrupt changes in political opportunities.

SHORT-TERM OPENING OF POLITICAL OPPORTUNITIES BY GOVERNOR PATTEN

Hong Kong did not have a democratic political system throughout most of its colonial history, as the Governor monopolized all important political powers. The colony had an executive-led political system, under which the Governor together with senior government officials controlled policy-making and implementation. In 1984, the British and Chinese governments signed the Sino-British Joint Declaration which stipulated that China would resume Hong Kong's sovereignty in July 1997. After settling the sovereignty issue, Britain (with Beijing's consensus) began to introduce gradual political reforms in Hong Kong. The main thrust of the reforms was to implement elections in the legislature. Before 1985, all legislative councilors were appointed by the Governor. In 1985, the colonial authorities introduced functional constituency elections through which various professional sectors elected their representatives to the legislature. However, functional constituency elections have a number of undemocratic elements.

First, only members of a profession have the right to vote and stand in elections, and the public are excluded. In the education sector, for example, teachers alone have the right to vote and stand in elections. Second, corporate voting is used in more than half of functional constituency elections (i.e., only employers have the right to vote and stand in elections). For instance, even though the banking sector in Hong Kong has a large working population, they are excluded from participating in electing their representative to the legislature. Third, the majority of functional constituency seats have been allocated to business sectors, which tend to oppose a faster pace of democratization. By contrast, the grassroots have merely got a small number of functional constituency seats.

The colonial government introduced geographical constituency elections (i.e., direct elections) to the legislature in 1991.[1] Each citizen casts one vote in the election. Benefiting from the strong

[1] In 1991, eighteen out of sixty seats in the legislature were filled by direct election. In 1995, the number of directly elected seats increased to twenty.

anti-Beijing sentiment in Hong Kong following the crackdown on the 1989 Tiananmen democracy movement, pro-democracy forces captured the majority of the directly elected seats in the 1991 legislative elections.

Summing up, in the second half of the 1980s and early 1990s, the British government partially opened up political opportunities in Hong Kong by expanding public participation in the legislative elections. The opening, however, had serious limitations. On the one hand, directly elected members accounted for merely one-third of all the legislators. Thus, although pro-democracy forces won the majority of the directly elected seats, they were still the minority in the legislature. On the other, only a very small group of the electorate was eligible to participate in functional constituency elections. This limited political participation was changed by Patten, the last Governor, who implemented more radical democratic reforms in Hong Kong.

After coming into office in 1992, Patten unilaterally introduced more radical democratic reforms in spite of Beijing's opposition.[2] By opening up numerous political opportunities, Patten's reforms enabled pro-democracy forces to attain an unprecedented influence in the legislature and more broadly in the political system.

First, in the 1995 legislative elections,[3] the reforms greatly expanded the franchise in functional constituency elections. All registered working populations in the nine newly added functional constituencies were given the right to vote and stand in elections, so as to make these elections more competitive and democratic.[4]

Second, an Election Committee was responsible for choosing ten legislators. The Basic Law, however, has not stipulated the composition of that Committee. To augment the democratic element in the legislature, Patten decided that the Election Committee would be mainly composed of directly elected District Board councilors.

Third, all appointed seats in the District Boards and the two municipal councils were abolished.[5] Finally, in 1993, Patten used his

[2] The discussion in the next two paragraphs is primarily based on Pepper (2002).

[3] In the 1995 legislative elections, all legislators were elected. The legislature was composed of thirty functional constituency seats, twenty directly elected seats, and ten Election Committee constituency seats.

[4] There were about one million voters in the nine newly added functional constituencies, which amounted to about one-sixth of the total population in Hong Kong.

[5] District Boards and the two municipal councils were responsible for advising and implementing the provision of public services at the local levels.

official power to appoint two prominent pro-democracy figures, Christine Loh[6] and Anna Wu, to the legislature. As will be discussed later, Loh and Wu played a leading role in passing two important laws, which provided the legal basis for legal mobilization in the post-1997 era.

Pro-democracy and grassroots interests were the major winners of the opening up of political opportunities by Patten. In the 1995 legislative election, for example, the expansion of franchise in the nine newly added functional constituency seats enabled them to win five out of nine seats.[7] In addition, pro-democracy parties also won three out of ten seats in the Election Committee elections. Overall, pro-democracy and grassroots interests captured half of the seats in the legislature.

After taking advantage of Patten's democratic reforms to significantly expand their influence in the legislature, pro-democracy forces used the legislature to advance grassroots interests and to improve the protection of civil rights. Three prominent cases are discussed here. First, legislators from the Confederation of Trade Unions initiated and passed a series of private member bills that sought to enhance the power of trade unions and promote housing rights for the lower class. Several liberal labor laws were enacted and provided labor unions with the following rights:[8] collective bargaining to negotiate for workers' compensation; to be consulted on changes to workers' employment terms and other business administration measures; and to claim against companies for anti-labor union discrimination. On housing rights, Leung Yiu-chung proposed the Housing (Amendment) Ordinance 1997, which greatly restricted the government's power to increase the rent of public housing.

Second, pro-democracy legislators took the lead in passing legislation that improved the protection of human rights and civil liberties. In spite of opposition from the colonial government, Anna Wu raised the Equal Opportunities Bill, which proposed the setting up of a

[6] When all appointed seats in the legislature were abolished in 1995, Loh ran for the 1995 legislative election and won in the geographical constituency election.

[7] They were Lee Cheuk-yan and Leung Yiu-chung (Confederation of Trade Unions); Tsang Kin-shing and Cheng Kar-foo (Democratic Party); and Elizabeth Wong. Tsang and Cheng were also members of the Confederation of Trade Unions.

[8] Trade Unions (Amendment) (No. 2) Ordinance 1997; Employee's Rights to Representation, Consultation and Collective Bargaining Ordinance; and Employment (Amendment) (No. 4) Ordinance 1997.

powerful Equal Opportunities Commission (EOC) to fight against discrimination.[9] After the legislature voted down the Equal Opportunities Bill, Wu put forward three private member's bills that tackled discrimination based on age, political affiliation, trade union membership, and religion. Although the bills were rejected, Wu's efforts prompted the government to enact three laws prohibiting sex, disability, and family status discrimination. Additionally, a less powerful EOC was set up and empowered to investigate and if necessary take legal action against discriminatory practices in both the public and private sectors.[10] The passage of three anti-discrimination laws and the establishment of the EOC opened up a new legal opportunity for post-colonial legal mobilization. In 2001, for example, the EOC forced the government to change a long-standing education policy through litigation. The Commission sued the Education Department's policy concerning the allocation of secondary school places to students completing primary education. Under the policy, boys had a better chance of being admitted to a preferred secondary school than girls, even if they had equal academic achievements. The court held that the policy violated the Sex Discrimination Ordinance and discriminated against female students.[11]

Third, environmental protection organizations made use of the opening up of the legislature to advance their cause. A case in point was the Society for the Protection of the Harbour (SPH), which advocated the passage of a law restricting the government's reclamation policies.[12] Formed in 1995, the major goal of the SPH is to protect the harbor from the government's excessive reclamation. Knowing that the government had planned a large-scale reclamation project and that there was no law regulating reclamation, legislator Christine Loh (a core member of the SPH) put forward the Protection

[9] Wu also proposed the establishment of a Human Rights Commission. The British government vetoed the proposal and argued that the Commission's remit would be too wide and that the Commission could not straddle the sovereignty handover. Author's interview with Anna Wu, March 4, 2008.

[10] Anna Wu proposed that the EOC should have the power of judicial review, but the government rejected the proposal. Author's interview with Anna Wu, March 4, 2008.

[11] *Equal Opportunities Commission* v. *Director of Education* [Court of First Instance 2001].

[12] The discussion in this paragraph is based on author's interview with Winston Chu, former chairman of the Society for the Protection of the Harbour, November 6, 2007.

of the Harbour Bill on behalf the SPH. With the support of pro-democracy legislators, the legislature passed the Protection of the Harbour Ordinance establishing the principle of minimal reclamation. The Ordinance provides the basis for the courts to regulate an important public policy – reclamation. The SPH used the Ordinance to successfully litigate against two crucial reclamation projects in 2003 and 2008.[13]

To conclude, Governor Patten expanded political opportunities in Hong Kong in the late colonial years through democratizing access to the legislature. As pro-democracy parties captured half of the legislative seats, the legislature became a major avenue through which pro-democracy and grassroots forces advanced their interests. However, the opening of political opportunities was short-lived because it was not sanctioned by the Chinese government. With the reversion of Hong Kong to Chinese sovereignty in July 1997, Patten's democratic reforms were also reversed (Sing 2004, pp. 163–90).

POST-COLONIAL REVERSAL OF THE OPENING OF POLITICAL OPPORTUNITIES

The Chinese government strongly opposed Patten's democratic reforms because it feared that the reforms allowed pro-democracy forces to expand their political influence and might weaken Beijing's control over Hong Kong. Arguing that Patten's reforms had violated the Basic Law, Beijing and the Tung Chee-hwa government decided to completely dismantle the reforms (see Table 5.1). By restricting the power of the legislature and marginalizing pro-democracy forces from it and other major decision-making bodies (see below), Beijing and Tung Chee-hwa have prompted aggrieved parties in society to turn to the courts to fight for their cause.

In dismantling Patten's democratic reforms, Beijing mainly targeted the legislature where most of the new political opportunities were laid. First, after the sovereignty handover, the Chinese government abolished the legislature elected under Patten's reforms. Instead, a Provisional Legislative Council (PLC) was set up. Incumbent legislators who supported the scrapping of Patten's reforms could keep their seats in the

[13] *Town Planning Board* v. *Society for the Protection of the Harbour Ltd* [Court of Final Appeal 2004]; *Society for the Protection of the Harbour* v. *Secretary for Justice (On behalf of Secretary for Transport and Housing)* [Court of First Instance 2008].

TABLE 5.1: Beijing's efforts to narrow political opportunities in the post-colonial era

Establishment of a provisional legislature
Changes of the election system of the legislature
Restrictions of the legislative power
Marginalization of pro-democracy forces from major decision-making and advisory bodies
Restoration of appointment system in the District Council
Abolition of liberal legislation

Sources: Chan (2002); Chan (2009); Cheung and Wong (2004); Pepper (2002); Sing (2004)

interim legislature.[14] Protesting against the legitimacy of the PLC, most pro-democracy legislators chose to stay out. As I will elaborate later, the absence of pro-democracy forces in the PLC enabled the Tung Chee-hwa administration to pass laws denying the constitutional right of abode to mainland-born children of Hong Kong permanent residents. These restrictive laws in turn led to a decade-long right-of-abode litigation.

Second, Beijing reshuffled the electoral system of the legislature, with a view to increasing the number of pro-Beijing and conservative legislators and to undermining the influence of pro-democracy forces in the legislature. The first-past-the-post electoral system, which was adopted in the 1991 and 1995 legislative elections, was replaced by a proportional representation system.[15] By guaranteeing that the number of seats each party will get is roughly equal to its vote share, the proportional representation system enabled pro-China parties to get more directly elected seats in the post-1997 legislature at the expense of pro-democracy parties. Finally, regarding the Election Committee elections, Beijing also eradicated the democratic elements introduced by Patten's reforms. Instead of being composed of popularly elected district councilors, the post-1997 Election Committee was constituted by 800 members, the vast majority of whom were pro-China and pro-business figures. These 800 members in turn were

[14] Under the Basic Law, all legislators elected in 1995 would become members of the first legislature of the HKSAR.

[15] Pro-democracy candidates frequently defeated their pro-China rivals in legislative elections under the first-past-the-post electoral system. See Baum (2000, pp. 446–7).

chosen by 200,000 electorates. This change in the electoral rule denied pro-democracy parties access to Election Committee seats, as they were wholly taken by pro-China parties.

Beijing's reshuffle of the electoral arrangements for the legislature succeeded in undermining the pro-democracy camp's influence in the legislature. In the 1998 legislative elections, pro-democracy forces only won twenty-three seats (out of sixty), down from their near majority (thirty seats) in 1995. They merely bounced back to twenty-five in the 2004 elections.

The sovereignty handover also imposed substantial constitutional constraints on the power of the legislature. As mentioned earlier, Patten's reforms allowed pro-democracy and pro-labor legislators to actively use the legislature to promote progressive policy change through private member's bills, amendment, or vetoing of government bills. The provisions of the Basic Law on private member's bills and voting-by-group, however, have made it more difficult for legislators to influence policy change through the legislature. Article 74 of the Basic Law prohibits legislators from introducing private bills relating to public expenditure, political structure, or the operation of the government. Legislators who want to introduce bills relating to government policy have to seek the written consent of the Chief Executive.

Annex II of the Basic Law also stipulates that the passage of motions, bills, or amendments to government bills introduced by individual legislators requires a simple majority of both members returned by geographical constituencies *and* those returned by functional constituencies (i.e., voting-by-group).[16] The passage of bills introduced by the government, however, merely requires a simple majority vote of all legislators.

The Tung Chee-hwa administration not only undermined the influence of pro-democracy and grassroots forces in the legislature, but also marginalized them from major power centers. Indeed, Tung disproportionately co-opted pro-Beijing and business elites into major policy-making and advisory bodies (Chan 2002, pp. 10–11). For example, Patten appointed several liberal figures as members of the Executive Council. After Tung took office, his cabinet no longer

[16] Pro-Beijing and pro-government figures captured the majority of the functional constituency seats. The practice of voting-by-group has allowed them to veto many of the motions initiated by pro-democracy legislators.

had any pro-democracy members. In their survey of political cooptation by the Hong Kong government, Cheung and Wong (2004, p. 882–83) find that, compared with the colonial period, the Tung government was more skewed in appointing business elites into major advisory committees and political offices. Chan (2009) concurs with the foregoing studies and suggests that since the sovereignty handover, appointment to major policy-making and advisory bodies has no longer been based on merit but on political affiliation.

Finally, taking advantage of the absence of pro-democracy forces in the interim legislature, the Tung administration repealed and amended a number of liberal laws passed by pro-democracy legislators in the last colonial year. The Bill of Rights (Amendment) Ordinance, which extended rights protection to disputes between individuals, was repealed. Three liberal labor laws which provided labor unions with the right to collective bargaining and to be consulted on changes to workers' employment terms were also abolished. Accordingly, the scope for labor unions to advance their interests was restricted in the post-1997 period.

The foregoing discussion highlighted the efforts of Beijing and the Tung administration to dismantle Patten's democratic reforms. This reversal fundamentally changed the political opportunities pro-democracy forces and civil society faced. First, changes in the legislative electoral arrangements, the restoration of the appointment system in the District Councils, and Tung Chee-hwa's disproportionate appointment of business and pro-Beijing elites to major policy-making and advisory bodies have substantially restricted access to political participation by pro-democracy and grassroots organizations. Second, as pro-democracy and grassroots parties no longer held half of the legislative seats, civil society groups, particularly grassroots organizations, have lost important allies within the governing elite. Accordingly, they have to find alternative institutions through which they can effectively promote their interests.

Finally, the weakening of the legislature vis-à-vis the executive branch has deprived pro-democracy groups and civil society of a useful platform to advance their cause.

While post-colonial political opportunities in the legislature and other power centers have become more adversarial to pro-democracy forces and civil society, the sovereignty handover has also opened up important legal opportunities (see Chapter 4). In short, there was a shift in political opportunities from the legislature to the judicial branch. A preexisting legal complex enables aggrieved social forces to take up legal opportunities and to go to the courts to address their concerns. The next section presents evidence of how politically disadvantaged parties, especially political and social activists, have increasingly mobilized the law after July 1997.

POLITICAL DISADVANTAGE AND LEGAL MOBILIZATION

"Political disadvantage" is a broad and imprecise term. As first articulated by Cortner (1968, p. 287), politically disadvantaged groups were defined as "groups that are temporarily or permanently disadvantaged in terms of their abilities to pursue successfully their goals through representative political institutions like the electoral process, the legislature or the bureaucracy. Thus, the courts become the only viable arenas for the politically disadvantaged." A wide range of groups such as the poor, racial minorities, prisoners, and politicians have been treated as politically disadvantaged in Cortner's and subsequent studies on interest-group litigation in US courts.[17] However, there may be substantial differences in terms of objectives, strategies, and impacts, between litigation launched by diverse disadvantaged groups. On the one hand, litigation launched by politicians or social activists tends to carry important political and/or policy objectives like a challenge to an administration or its policies. Accordingly, the issues involved are generally more politically sensitive and have wider socio-political impacts. On the other hand, individual litigation often aims at solving individual immediate problems, rather than challenging a government policy per se. For example, the immediate goal of many cases brought by prisoners is to overturn their convictions rather than pursuing any political or policy reform.

In discussing the impact of shifting political opportunities on legal mobilization in authoritarian Hong Kong, this book focuses on two sub-groups within the politically disadvantaged – pro-democracy politicians and social activists. This is because Beijing's closing down of political opportunities in post-colonial Hong Kong has a greater negative impact on these two sub-groups and therefore prompted

[17] For a good summary, see Olson (1990, pp. 854–8).

them to turn to the courts. Given that the legislature is a major arena where pro-democracy politicians can exercise their influence, shifting political opportunities like the weakening of the legislature have forced pro-democracy politicians to find other viable means to accomplish their goals. As their supporters (pro-democracy politicians) have become less influential in the legislature, social activists have to find alternative institutions to advance their cause as well. A preexisting legal complex and the opening of new legal opportunities during the process of the sovereignty transition make legal mobilization a sound choice for pro-democracy politicians and social activists. By contrast, shifting political opportunities has less impact on other disadvantaged groups, such as criminal suspects. Regardless of how open the political system is, for example, the courts are the major institutions through which criminals can address their concerns.

To evaluate the argument that Beijing's tightening of political opportunities forced pro-democracy politicians and social activists to go to the courts to promote their cause and therefore contributed to legal mobilization, I first review and compare the socio-political background of litigants in important human rights and public policy litigation before and after July 1997. The objective is to assess whether there are substantial changes regarding the background of litigants over time, and particularly whether pro-democracy politicians and social activists have increasingly participated in litigation. Second, through my interviews and media report, I seek to understand litigants' motivations and examine whether their political marginalization has been a crucial factor behind the decisions to sue the government.

In the following sections, I will demonstrate that post-colonial human rights and public policy litigation is marked by increasing participation by pro-democracy politicians and social activists. Additionally, political marginalization is a critical reason for their use of the courts.

Increasing use of courts by pro-democracy politicians and social activists

Appendix 1 (column 2) reports the background of litigants in human rights and public policy litigation that the Privy Council and the Court of Final Appeal (CFA) decided between 1981 and 2010. A trend is clear: pro-democracy politicians and social activists have increasingly resorted to courts to attain their goals since the sovereignty handover. From 1981 to June 1997, none of the litigants in human rights cases had activist backgrounds. They were either ordinary citizens who were convicted of criminal offences or illegal immigrants from China or Vietnam.

The background of litigants in the post-handover period, however, has diversified considerably. Appendix 1 demonstrates that pro-democracy politicians and social activists have increasingly used litigation to pursue their agendas. They were plaintiffs or sponsors or both in 29 percent of human rights cases (fourteen out of forty-eight) that the CFA decided between 1998 and 2010. The Society for Community Organization (SoCO) organized mainland-born children and adopted children of Hong Kong permanent residents to fight for the right of abode in Hong Kong. The litigation lasted for a decade. A veteran activist-cum-legislator, Leung Kwok-hung and his fellow members of the April 5th Action Group,[18] challenged the National and Regional Flag Ordinance (freedom of expression, national flag desecration), the Public Order (Amendment) Ordinance (the right of peaceful assembly), and the power of the law enforcement agencies to conduct covert surveillance. Finally, sexual minorities have also begun to use the judicial process to advocate their rights. In *Secretary for Justice* v. *Yau Yuk Lung Zigo and Another*,[19] CRSD played a critical role in helping two gay men to fight against the charge of committing homosexual buggery in a public place (see Chapter 8).

Pro-democracy politicians and social activists have actively used litigation to promote changes in public policy as well. Between 1981 and June 1997, the Privy Council only decided one public policy lawsuit, in which two Filipino domestic helpers litigated against an immigration policy concerning foreign domestic helpers in Hong Kong. In the post-colonial period, pro-democracy politicians and social activists litigated against important public policies before the CFA. Between 2002 and 2005, the Alliance for Defending Grassroots Right to Housing, and the Neighbourhood and Workers' Service Centre[20] organized two lawsuits against the

[18] The April 5th Action Group is a Marxist, radical social action organization. Leung Kwok-hung is a core member.

[19] *Secretary for Justice* v. *Yau Yuk Lung Zigo and Another* [Court of Final Appeal 2007].

[20] Founded in the mid 1980s and led by legislator Leung Yiu-chung, the Neighbourhood and Workers' Service Centre is a grassroots rights organization.

government's public housing rental policy and the privatization of shopping and car-park facilities within public housing estates. A number of pro-democracy legislators including Chan Wai-yip, Albert Cheng King-hon, and Leung Kwok-hung also supported the privatization lawsuit. In 2003, the Society for the Protection of the Harbour successfully challenged a crucial reclamation project before the CFA.

The increasing participation of pro-democracy politicians and social activists in the judicial process is not limited to the highest court. Indeed, they have also actively used the lower courts. Appendix 2 reports important human rights, public policy, and politically charged lawsuits that pro-democracy politicians and social activists brought to the Court of Appeal and the Court of First Instance. Several phenomena are noteworthy. First, most cases were launched after July 1997 and this suggests the impact of Beijing's tightening of political opportunities in the legislature and other major power centers.[21] Second, social activists have increasingly used litigation to push for progressive public policy change, like the introduction of a minimum wage and the democratization of the process of urban planning. Finally, the Democratic Party's active mobilization of the law not only reflects its narrower political space in the post-1997 legislature, but also its considerable legal resources. Its founding chairman, Martin Lee, is a senior counsel; the current chairman Ho Chun-yan owns a law firm (Ho, Tse, Wai and Partners). As columns 2 and 7 of Appendix 2 demonstrate, Lee and Ho represented all their party's litigation against the government.

After presenting evidence of an increasing usage of litigation by pro-democracy politicians and social activists in the post-1997 period, through my interviews and media report, I will show that

[21] The implementation of the Basic Law also matters. It alone, however, is insufficient in explaining why pro-democracy politicians and social activists have increasingly mobilized the law after the sovereignty handover. First, the HKBORO also provided a legal basis to sue the government (e.g., *Leung TC William Roy* v. *Secretary for Justice* [Court of Appeal 2006]). Second, a number of important policy-oriented cases (e.g., *Town Planning Board* v. *Society for the Protection of the Harbour Ltd* [Court of Final Appeal 2004], and *Ho Choi Wan* v. *HKSAR* [Court of Final Appeal 2005]) did not involve the Basic Law (see column 4 in Appendices 1 and 2).

political marginalization has significantly motivated them to take up the law as their weapon.

Political marginalization of pro-democracy politicians and legal mobilization

The pro-democracy politicians and social activists that I interviewed unanimously claimed that a shift of political opportunities from the legislature to the judiciary in the post-handover era is *the* central motivation for them to mobilize the law. Pro-democracy politicians lost their near-majority status in the legislature. More important, the Basic Law sets substantial restrictions on the legislators' policy-making power. Article 74 of the Basic Law, for example, prohibits legislators from introducing private bills relating to public expenditure, political structure, or the operation of the government. Being politically marginalized, pro-democracy politicians have to take up the new legal opportunities to advance their agendas. Martin Lee remarked that:

> On the one hand pro-democracy parties in the legislature were undermined after July 1997 and therefore they did not have enough votes to make the government listen to their demands. The government often secured enough support from the pro-Beijing and pro-government legislators. On the other, a strong tradition of the rule of law, a competent judiciary and respected barristers in Hong Kong enabled them to turn to the courts to fight for citizens' interests.[22]

Ho Chun-yan also echoed Lee's standpoint. He claimed:

> Pro-democracy parties have become minorities in the post-1997 legislature. The government can more easily bypass the legislature in formulating policy. Under these circumstances, legal mobilization and social movements become the remaining viable options for pro-democracy forces to fight for democracy and to influence government policy. For us, legal mobilization is a more viable choice. This is because we have a strong legacy of the rule of law. The judiciary has commanded a high level of respect from the government since the colonial period. Additionally, we have a Bill of Rights and a functioning legal aid system in Hong Kong. The latter helps to narrow the advantage of the government over social groups in litigation.[23]

[22] Author's interview with Martin Lee, February 20, 2008.
[23] Author's interview with Ho Chun-yan, September 21, 2006.

The stricter limitation of the legislative power has also caused a legislator-cum-social activist, Leung Kwok-hung, to resort to litigation. Leung argues:

> Under article 74 of the Basic Law and the practice of voting-by-group, the chance of legislators to propose private bills relating to public policy is almost equal to zero. Motions passed by the legislature are not binding on the government. In short, our legislature only has the veto power. These structural constraints on the legislature have stymied my efforts to transform citizen preferences into government policy. Litigation, therefore, becomes my alternative choice.[24]

The foregoing comments by three prominent pro-democracy politicians highlight that their political marginalization and the weakening of the legislature vis-à-vis the executive have caused them to increasingly turn to the courts to advance their goals. Leung Kwok-hung's legal challenge of the president of the legislature in 2006 is an illustration of the impact of shifting political opportunities on legal mobilization.

In *Leung Kwok Hung* v. *The President of the Legislative Council of the HKSAR and Another*,[25] Leung challenged Rita Fan's[26] decision to block pro-democracy legislators' amendments to a covert surveillance bill in August 2006.[27] Fan defended her decision on the ground that article 74 of the Basic Law prohibits legislators from proposing amendments which would incur government expenditure. Dissatisfied with Fan's decision to block pro-democracy legislators' amendments to the covert surveillance bill and more broadly with the Basic Law's constraints on legislative power, Leung decided to sue Fan and the government.[28]

[24] Author's interview with Leung Kwok-hung, January 3, 2008.

[25] *Leung Kwok Hung* v. *The President of the Legislative Council of the HKSAR and Another* [Court of First Instance 2007].

[26] Rita Fan, a pro-Beijing politician, was the president of the Legislative Council between July 1997 and July 2008. In March 2008, Beijing appointed her as a member of the Standing Committee of the National People's Congress.

[27] According to the Legislative Council's Rules of Procedure, legislators who want to amend government bills or propose private bills must seek approval from the president of the legislature.

[28] Author's interview with Leung Kwok-hung, January 3, 2008.

Weakening of allies in the legislature and legal mobilization

Beijing's tightening of post-1997 political opportunities has not only affected pro-democracy parties but also social activists and civil society groups, given that pro-democracy parties have long been their important allies. As their allies in the legislature have been weakened, social activists and civil society groups have to find alternative channels to advance their cause. As a veteran social activist commented:

> After July 1997, the legislature cannot effectively check and balance the Tung Chee-hwa administration's excessively rightist economic and social policies. On the one hand, pro-democracy forces, who are more sympathetic with the disadvantaged, become legislative minorities. The practice of voting-by-group enables the business sector to veto any pro-poor policies. What is more, it seems that the government has already become accustomed to protests and demonstration. On the other hand, Hong Kong has a competent and relatively impartial judiciary. Therefore, apart from judicial reviews, we have no viable alternative to advance the cause of the poor. This explains why the Society for Community Organization has increasingly litigated against the post-1997 government.[29]

Fernando Cheung Chiu-hung, a veteran advocate of disability rights, made similar comment as well:

> The post-colonial Hong Kong government's rightist social policy has adversely affected the disability welfare. In summer 2009, the government implemented the policy of not allowing students with disabilities to continue their studies in special schools, if they are 18 years old or above. On the one hand, we lobbied the legislature to oppose this discriminatory policy. Legislators from the pro-government political parties, however, were not sympathetic to our cause. Only the pro-democracy legislators (the legislative minorities) had actively helped us. On the other hand, Hong Kong has a competent and relatively impartial judiciary. Judicial review, therefore, became our last resort to defend disabled students' rights

[29] Author's interview with Fung Ho-lup, Chairman of the Board of Directors of the Society for Community Organization (SoCO), February 29, 2008. Chapter 8 of this book will elaborate the history of the SoCO and its role in legal mobilization.

> to education. This explained why we took the government to court in August 2009.[30]

The four case studies below seek to illuminate how the weakening of their pro-democracy allies in the legislature has caused social activists to mobilize the law to pursue their interests.

Protesting against Beijing's replacement of an elected legislature with a Provisional Legislative Council (PLC) after the sovereignty handover, the majority of pro-democracy parties refused to join the PLC.[31] Accordingly, pro-Beijing and pro-government forces dominated the PLC. The absence of pro-democracy parties in the interim legislature enabled the Tung administration to pass emergency laws which denied the constitutional right of abode to mainland-born children of Hong Kong permanent residents. Moreover, the PLC repealed two liberal labor laws which granted labor unions collective bargaining rights and outlawed discrimination against union activists. The laws were sponsored by the pro-democracy Confederation of Trade Unions (CTU) and passed by the last colonial legislature. These two acts of the PLC in turn led the Society for Community Organization (SoCO) and the CTU to resort to litigation.

The Basic Law states that mainland-born children of Hong Kong permanent residents have a right of abode in Hong Kong. Seeking to obtain a right of abode, many mainland-born children were smuggled into Hong Kong before the sovereignty handover. Shortly after July 1, 1997, SoCO organized several hundred illegal child immigrants to press the government for a right of abode.[32] Fearing that granting these illegal child immigrants a right of abode would trigger an influx of immigration from China and overload the welfare system of Hong Kong, the Tung Chee-hwa administration requested the PLC to pass an emergency law to deny the constitutional right of abode to these illegal child immigrants. Given that the PLC was

[30] Author's interview with Fernando Cheung Chiu-hung, a core member of the Grand Alliance of Parents for the Rights of Students with Special Educational Needs and the Labour Party of Hong Kong, December 19, 2011. For more background of this judicial review, see Yvonne Tsui, "Disabled Pupil Seeks 'Discrimination' Review," *South China Morning Post*, August 5, 2009, p. A2; and *Tong Wai Ting* v. *Secretary for Education and Another* [Court of First Instance 2009].

[31] The term of the Provisional Legislative Council only lasted for a year. In September 1998, elections were held for the first legislature of the HKSAR.

[32] Staff Reporters, "Policy shift sparks fear of children flooding in," *South China Morning Post*, July 4, 1997, p.1.

controlled by pro-Beijing and pro-government figures, it complied with Tung's request. The PLC passed the Immigration (Amendment) Ordinance, which required these illegal child immigrants to be repatriated back to China and to hold a certificate of entitlement (issued by the Chinese government) before they could enjoy the constitutional right of abode in Hong Kong (Fung 2004, pp. 103–04). Contending that the Ordinance had infringed their constitutional rights, SoCO helped these illegal child immigrants to litigate against the government. The litigation lasted for a decade.

The foregoing discussion highlights the impact of the political marginalization of pro-democracy forces on the rise of legal mobilization. Pro-democracy politicians supported the claims of illegal child immigrants from China and opposed the passage of any emergency law by the PLC. If Beijing had not dismantled Patten's democratic reforms and pro-democracy parties could have kept the near-majority status in the legislature, the Tung Chee-hwa administration would have faced much more difficulty in passing the emergency law. Instead, Tung might have to negotiate and compromise with the legislature, illegal child immigrants, and SoCO in order to resolve the problem. In this way, the right-of-abode litigation might have been avoided. Beijing's tightening of post-1997 political opportunities, however, completely deprived SoCO and illegal child immigrants of important allies in the legislature. The lack of influential allies within the governing elite, in turn, caused SoCO and its clients to turn to the courts to defend their interests.

The marginalization of pro-democracy parties from the PLC almost caused another lawsuit by a pro-democracy labor union as well. Taking advantage of the absence of pro-democracy parties in the PLC, the Tung Chee-hwa administration repealed two liberal labor laws which granted labor unions collective bargaining rights and outlawed discrimination against union activists. The CTU sponsored the laws during the final colonial year.[33] After his return to the legislature in 1998, Lee Cheuk-yan of the CTU tried to reinstate the two liberal labor laws through private member's bills. Rita Fan rejected Lee's proposal of private member's bills on the ground that the bills would incur substantial government expenditure and therefore violated article 74 of the Basic Law.

[33] Established in 1990, the Confederation of Trade Unions (CTU) is pro-democracy and the second largest labor union in Hong Kong. The CTU often uses radical means like strikes to promote labor interests. Lee Cheuk-yan is the secretary-general of the CTU.

Lee had considered initiating a judicial review against Fan's refusal of his proposal to introduce private member's bills. He not only aimed at reinstating the two liberal labor laws, but also at expanding the power of the legislature vis-à-vis the executive. As Lee said: "If the government won (i.e., rejecting his proposal for private member's bills), there won't be a balance between the executive and the legislature anymore. The executive would become more autocratic."[34] Lee finally gave up his plan of litigation because of financial concerns. As a lawmaker, Lee's generous income made him ineligible to apply for government-funded legal aid. What is more, he feared that if he lost the legal battle, he would be unable to pay for the litigation costs and might need to declare bankruptcy.[35] If Lee had not been afraid of bankruptcy and the subsequent possibility of being barred from standing for future elections, a politically charged lawsuit might have happened.

The right-of-abode litigation by SoCO and the aborted litigation by the CTU illustrate the impact of political marginalization of pro-democracy forces on the rise of legal mobilization. As pro-democracy parties did not join the PLC, rights advocacy groups and their disadvantaged clients lost important allies among the governing elite during 1997–98. The judicial branch became another channel for these groups to advance their cause. Even though the PLC was replaced by an elected legislature in 1998, Beijing's reshuffle of the electoral arrangements has made it difficult for pro-democracy forces to regain their pre-1997 near-majority status. As their legislative allies are weakened, rights advocacy groups have to continue to mobilize the law. Two prominent lawsuits – the demolition of the Queen's Pier and the school management reform – demonstrate how the minority status of pro-democracy forces in the legislature has prompted social activists to use the courts to attain their goals.

In *Chu Hoi Dick and Another* v. *Secretary for Home Affairs*, two environmental protection activists from Local Action Group challenged the government's decision to demolish the historic Queen's Pier.[36] They argued that the government should not demolish the

[34] No Kwai-Yan, "Unionists may seek judicial review," *South China Morning Post*, April 27, 1999, p. 6.

[35] Angela Li, "Unionist weighs cost of lawsuit," *South China Morning Post*, July 29, 1999, p. 2.

[36] *Chu Hoi Dick and Another* v. *Secretary for Home Affairs* [Court of First Instance 2007].

pier for the construction of a highway.[37] More broadly, the activists sought to change the government's heritage conservation and urban planning policies so that the public can have greater participation in the processes.

The activists initiated the judicial review *after* pro-democracy legislators repeatedly failed to block the government's demolition decision through the legislature. In May 2007, Civic Party legislator Alan Leong put forward a motion which demanded the government preserve the pier. The motion, however, was defeated by pro-government legislators.[38] Pro-democracy legislators had twice opposed the government's appropriation requests for the demolition. Their efforts again were vetoed by pro-government parties, who are the majority in the legislature.[39] If pro-democracy parties had held the majority of votes in the legislature, they could have blocked the government's demolition decision and Local Action Group would not have needed to mobilize the law. The adoption of the proportional representation system after July 1997, however, makes it difficult for pro-democracy parties to gain majority status in the legislature. As a core member of Local Action Group comments:

> Because legislators are not completely elected by democratic methods and pro-democracy parties are minorities within the legislature, we cannot rely on the legislature to promote progressive reforms of the heritage conservation policy. This explains why we chose judicial review to advance our cause.[40]

The litigation between the Catholic Church of Hong Kong and the government over the 2004 school management reform also illustrates the impact of the weakening of pro-democracy forces in the legislature on legal mobilization.[41] The Catholic Church opposed the 2004 school management reform bill, which required every government-aided school to establish an incorporated school

[37] Built in 1954, the Queen's Pier had been the landing place for new colonial governors and a public pier.

[38] Chloe Lai, "Expert to run pier demolition," *South China Morning Post*, May 3, 2007, p. 3.

[39] Chloe Lai, "Funding to raze icon passes Legco hurdle," *South China Morning Post*, May 24, 2007, p. 1; idem, "Legco gives green light to demolition of Queen's Pier," *South China Morning Post*, June 16, 2007, p. 5.

[40] Author's interview with Szeto May, November 2, 2007.

[41] *The Catholic Diocese of Hong Kong* v. *Secretary for Justice* [Court of First Instance 2006].

management committee (SMC) by 2012. Under the reform, a school-sponsoring body (e.g., Catholic Church) can only appoint up to 60 percent of the members of the SMC. All incorporated SMCs must include elected teacher and parent representatives. What is more, the government has the power to appoint members to the SMC if it finds problems with the management of a school.[42]

By contrast, before the reform, school-sponsoring bodies had complete control over the membership of the SMC. The Catholic Church, which runs more than 300 schools in Hong Kong, argued that the government's appointment power would undermine its autonomy in running schools and academic freedom. The Church made representations to the legislature and sought to persuade lawmakers not to pass the bill. It turned out that only pro-democracy parties were willing to support the Church. When the bill was debated in the legislature, pro-democracy lawmakers proposed numerous amendments to minimize the government's grip on the SMCs. Their efforts, however, were vetoed by pro-government parties. In the end, the school management reform bill was passed into law with the support of pro-government parties.[43] As pro-democracy parties failed to protect its interest through the legislature, the Catholic Church had to turn to the court and litigate against the government.

CONCLUSION

Governor Patten's democratic reforms enabled pro-democracy forces to expand their political influence during the last colonial years. Pro-democracy parties, for example, captured half of the seats in the 1995 legislative elections. They actively took advantage of their influence in the legislature to advance their agendas. The opening of political opportunities, however, was short-lived. Shortly after the sovereignty handover, Beijing and the Tung Chee-hwa administration dismantled Patten's democratic reforms and marginalized pro-democracy parties from the legislature and other major power centers. Political opportunities in the legislature have become more

[42] "School reform bill in race against time," *South China Morning Post*, May 8, 2004, p. 5.

[43] Polly Hui and May Chan, "Education chief under attack as school bill is passed," *South China Morning Post*, July 9, 2004, p. 1. See also Hansard of the Legislative Council, July 8, 2004, pp. 8861–2.

unfavorable to pro-democracy parties and their allies in civil society. Meanwhile, the process of the sovereignty transition also opened up important legal opportunities, notably the promulgation of the Hong Kong Bill of Rights Ordinance (HKBORO) and the Basic Law and the establishment of a new final appellate court. In short, there was a shift in political opportunities from the legislature to the judicial branch during the process of the sovereignty transition. A preexisting legal complex enabled pro-democracy forces and civil society groups to take up the legal opportunities and to go to the courts to address their concerns.

My analysis of the background of litigants in the post-handover period demonstrates that pro-democracy politicians and social activists have increasingly used litigation to pursue their agendas (see column 2 in Appendices 1 and 2). Through my interviews and media report, I find that political marginalization is the major reason why pro-democracy politicians and social activists have increasingly mobilized the law.

Agency is required to seize upon and transform the shifting political opportunities into legal mobilization. In the next three chapters, I will study how cause lawyers and rights advocacy groups have acted as transformative agents in that regard.

PART III

6

THE POLITICAL ORIGINS OF CAUSE LAWYERING IN HONG KONG

Epp (1998, 1999) contends that successful legal mobilization requires a support structure – consisting of activist lawyers and rights advocacy groups – to bring rights cases onto the judiciary's agenda and produce judicial activism. This book goes one step further than Epp, however. This chapter and those that follow examine the political origins of the rise of cause lawyering in Hong Kong and what cause lawyers have done to advance legal mobilization. In this chapter, I argue that the process of the sovereignty transition led to the rise of cause lawyering in three important ways.[1] First, the process opened up a favorable legal opportunity structure: the implementation of the Hong Kong Bill of Rights Ordinance (HKBORO) and the Basic Law and the establishment of a final appellate court (the Court of Final Appeal (CFA)) located in Hong Kong. The new legal opportunities have provided lawyers with the necessary legal basis to engage in cause lawyering. Second, concern over civil liberties prompted a few international human rights lawyers to move their practice to Hong Kong. Third, Beijing's tightening of political opportunities in the post-1997 legislature prompted several prominent liberal lawyers-cum-politicians to use their legal expertise to promote democratic changes through the courts. In addition to the aforementioned three factors, a rights-receptive judiciary has facilitated cause lawyering as well.

[1] Portions of Chapter 6 appeared earlier in Tam (2010).

This chapter proceeds as follows. First, I discuss the socio-political background of Hong Kong cause lawyers. Second, I analyze how the process of the sovereignty transition contributed to the rise of cause lawyering. Third, I examine the role of a rights-receptive judiciary in facilitating cause lawyering. Fourth, I study the interplay of opportunities and constraints for practicing cause lawyering in Hong Kong. The final section concludes.

SOCIO-POLITICAL BACKGROUND OF CAUSE LAWYERS

Table 6.1 presents data on the socio-political background of cause lawyers who have consistently represented citizens and social groups in pivotal human rights and public policy litigation. This is not an exhaustive list of cause lawyers in Hong Kong; others have actively fought for civil liberties and democracy outside the courts.[2]

These cause lawyers share a number of characteristic features. First, although many of them were admitted to practice in Hong Kong between the mid 1960s and the 1980s (see Table 6.1, column 2), they did not actively engage in cause lawyering during that period of time. This fact indicates that other favorable conditions are required for these lawyers to take up cause lawyering. The section below discusses these conditions. Second, the majority of cause lawyers are active in promoting civil liberties, democracy, and social justice through other non-court settings (Table 6.1, column 3). For example, about half are the core members of either the Civic Party or the Democratic Party: Paul Harris, Philip Dykes, Johannes Chan, and John Clancy founded the Hong Kong Human Rights Monitor; and Michael Vidler and Hectar Pun have been actively involved in social movements. The long-standing political activism of all of these lawyers has expanded their social capital in areas such as social networks, reputation, and political power.[3] They have frequently used this social capital to

[2] For example, Ronny Tong and Alan Leong (former chairmen of the Hong Kong Bar Association) led the Bar to fight against the Tung Chee-hwa administration's proposal for a national security law during 2002–2003. The proposed law contained various illiberal provisions that might have seriously curtailed civil liberties.

[3] With respect to the major arenas where cause lawyers develop their social capital, Hong Kong cause lawyers are somewhat different from their counterparts in India (another former British colony). Hong Kong cause lawyers develop their social capital primarily through their political activism *outside* the state. By contrast,

TABLE 6.1: Background of cause lawyers listed by year of admission to practice in Hong Kong

	Year	Political affiliation, participation, and/or law firm
Martin Lee, SC	1966	Democratic Party; legislator (1985–2008)
Denis Chang, SC	1970	Civic Party
Wong Hin-lee	1976	Former legal advisor to Hong Kong Federation of Students;[1] Campaign manager of Audrey Eu (legislative by-election 2000)
Ho Chun-yan	1977	Democratic Party; legislator (1995–present); Chairperson of China Human Rights Lawyers Concern Group; board of directors of the Society for Community Organization (SoCO);[2] Ho, Tse, Wai and Partners
Audrey Eu, SC	1978	Civic Party; legislator (2000–present); legal advisor to SoCO
Gladys Li, SC	1978	Civic Party
Johannes Chan, SC	1982	Civic Party; Hong Kong Human Rights Monitor; Dean of Law School, University of Hong Kong
Philip Dykes, SC	1985	Hong Kong Human Rights Monitor; legal advisor to SoCO
Margaret Ng	1988	Civic Party, legislator (1995–2012)
Michael Vidler	1992	Amnesty International (Hong Kong); Hong Kong Human Rights Monitor; former board member of Aids Concern; Vidler and Co. Solicitors
Pamela Baker	1993	Pam Baker and Co.
Paul Harris, SC	1993	Hong Kong Human Rights Monitor
Hectar Pun	1995	Former president of the student union at City University of Hong Kong
Mark Daly	1997	Civic Party; Amnesty International's Lawyers' Network; Barnes and Daly
John Clancey	1997	Asian Human Rights Commission; China Human Rights Lawyers Concern Group; formerly on board of directors of SoCO; Ho, Tse, Wai and Partners
Stanley H.F. Ma	2000	Legal advisor to SoCO
Jocelyn Leung	2005	Denis Chang's Chambers

Note: Cause lawyers A and B are not included in this table for anonymity purposes.

[1] Established in 1958, the Hong Kong Federation of Students is a leftist student organization using radical means to promote progressive socio-political changes.

[2] Established in 1972, SoCO is a non-governmental organization seeking to promote grassroots interests through social action.

further their work, for example, in mobilizing their political influence to help disadvantaged clients (see below).

Third, Hong Kong cause lawyers practice in different settings. Audrey Eu, Margaret Ng, Denis Chang, Philip Dykes, Hectar Pun, and Jocelyn Leung practice in large chambers, while a number of cause lawyers practice in small law firms. Barnes and Daly, where Mark Daly is a partner, has three employees: the two partners and a trainee lawyer.[4] Ho, Tse, Wai and Partners, where Ho Chun-yan and John Clancey practice, has seven lawyers. Cause lawyer B practices in a small firm that employs three lawyers. Compared with large law firms, small firms allow cause lawyers to enjoy more freedom to choose their causes, colleagues, and strategies (Sarat and Scheingold 2005, pp. 11–12). As an example, before starting his own law firm in 1995, Ho Chun-yan was a partner elsewhere (which he requested be unnamed). At that time Ho found it difficult to engage in cause lawyering for two reasons. First, law firms in Hong Kong tend to avoid politics; and, second, Ho's support for democratic movements in China since the 1989 Tiananmen crackdown angered Beijing, and therefore his partners felt intense political pressure from the Chinese government.[5] By establishing his own law firm and hiring colleagues with similar political and ideological beliefs, Ho has a more supportive setting to practice his cause lawyering work. Finally, apart from practicing in law firms, cause lawyers in Hong Kong are also found working as law professors. Johannes Chan, for example, teaches constitutional and public law at the University of Hong Kong.

NEW LEGAL OPPORTUNITIES AND CAUSE LAWYERING

Although many cause lawyers were admitted to practice in Hong Kong between the mid 1960s and the 1980s, a lack of legal opportunities made it difficult for them to actively pursue liberal causes in courts during that period.[6] However, they have become more active since the

Indian cause lawyers draw their social capital mainly from their practice sites (that is, high courts and the Supreme Court). For a discussion of how different practice sites (different levels of courts) affect the ability of Indian cause lawyers to develop social capital, see Krishnan (2005).

4 Author's interview with Mark Daly, December 6, 2007.

5 Author's interview with Ho Chun-yan, February 20, 2008.

6 From the mid 1960s to the early 1980s, the most prominent cause lawyer in Hong Kong was Henry Litton, currently a non-permanent judge of the CFA. Litton

1990s. I argue that the process of the sovereignty transition and the associated opening of new legal opportunities in the 1990s provided the necessary conditions for the rise of cause lawyering. The sovereignty transition changed the legal opportunity structure by creating two new legal opportunities: the promulgation of the HKBORO and the Basic Law, and the setting up of the CFA in Hong Kong.

HKBORO, Basic Law, and cause lawyering

The colonial constitution – the Letters Patent and the Royal Instructions – had few provisions safeguarding fundamental human rights. Accordingly, during the majority of the colonial period, liberal lawyers did not have a sound legal basis on which to defend citizens' rights in the courts. As Martin Lee said:

> Without the HKBORO and the Basic Law that guarantee important rights and freedoms, it would have been extremely difficult for me to defend citizens whose rights have been infringed by the government. In an undemocratic state like Hong Kong, the government has numerous powers to pass a draconian law that violates civil rights.[7]

In the aftermath of the Cultural Revolution in the late 1960s, the police framed a pro-Beijing coolie (unskilled laborer) for possessing dangerous drugs. In defending this client, Martin Lee did not adopt any human rights arguments, due to lack of constitutional entrenchment of human rights. Instead, he raised a procedural challenge to the legality of the prosecution's action and argued that the physical environment made it unlikely for the police to gather convincing evidence against the accused.[8]

The lack of a constitutional safeguard of civil rights also led judges to downplay human rights arguments put forward by lawyers. As mentioned by Wong Hin-lee, a veteran cause lawyer:

> The most serious challenge of practicing cause lawyering in Hong Kong is that before the implementation of the HKBORO, it was very difficult

actively defended the poor who were arrested for unlawful assembly and for assaulting the police when they were protesting against the colonial government's resettlement and housing application policies. During that period, Wong Hin-lee helped Litton to defend the poor in the courts. Author's interviews with John Clancey, November 7, 2007; and Wong Hin-lee, February 22, 2008.

7 Author's interview with Martin Lee, February 20, 2008.

8 Author's interview with Martin Lee, February 20, 2008.

> to convince the judges to accept foreign court judgments on human rights, particularly those from the United States and Canada.[9]

When presenting foreign jurisprudence on human rights before the judges, Wong was often ignored and in one case was even told by a judge not to cite foreign human rights cases. Wong observed that trying to use human rights arguments to defend his disadvantaged clients was like arguing before a blank wall, hearing only the echo of his own voice while the judges often showed no response whatsoever.[10] Cause lawyer A concurred that:

> the Letters Patent was the only constitutional document during the colonial era and it had very few provisions protecting rights and freedoms. Accordingly, it was hard for lawyers to find a sound legal basis to effectively defend citizens' rights and freedoms against government infringement during the majority of the colonial period.[11]

The remarks by Martin Lee, Wong Hin-lee, and cause lawyer A demonstrate that before the 1990s, lawyers lacked a necessary legal tool – human rights laws – to make effective rights-based claims in the courts. The implementation of the HKBORO in 1991 and the Basic Law in July 1997, however, has fundamentally changed this situation. By establishing various civil, political, and social rights, the HKBORO and the Basic Law provide lawyers with a more conducive environment for cause lawyering.

The enactment of the HKBORO and the Basic Law was a product of the sovereignty transition. Beijing's military crackdown on the democratic movement in June 1989 precipitated a confidence crisis in Hong Kong. To restore public confidence and to provide an alternative to granting British citizenship to all the people of Hong Kong, London introduced the HKBORO in Hong Kong shortly after the crackdown. The HKBORO incorporates the International Covenant on Civil and Political Rights (ICCPR) into Hong Kong's law (with some reservations). It repeals all the preexisting laws that contravene the ICCPR and prohibits the legislature from creating any laws that are incompatible with provisions of the ICCPR.

After China resumed sovereignty over Hong Kong in July 1997, the Basic Law became Hong Kong's constitution. The new

[9] Author's interview with Wong Hin-lee, February 22, 2008.

[10] Author's interview with Wong Hin-lee, February 22, 2008.

[11] Author's interview with cause lawyer A, September 19, 2007.

constitution has an entire chapter on the protection of fundamental political and civil rights. The scope of protection is also much broader than that contained in the HKBORO. Justice Michael Hartmann highlighted the importance of the new constitution to rights protection. As he mentioned, "The Basic Law has awakened the people of Hong Kong that there is a constitution to protect their fundamental rights."[12]

Constitutional entrenchment of civil rights has provided lawyers with an essential tool (i.e., human rights laws) to undertake cause lawyering. They have a stronger legal basis to present human rights arguments in the courts. All the cause lawyers that I interviewed claimed that because of the passage of the HKBORO and the Basic Law, they have been able to take advantage of the new legal opportunities and to actively engage in cause lawyering, armed with crucial resources afforded them by the new legal environment. For example, Ho Chun-yan could focus on human rights law when he founded his own law firm in 1995. Before then, he practiced banking, trust, inheritance, and family law.[13]

The CFA and cause lawyering

The sovereignty transition not only caused the implementation of the HKBORO and the Basic Law, but it also led to the establishment of a final appellate court in Hong Kong – the CFA. The CFA has expanded the opportunities for lawyers in Hong Kong to acquire litigation experience before the highest court and has helped to nurture an experienced team of cause lawyers.

Before July 1997, when litigants from Hong Kong brought a case to the Privy Council, they had to first hire a Hong Kong law firm. However, Hong Kong law firms generally did not handle the litigation themselves because the majority of them did not have branches in Britain. Thus, they often assigned lawyers in Britain to conduct the litigation.[14] As Justice Kemal Bokhary remarked, "Counsel in Britain could simply take the subway to the Privy Council, whereas counsel in Hong Kong had to take a long and expensive flight to London to conduct the litigation."[15]

[12] Author's interview with Justice Michael Hartmann, March 5, 2008.
[13] Author's interview with Ho Chun-yan, February 20, 2008.
[14] Author's interview with barrister B, February 19, 2008.
[15] Author's interview with Justice Kemal Bokhary, February 28, 2008.

Since lawyers in Britain were often assigned to arguing before the Privy Council, Hong Kong's lawyers were less likely to develop expertise in constitutional litigation. This led to difficulty in building up a competent team of local cause lawyers.[16]

The setting up of the CFA changed the situation. Local lawyers have taken up most of the litigation work before the new final appellate court, especially in human rights and public policy cases. Thus, the CFA helps to nurture an experienced team of cause lawyers.

CONCERN OVER CIVIL LIBERTIES AND FOREIGN CAUSE LAWYERS

The process of the sovereignty transition raised widespread concern about whether the rule of law and civil liberties in Hong Kong could be maintained after July 1997. Beijing's military suppression of the 1989 Tiananmen democratic movement exacerbated this concern. In the mid 1990s, several international human rights lawyers, including Paul Harris and Mark Daly, moved to Hong Kong seeking to defend the rule of law and human rights in the post-1997 era.

Paul Harris, the first chairman of the Human Rights Committee of the English Bar, which was created in 1991, practiced law in London.[17] The 1989 Tiananmen crackdown aroused his concern about civil liberties and the rule of law in post-colonial Hong Kong. As committee chairman, Harris made the maintenance of the rule of law in post-1997 Hong Kong a priority. In 1993 he visited Hong Kong and met pro-democracy forces and lawyers like Martin Lee, who persuaded Harris to establish an independent human rights organization in Hong Kong to safeguard human rights. In 1994 Harris moved to Hong Kong, established the Hong Kong Human Rights Monitor, and continued his cause lawyering.

Mark Daly got his law degree in Canada in 1992 and came to Hong Kong three years later because of uncertainty about civil liberties in post-1997 Hong Kong. As Daly remarked:

[16] Author's interview with Justice Kemal Bokhary, February 28, 2008.

[17] The following discussion is based on a talk delivered by Paul Harris at the Center for Comparative and Public Law, the University of Hong Kong, September 12, 2007; and in Harris (2007, pp. 1–3).

> Hong Kong needed more human rights lawyers to safeguard the rule of law and civil liberties when the sovereignty handover was approaching. As human rights lawyering was under-developed in Hong Kong, there were more opportunities for me to engage in human rights lawyering here than in Canada, where human rights lawyering was well-developed.[18]

The arrival of these Canadian and British human rights lawyers helped to jumpstart the process of human rights litigation. In his early years in Hong Kong, while pioneering asylum-seeker litigation, Daly worked closely with the late Pam Baker[19] on Vietnamese refugee cases. After establishing his own law firm in 1999, Daly launched a number of landmark asylum-seeker judicial reviews based on the United Nations Convention against Torture, establishing the right of asylum claimants to a fair and independent assessment of their claims (for example, see *Secretary for Security* v. *Sakthevel Prabakar* and *FB* v. *Director of Immigration and Another*).[20] These landmark cases laid the foundation for subsequent litigation advancing the rights of asylum seekers such as freedom from unlawful administrative detention (see "A" v. *Director of Immigration*) and the right to work while waiting for verification of their refugee claims (see *Iqbal Shahid and Others* v. *Secretary for Justice*).[21] Paul Harris also helped to jumpstart human rights litigation. He conducted research and provided legal advice for the United Ants, which litigated against the undemocratic functional constituency arrangement in the legislature in 1994 and 1995 (see *Lee Miu Ling and Another* v. *The Attorney General*).[22] This case represented the first attempt by political activists in Hong Kong to democratize the political system through human rights litigation. Additionally, Harris was one of the lawyers

[18] Author's interview with Mark Daly, December 6, 2007.

[19] In 1982, Pamela Baker moved from Britain to Hong Kong, and worked in the Department of Legal Aid until 1991. Disappointed with the government's policy toward the Vietnamese refugees, in 1993 she established Pam Baker and Co., which specialized in helping Vietnamese boat people and right-of-abode seekers from China. She passed away in 2002.

[20] *Secretary for Security* v. *Sakthevel Prabakar* [Court of Final Appeal 2004] and *FB* v. *Director of Immigration and Another* [Court of First Instance 2008].

[21] "A" v. *Director of Immigration* [Court of Appeal 2008] and *Iqbal Shahid and Others* v. *Secretary for Justice* [Court of First Instance 2009].

[22] *Lee Miu Ling and Another* v. *The Attorney General* [Court of Appeal 1995]. Author's interview with Law Yuk-kai, Director of the Hong Kong Human Rights Monitor and spokesperson of the United Ants, February 15, 2008.

representing the first post-colonial constitutional litigation, which challenged the legality of the Provisional Legislative Council.[23]

BEIJING'S TIGHTENING OF POLITICAL OPPORTUNITIES AND CAUSE LAWYERING

An analysis of the emergence of cause lawyering in Hong Kong would be incomplete without discussing the role of shifting political opportunities. Beijing's tightening of political opportunities after July 1997 motivated several prominent liberal lawyers-cum-politicians to take up the new legal opportunities. In the last chapter, I examined how Beijing and the Tung Chee-hwa administration reversed Patten's democratic reforms and marginalized pro-democracy forces from the legislature and important power centers. Faced with a more constricted political space, several pro-democracy lawyers-cum-politicians decided to use their legal expertise to promote democratic changes through the courts. Martin Lee and Ho Chun-yan argued that after July 1997, the legislature is no longer a viable institution for pro-democracy parties to fight for their causes. The legislature has been weakened and pro-democracy parties do not have enough votes to push for democratic changes through the legislature. However, the implementation of the HKBORO and the Basic Law, and the setting up of the CFA provided a more conducive legal environment for them to use their legal expertise to fight for greater democracy and civil liberties through the courts.[24]

Finally, Gladys Li also argues that her cause lawyering provides an alternative to an undemocratic legislature in civil society's struggle for greater democracy and social justice. As Li puts it:

> We (cause lawyers) are there, available to be used by civil society when the political process does not work. We do not spearhead any political or social campaigns. When a campaign fits into a legal context, however, I will use my legal expertise to bring this campaign to the court.[25]

[23] The legality of the Provisional Legislative Council was contested because it was not provided for in the Basic Law. See *HKSAR* v. *Ma Wai Kwan David and Others* [Court of Appeal 1997].

[24] Author's interviews with Martin Lee, February 20, 2008; and Ho Chun-yan, September 21, 2006.

[25] Author's interview with Gladys Li, February 21, 2008.

To conclude, political marginalization and the opening up of legal opportunities have led several liberal lawyers-cum-politicians to turn their legal expertise into political capital to pursue democratic changes. Instead of merely depending on the legislature, they have increasingly used cause lawyering as a supplementary form of political participation. This process in turn encouraged the rise of cause lawyering in Hong Kong.

Summing up, the process of the sovereignty transition contributed to the rise of cause lawyering in three ways. First, it opened up two important legal opportunities, namely the implementation of the HKBORO and the Basic Law, and the establishment of a final appellate court in Hong Kong. Constitutional entrenchment of civil rights provides lawyers with an important tool – human rights laws – to widen the scope for cause lawyering. With the setting up of the CFA, local lawyers have taken up most litigation work before the new final appellate court, especially in human rights and public policy cases, and this helped nurture an experienced team of cause lawyers. Second, a few prominent foreign human rights lawyers moved their practice to Hong Kong to seek to maintain civil liberties and the rule of law in post-colonial Hong Kong. Third, Beijing's tightening of political opportunities in the post-1997 legislature prompted several prominent liberal lawyers-cum-politicians to use their legal expertise to advance democratic changes through the courts.

A RIGHTS-RECEPTIVE JUDICIARY

The opening up of legal opportunities, however, only provides the necessary conditions for the rise of cause lawyering. The new legal opportunities by themselves are insufficient for cause lawyering to flourish. Judges must be receptive to human rights arguments and actively use the new legal tools (the HKBORO and the Basic Law) in response to cases brought by cause lawyers. Otherwise, cause lawyers are likely to encounter considerable difficulties in promoting their causes in the courts, and indeed this happened to asylum cause lawyers in Britain. In his study of the impact of the 1998 Human Rights Act on asylum cause lawyering in Britain, Maiman (2005) finds that the Human Rights Act had not changed the fundamental hostility of appellate judges toward asylum seekers' legal arguments. Continued judicial resistance to rights-based claims significantly undermined the cause lawyering efforts.

Maiman's finding suggests that successful development of cause lawyering not only requires a favorable legal opportunity structure but also a supportive judiciary. In Chapter 4, I studied the role conceptions of the post-1997 judiciary and its performance in safeguarding the rule of law and human rights. I found that the judiciary, led by the CFA, has defined its role as guardians of fundamental rights and the rule of law. Moreover, the judiciary has actively adopted international human rights treaties and judgments in its constitutional interpretation.[26] This active embrace of a universal standard of human rights has often put the government on the losing side of litigation (Petersen 2007, pp. 34–9). In short, the judiciary has assertively defended individual rights and freedoms since July 1997.

The receptivity of the Hong Kong judiciary to human rights claims and its active use of the HKBORO and the Basic Law (particularly in civil and political rights litigation) has facilitated cause lawyering. Many cause lawyers that I interviewed mentioned that the judiciary's (especially the CFA's) responsiveness to their rights claims enlarged the room for argument as they promoted the rights of their disadvantaged clients in the courts.[27] Hectar Pun summarized the importance of a supportive judiciary to cause lawyering:

> Without an independent and rights-friendly judiciary in Hong Kong, my cause lawyering would not have flourished. Even though the HKBORO and the Basic Law have provided us with the necessary legal basis to present human rights claims, these claims would not work in front of a rights-resistant judiciary.[28]

This comment echoes Maiman's finding that a bill of rights by itself is not a sufficient condition for the success of a cause before the judiciary. Instead, judicial ideology plays an equal, if not more important, role in determining the outcome of cause lawyering work.

[26] Audrey Eu noted that in hearing human rights cases, the CFA judges have increasingly taken the initiative to ask lawyers about the relevant foreign jurisprudence. Author's interview with Audrey Eu, February 27, 2008.

[27] Author's interviews with Philip Dykes, November 29, 2007; Audrey Eu, February 27, 2008; Ho Chun-yan, September 21, 2006; Martin Lee, February 20, 2008; Gladys Li, February 21, 2008; Hectar Pun, February 13, 2008; and Wong Hin-lee, February 22, 2008.

[28] Author's interview with Hectar Pun, February 13, 2008.

OPPORTUNITIES AND CONSTRAINTS

Cause lawyering often entails political, economic, and professional risk to cause lawyers, because it inevitably challenges the state and other vested interests. The risk is particularly grave in undemocratic regimes. O'Brien and Li (2004, p. 79), for example, document how local officials in China threatened lawyers who helped villagers to sue them for unlawful tax and fee collections. With a strong legacy of the rule of law left by the British colonial government and under the shadow of the authoritarian communist rule since July 1997, cause lawyers in Hong Kong face a unique combination of opportunities and constraints for their work. In this section, I study the interplay of opportunities and constraints for practicing cause lawyering in Hong Kong.

An autonomous and organized legal profession

An autonomous and organized legal profession is crucial to cause lawyering. To be independent of state control, a bar must be capable of governing itself and hold disciplinary powers over its members. Human rights and public policy litigation frequently pits civil society against the government and/or powerful groups. An autonomous and unified bar can protect cause lawyers who take up politically charged cases from state harassment and crackdown.

In Chapter 3, I discussed how the British colonial authorities helped cultivate an autonomous and organized legal profession in Hong Kong. The legal profession was allowed to organize itself into voluntary associations for self-governance. They have effective control over matters crucial to professional independence, including: the size of the profession; fee schedules; admission and educational requirements; modes of organization; and disciplinary powers over their members.

An autonomous Bar Association has played a significant role in supporting cause lawyering and legal mobilization. This is evident in the right-of-abode litigation shortly after the sovereignty handover. The Bar Association actively mobilized its members to offer pro bono legal services to litigants who failed to get government-funded legal aid.[29] The move by the Bar, however, was criticized by some pro-China figures as a confrontation with the Hong Kong government.

[29] Author's interview with Gladys Li, a former chairwoman of the Hong Kong Bar Association, February 21, 2008.

Then Bar chairwoman Audrey Eu openly defended the Bar against the criticism.[30] If the Bar Association had been tightly controlled by the government, like its counterparts in China, it might not have adopted a firm stand in helping the litigants.

Political activism and social capital

The majority of Hong Kong cause lawyers are active in promoting democracy, civil liberties, and rights of marginalized groups through other non-court settings (Table 6.1, column 3). Their long-standing political activism has expanded their social capital in areas such as social networks, credibility, and political power. They have frequently used this social capital to further their work.

First, the social networks of these cause lawyers provide more opportunities for them to contact and interact with the marginalized groups so that they can explore the possibilities of litigation. The two cases below illustrate the important roles of these social networks. The first case concerns gay rights litigation. After exhausting all means to press the Broadcasting Authority to change its decision to censure a TV program on the love affairs of gay and lesbian couples in 2006, a gay rights activist (Joseph Cho) contacted his friend at Amnesty International Hong Kong and enquired about the feasibility of litigating against the Authority's decision. More important, Cho asked his friend to recommend lawyers for help. Cho's friend introduced him to Michael Vidler, who is a member of Amnesty International's Lawyers' Network.[31] Vidler became Cho's lawyer and they established a cordial lawyer–client relationship.

The second case concerns a housing rights case launched by the Evangelical Lutheran Church in 1999 on behalf of emigrant families from China (see Chapter 2). The Church retained Ho Chun-yan as its lawyer. Two social workers of the Church explained how and why they retained Ho to litigate for them, as they noted:

> When we lobbied the legislature against the government's discriminatory housing allocation policy, Ho Chun-yan was one of the legislators we met. During various meetings, Ho showed his sympathy with our cause. After deciding to sue the government, we turned to Ho for legal

[30] Linda Choy, "Rita Fan lands in 'II' legal aid row," *South China Morning Post*, July 15, 1997, p. 1.

[31] Author's interview with Joseph Cho Man-kit, November 20, 2007.

> advice because we had already established contact and knew that he was supportive to our cause.[32]

In short, the extensive social networks of cause lawyers have facilitated their interactions with marginalized groups who want to use the law to advance their interests.

Second, the political influence attached to the networks of cause lawyers has facilitated their work as well. They can mobilize their political influence to help their clients. In the litigation against the government's public housing rental policy in 2003–04, for example, the rights advocacy groups retained Ho Chun-yan because they sought to use Ho's expansive political networks to further the movement of affordable public housing. As an activist said, "We instructed Ho Chun-yan as our legal representation because he, as a core member of the Democratic Party, could help us to persuade the Party to support our movement."[33]

Finally, the track record of cause lawyers in promoting democracy and defending the rights of marginalized groups has helped them to establish trust and credibility within civil society. Human rights and public policy litigation is generally politically charged and thereby demands greater trust and cooperation between the litigants and their lawyers. As a cause lawyer remarked:

> In high-profile judicial reviews, litigants often have their strategies in mind. Thus, they need trustworthy lawyers who understand and are willing to litigate from their perspectives. Moreover, public policy litigation requires substantial information about the policy such as the policy-making process and government's standpoint. In that regard, litigants (who are often social activists) are more resourceful.[34]

The following comments by three political activists illustrate the importance of a trusting relationship between litigants and their lawyers in politically sensitive litigation. In their litigation against the government's decision to privatize shopping and car park facilities within public housing estates in 2004–05, the rights advocacy groups retained Philip Dykes and Hectar Pun because of their trust in them. As an activist explained their decision:

32 Author's interview with Wong Kwok-kei and Wong Chui-shan, December 19, 2007.

33 Author's interview with a core member of the Neighbourhood and Worker's Service Center, October 26, 2007.

34 Author's interview with Jocelyn Leung, February 26, 2008.

> We chose Philip Dykes and Hectar Pun to be our lawyers because, apart from their legal expertise, we had a cordial working relationship before. Dykes was famous for representing civil society organizations in human rights litigation; and Pun and I knew each other when we were student activists in the late 1980s and early 1990s.[35]

Leung Kwok-hung, who has filed a number of high-profile lawsuits against the government after the sovereignty handover, also emphasized the significance of having trustworthy lawyers in litigation. As he noted, "It is crucial that my lawyers are able to sympathize with my political viewpoints. Otherwise, they can hardly advocate my case enthusiastically."[36] Fernando Cheung Chiu-hung, who organized a judicial review defending disabled students' rights to special education in 2009, mentioned that he chose Martin Lee, Hectar Pun, and Dennis Kwok as his lawyers because of both their expertise in human rights cases and their credibility in championing human rights.[37]

In brief, my interviews find that human rights and public policy litigants require a higher level of trust in their lawyers because of the political salience of their cases. The track record of cause lawyers in promoting democracy and civil rights helps them to gain the confidence of potential litigants.

Government-funded legal aid

Litigation is prohibitive and the loser-pays system in Hong Kong further increases the barriers to access to courts for the lower class. Established by the colonial government in 1966, the government-funded legal aid system has facilitated cause lawyering by financing the lower class to use the courts to defend their rights. The last column in Appendices 1 and 2 shows that the majority of human rights and public policy litigation was supported by government legal aid. All legal aid applicants have to pass the means and merit tests. The means test requires an applicant's financial resources not to exceed the limit set by the government. It is waived for applications which involve the HKBORO. The merit test is more controversial (see Chapter 7) and an applicant has to demonstrate that his claim in the court has a

[35] Author's interview with Wan Siu-kin of the Neighbourhood and Worker's Service Center, November 28, 2007. Wan and Pun were core members of the student union at City University of Hong Kong in the late 1980s and early 1990s.

[36] Author's interview with Leung Kwok-hung, January 3, 2008.

[37] Author's interview with Fernando Cheung Chiu-hung, December 19, 2011.

reasonable prospect of success.[38] Once granted, legal aid not only covers the costs of the recipient, but also pays for the opposing party who wins the case.

Government-funded legal aid in Hong Kong has two salient features which facilitate the development of cause lawyering and, more broadly, legal mobilization. First, there is no predetermined funding cap for each individual case.[39] Thus, cause lawyers in legal aid cases have more room to mobilize and deploy resources to fight for their clients. For example, they can secure expert witnesses or invite their prominent foreign counterparts to join the case.[40] This is conducive to cause lawyering. After a case has started, the expense may exceed the amount that was initially predicted and therefore litigants and their lawyers have to constantly obtain more resources. This happened in race relations litigation in America.[41] Unlike their American counterparts, cause lawyers in Hong Kong need not constantly mobilize additional resources for their legal aid cases.

Second, for the sake of enhancing the independence of the Legal Aid Department from undue government intervention, the following types of legal aid cases are assigned to lawyers in private practice:[42] applications for writ of habeas corpus; judicial review; cases involving the government or a public body as a defendant; and cases where a human rights or Basic Law issue is raised.[43] By making lawyers within civil society responsible for most human rights litigation, the foregoing practice has fostered cause lawyering. Cause lawyering *within the state* tends to encounter more restrictions, given that it often challenges the

[38] Legal Aid Services Council (2006, p. 117).

[39] Legal Aid Services Council (2006, p. 53).

[40] For example, in 2001 Pamela Baker invited Geoffrey Robertson, a veteran British human rights lawyer, to lead an important right-of-abode case heard by the CFA. The case involved more than 5,000 mainland-born children of Hong Kong permanent residents (*Ng Siu Tung and Others* v. *The Director of Immigration* 2002). Robertson visited communist countries on behalf of Amnesty International in the 1970s and defended political dissidents in the former communist Czechoslovakia. See Cliff Buddle, "Rights QC counts gains, losses," *South China Morning Post*, September 17, 2001, p. 14.

[41] See Wasby (1995, p. 78). Many overseas jurisdictions like New South Wales, Ontario, and civil legal aid in England and Wales have imposed a cap on legal aid spending as well. Legal Aid Services Council (2006, p. 241).

[42] The Legal Aid Department has several hundred in-house counsel, who handle non-judicial review cases like marital disputes and personal injury.

[43] Legal Aid Services Council (2006, p. 61).

state or powerful groups.[44] In Hong Kong, this is no exception and most litigation against the government is highly politically contested. It is doubtful whether lawyers in the Legal Aid Department possess sufficient autonomy to actively promote the causes of the disadvantaged against their boss – the government. Indeed, the next chapter will examine the inadequacies of the Legal Aid Department in handling politically sensitive legal aid applications.

Whereas a legal complex and social capital of cause lawyers have provided important opportunities for cause lawyering in Hong Kong, the shadow of communist rule since July 1997 and the lack of alternative practice sites have imposed constraints as well. I discuss these constraints below.

Economic pressure

Economic pressure of the Chinese government and its business allies in Hong Kong has posed substantial financial difficulty for several cause lawyers.[45] With deeper economic integration between Hong Kong and China, and subsequent greater economic dependence on China, the threat of economic pressure has intensified. As discussed above, Hong Kong's cause lawyers mainly work in small law firms or as sole practitioners. Although small law firms have features that facilitate cause lawyering, they are also more vulnerable to economic pressure. The difficulty faced by Ho Chun-yan's law firm is an illustration. Because of his support for the pro-democracy movement in China and his cause lawyering activities, the Chinese authorities have imposed economic pressure on Ho's law firm. All Chinese state-owned corporations or local business firms that have good relationships with

[44] White (2001) discusses how the institutional roles of young Ghanaian lawyer-bureaucrats have constrained their cause in changing the development policy. Dotan (2001) suggests that cause lawyering for the rule of law exists within the state and among state lawyers in Israel. Dotan, however, also notes the potential dangers of cause lawyering within the state, like cultivation of a discourse in which formalistic legal values supersede human concerns and social values. Finally, Liu and Halliday (2008) show that the dependence of Chinese criminal defense lawyers on the state has significantly constrained their capacity to mobilize for protection of basic legal freedoms of citizens.

[45] Among the sixteen cause lawyers that I interviewed, Ho Chun-yan, Martin Lee, cause lawyer B, and cause lawyer Z (who requested to be unnamed concerning the issue of economic pressure from Hong Kong large business corporations) mentioned that they have faced economic pressure from Beijing and/or large business corporations in Hong Kong.

China have refused to hire Ho's law firm as their legal representatives. Chinese state-owned banks have even indicated to Ho's clients that they will not get any mortgages if they retain Ho's firm.[46]

Martin Lee and cause lawyers B and Z have also encountered economic pressure from large business corporations in Hong Kong. Cause lawyer Z observed:

> In the 1980s, I often represented large property developers in cases like town planning. My cause lawyering work, however, cost me these business opportunities. My colleagues told me that many large property developers did not like my high-profile defense of pro-democracy activists in the courts. Since the mid-1990s, very few large developers are willing to retain me and I no longer take any town planning cases.[47]

Finally, another pro-democracy lawyer, Ronny Tong, also claimed that after he was elected to the legislature in 2004, many of his former clients told him that they would no longer retain him because of their business interests in China.[48]

Summing up, while the sovereignty handover opened up new legal opportunities for cause lawyering, it also imposed a political constraint. Economic pressure of Beijing and its business allies in Hong Kong has made several cause lawyers pay a cost for their activism. This cost can be lessened by the existence of more protective practice settings – law school clinics. Hong Kong universities, however, so far have not established any viable law school clinic for public interest litigation.

Lack of protective practice settings

Lack of well-established law school clinics for public interest litigation in Hong Kong deprives cause lawyers of an important institutional support and thereby exposes them to greater political and economic pressure. Legal clinics in universities have played a significant role in sustaining cause lawyering in the United States (Lawrence 1990, p. 23; Jones 2005, p. 211) and especially in authoritarian regimes (Fu and Cullen 2008, p. 115; Liu and Halliday 2008). First, by insulating practitioners from the marketplace, legal clinics in universities

[46] Author's interview with Ho Chun-yan, February 20, 2008.

[47] Author's interview with cause lawyer Z, February 2008.

[48] Albert Wong, "Politics exacts price for lawyer," *South China Morning Post*, January 27, 2008, p. A4.

minimize the risk associated with cause lawyering. Second, legal clinics serve as training bases for future cause lawyers and provide crucial logistic support, like law students and venues for mobilization.

Hong Kong has three law schools and none of them so far has set up a legal clinic for public interest litigation. Although the Law School at the University of Hong Kong established a legal clinic in January 2009, public interest litigation is not its focus. Instead, its main purposes are for legal education and provision of advisory services for those areas that have not received much attention from the legal profession.[49] The absence of viable legal clinics deprives cause lawyers of important protective practice settings. Indeed, among the sixteen cause lawyers that I interviewed, only Johannes Chan (a public law professor) bases his practice at university.

CONCLUSION

In this chapter, I have discussed the political origins of the rise of cause lawyering in Hong Kong. Many cause lawyers were admitted to practice in Hong Kong between the mid 1960s and the 1980s – long before the rise of legal mobilization in the 1990s. In other words, these liberal lawyers wormed their way into the system over a long period of time. I argue that the process of the sovereignty transition and the subsequent opening up of new legal opportunities created the necessary conditions for these liberal lawyers to actively use the law to pursue progressive socio-political changes under authoritarianism. This indicates that legal mobilization in post-colonial Hong Kong did not happen abruptly with the sovereignty transition from Britain to China in July 1997. Instead, we should also examine *historical* factors preceding the sovereignty transition. In the next chapter, I study how cause lawyers have served as transformative agents and actively seized upon the new legal opportunities and other favorable conditions to advance legal mobilization in Hong Kong.

49 Author's interview with Johannes Chan, Dean of Faulty of Law, the University of Hong Kong, October 9, 2007.

7

CAUSE LAWYERS AS TRANSFORMATIVE AGENTS

Legal mobilization in post-colonial Hong Kong, a seemingly sudden political change, depends on transformative agents like cause lawyers and rights advocacy groups to bring rights cases onto the judiciary's agenda and transform formal constitutional rights into political reality. Without these transformative agents, constitutional rights will remain as dead letters of the law.[1] Columns 2 and 7 in Appendices 1 and 2 demonstrate that elite cause lawyers and the disadvantaged have formed a cross-class coalition to pursue legal mobilization in Hong Kong since the mid 1990s. In the majority of human rights and public policy cases, disadvantaged litigants received government-funded legal aid and retained cause lawyers to sue the government. This chapter studies how a group of cause lawyers have taken up the shifting political opportunities associated with the process of the sovereignty transition and often worked behind the scenes to promote legal mobilization (and gradual political changes) in Hong Kong. The chapter proceeds as follows. First, I study the roles of cause lawyers in different phases of litigation. Second, I examine how the participatory work style of cause lawyers and their ability to harmonize the objectives and strategies with their disadvantaged clients have contributed to legal mobilization. The final section concludes and reflects how my study of Hong Kong cause lawyers informs the literature on economic modernization and democratization, particularly the role of the middle class.

[1] Transformative agents are the actual actors who change institutions. See Mahoney and Thelen (2010).

CAUSE LAWYERS AS GATEKEEPERS

Through providing pro bono legal advice on the prospect of litigation outcome, cause lawyers have often significantly influenced rights advocacy groups in deciding whether to initiate lawsuits against the government. In this sense, cause lawyers have served as gatekeepers who control the flow of political disputes into the courts.[2] For many rights advocacy groups, the first step of legal mobilization is to take legal advice concerning the legal basis for suing the government and the prospect of success. Provision of pro bono legal advice by cause lawyers is crucial, because at the initial phase, rights advocacy groups generally have not applied for legal aid, and seeking advice from other lawyers is beyond their reach.[3]

Most public policy litigation started with consultation with cause lawyers. In the public housing rental litigation, the activists consulted Audrey Eu and Liu Sing-lee.[4] In the litigation against privatization of shopping and parking facilities within public housing estates, the activists invited cause lawyer B to attend one of their brainstorming meetings on formulation of strategies against the government's policy. Before that meeting, the activists had not considered judicial review as a strategy, because they believed that the privatization decision was only a commercial dispute between retailers and the government. At that meeting, cause lawyer B highlighted that retailers in public housing estates paid below-market rents because the government wanted them to provide affordable services to the residents. However, retailers had to pay higher rent after privatization. Thus, cause lawyer B suggested that the activists had the legal basis to invoke the Housing Ordinance (which obliges the government to provide affordable housing services to residents) to challenge the government's privatization plan.[5]

The housing rights lawsuit launched by the Evangelical Lutheran Church in 1999 on behalf of emigrant families from China also illustrates the importance of cause lawyers in controlling the flow of

[2] Kritzer (1997) describes American lawyers, particularly contingency fee lawyers, as gatekeepers who control the flow of civil cases into the courts.

[3] Author's interviews with Wan Siu-kin, November 28, 2007 and Fernando Cheung Chiu-hung, December 19, 2011.

[4] Author's interview with Wan Siu-kin, November 28, 2007. Liu Sing-lee is a core member of a pro-democracy organization, the Association for Democracy and People's Livelihood.

[5] Author's interview with cause lawyer B, December 28, 2007.

political disputes into the courts. In that litigation, the Church consulted Johannes Chan on whether the government's housing allocation policy contravened the Basic Law. As an activist recounted, "We had scant knowledge about the whole process of judicial review. If Johannes Chan had not provided pro bono legal advice to us at the initial phase, we would not have had the courage and knowledge to start the litigation."[6]

In *Leung TC William Roy* v. *Secretary for Justice*, a young gay man sued the government for discrimination. He argued that section 118C of the Crimes Ordinance infringed homosexual rights to equality and privacy, because it set the minimum age for buggery at 21, whereas the minimum age for heterosexual intercourse was 16. Although the gay man was aware of the adverse impact of the Ordinance on his sexual life when he was 17, he was uncertain what he could do to protect his interests. He took legal action only after meeting Michael Vidler, who suggested that he could challenge section 118C through judicial review.[7]

Finally, cause lawyers can *discourage* rights advocacy groups from bringing political disputes into the courts as well. In 2005, the Society for Community Organization (SoCO) had considered suing the government's new housing application and allocation system for discriminating against young single adults.[8] In the end, SoCO gave up the litigation plan, because many cause lawyers highlighted the poor prospect of winning the case.[9]

MOBILIZING RESOURCES: BATTLE FOR LEGAL AID

Having decided to sue the government, seeking government-funded legal aid is the second step, given that most litigants lack the financial means to pursue litigation. Cause lawyers play a significant

[6] Author's interview with Wong Kwok-kei of the Evangelical Lutheran Church of Hong Kong, December 19, 2007.

[7] Author's interview with Leung William Roy, January 31, 2008.

[8] The new system replaces the first-come-first-served arrangement and gives priority to older applicants. The system allocates public housing according to the points accumulated by the applicants. The number of points an applicant gets will primarily depend on his age. See Chloe Lai, "Flats curb on young singles imminent," *South China Morning Post*, September 27, 2005, p. A1.

[9] Author's interview with Sze Lai-shan, community organizer of SoCO, December 19, 2007.

role in this process of resource mobilization. As mentioned previously, the legal aid system has several features that are favorable to legal mobilization (e.g., no predetermined financial limit on individual cases). Appendices 1 and 2 (last column) demonstrate that a majority of human rights and public policy litigation was funded by legal aid. In reality, it is very difficult to get legal aid for politically sensitive cases. The discussion below examines how cause lawyers have helped litigants circumvent the difficulties and obtain legal aid.

Although the government stresses that the Legal Aid Department (LAD) is operationally independent, cause lawyers, rights advocacy groups, and several non-partisan legal professions claim that the reality is different. They highlight that the LAD has declined legal aid to various politically charged cases because of political pressure.[10] The LAD is a government department and is subject to pressure from above. The government has power over LAD personnel and therefore critics argue that lawyers there are reluctant to grant legal aid to politically sensitive litigation out of concern for their career prospects. Their concern is not without merit. It is widely believed that in 1992 the government did not renew the contract of the then LAD director, Patrick Moss, because he approved legal aid to Vietnamese boat people to litigate against the government.

Indeed, the rise of legal mobilization has increasingly put the LAD under political pressure. It has not only faced pressure from the government but also from pro-China figures. Shortly after the sovereignty handover, for example, Rita Fan (then president of the provisional legislature) openly questioned whether the LAD should use government money to help right-of-abode seekers from China to litigate against the government's deportation order.[11] A non-partisan barrister and previous member of the Legal Aid Services Council

[10] In 1994 an activist group, the United Ants, applied for legal aid to challenge the functional constituency arrangement in the legislative elections. The LAD initially rejected the application on the ground that the litigation was a class action. Author's interview with Law Yuk-kai, February 15, 2008. In July 1997, the LAD refused legal aid to mainland-born children of Hong Kong permanent residents who sought to litigate against the government's deportation order.

[11] Linda Choy, "Rita Fan lands in 'II' legal aid row," *South China Morning Post*, July 15, 1997, p. 1.

observed that, "After July 1997, growing political pressure has made the LAD become less self-confident."[12]

Cause lawyers have played two crucial roles in helping litigants to mobilize legal aid to sue the government, namely writing legal opinions and/or directly applying for leave (*certiorari*) to appeal from the courts. Both acts are done on a (semi) pro bono basis. Legal aid applications need to pass a merit test, which means an applicant needs to demonstrate that his claim in the court has a reasonable prospect of success. A favorable opinion from an experienced lawyer is often required to persuade the LAD that an application (especially a politically sensitive one) has merit.[13] As litigants have not received legal aid at that stage, it is beyond their reach to pay a lawyer at market rates to write an opinion for their applications. Cause lawyers have actively assisted litigants to cross this hurdle by writing legal opinions on a (semi) pro bono basis. In the public housing rental litigation in 2003–04, for example, Johannes Chan wrote a legal opinion to support activists' application for legal aid.[14] A pro bono legal opinion is important because the majority of litigants lack the necessary legal expertise to write a convincing application. As a community organizer noted:

> Many disadvantaged that we helped initially failed to obtain legal aid, because they could not effectively present their claims to the LAD. When they received legal opinions from cause lawyers, however, most of their applications succeeded.[15]

Having a favorable legal opinion from cause lawyers is often not sufficient to prompt the LAD to grant legal aid to politically charged cases, because the LAD has also sought legal opinions from other lawyers that justified its decisions. The Legal Aid Ordinance stipulates that under certain circumstances,[16] the Director of the LAD may seek

[12] Author's interview with Ruy Barretto, February 15, 2008. Barretto served on the Legal Aid Services Council from 2000 to 2006. Established in 1996, the Council is responsible for monitoring the performance of the LAD and advising the government on legal aid policy.

[13] Author's interviews with Ho Chun-yan, September 21, 2006 and Wong Chi-yuen of the SoCO, December 19, 2007.

[14] Author's interview with Ho Chun-yan, September 21, 2006.

[15] Author's interview with Wong Chi-yuen, December 19, 2007.

[16] The circumstances include: when there is no precedent or decided cases on the subject; or the case is complex and raises a novel point of law (Legal Aid Services Council 2006, p. 111). The Director of the LAD may also seek outside legal opinions when an application involves politically sensitive issues. Author's

opinions from lawyers in private practice regarding the merits of a legal aid application before deciding whether to offer legal aid. Critics have argued that the LAD has turned the requirement into an excuse to refuse politically unpopular applications, given that the LAD has wide discretion in choosing which lawyers it consults. A public law professor observed that:

> LAD's choice of outside lawyers for legal opinions partly depends on expertise and fee. However, the Department still has very large discretion. It can consult Gladys Li (a liberal lawyer) or Joseph Fok (a pro-government lawyer).[17] The opinions given by these two lawyers on the same application can be very different.[18]

A social activist, Richard Tsoi, who has helped SoCO to appeal to the High Court against the LAD's refusal of legal aid, also highlighted that the LAD has used outside legal opinions to justify its decision before the court.[19]

To circumvent the foregoing tactics by the LAD, many cause lawyers have first applied for leave to appeal from the courts. After getting leave, they will present it and request the LAD to provide legal aid. Under this circumstance, the LAD has to approve legal aid, because judges have indicated that the case has a reasonable prospect of success by granting leave to the applicant. Indeed, some LAD lawyers have encouraged such practice, as one of them told Mark Daly to obtain leave to appeal first and then returned to the LAD for legal aid.[20] It seems that these LAD lawyers wanted to pass the buck to the courts so as to avoid making unpopular decisions.

The foregoing strategy requires cause lawyers to do extra work on a (semi) pro bono basis. Many, however, have been willing to undertake such work with a view to helping disadvantaged litigants to mobilize the necessary resources to advance their claims in the courts. Michael Vidler, for example, adopted the practice in two

interview with Thomas E. Kwong, Deputy Director of the Legal Aid Department, December 4, 2007.

17 Joseph Fok was appointed as a Court of First Instance judge in 2010.

18 Author's interview with a public law professor in Hong Kong, late 2007.

19 Author's interview with Richard Tsoi, August 9, 2007. Tsoi is the executive director of the Community Law Center of SoCO.

20 Author's interview with Mark Daly, December 6, 2007.

prominent gay rights lawsuits.[21] If Vidler had not worked on a pro bono basis, gay rights activists might not have scored important victories in the courts.

The right-of-abode litigation also demonstrates the significant role of cause lawyers in mobilizing resources for the disadvantaged. Shortly after the sovereignty handover in July 1997, the LAD refused legal aid to right-of-abode seekers from China to litigate against the government's deportation orders. To prompt the LAD to grant legal aid, Gladys Li applied for leave to appeal from the court on a pro bono basis.[22] In the end, the right-of-abode seekers received legal aid and won an important battle in the Court of Final Appeal (CFA).[23]

The strategy of applying for leave to appeal first can entail substantial economic risk, however. The government can apply to the court to strike down the application. If the potential litigant loses and the government seeks costs against him, he will not only fail to receive legal aid to advance his interests, but will also owe the government a large sum of money.

Summing up, cause lawyers have played a crucial role in initiating and mobilizing resources for legal mobilization. Very few lawyers in Hong Kong are willing to sacrifice lucrative commercial and conveyance practices and volunteer their services to the disadvantaged in human rights and public policy litigation. Michael Vidler, for example, has encountered difficulty in recruiting lawyers to join his law firm, because of its emphasis on pro bono services.[24]

ARGUING IN THE COURTS

Political issues often lie at the heart of human rights and public policy litigation. Representation by cause lawyers is important for two reasons. First, following the British legal tradition, judges in Hong

[21] *Leung TC William Roy* v. *Secretary for Justice* [Court of First Instance 2005]; *Cho Man Kit* v. *Broadcasting Authority* [Court of First Instance 2008].

[22] Author's interview with Gladys Li, February 21, 2008.

[23] *Chan Kam Nga* v. *Director of Immigration* [Court of Final Appeal 1999]. In *Lau Kong Yung and Others* v. *The Director of Immigration* [Court of Final Appeal 1999], another cause lawyer, Margaret Ng, also used the same strategy to help her disadvantaged client to receive legal aid. Author's interview with Margaret Ng, February 15, 2008.

[24] At the time of my interview, Vidler's law firm only had one solicitor trainee. Author's interview with Michael Vidler, November 28, 2007.

Kong primarily consider legal and procedural questions in hearing and deciding cases.[25] Litigants need capable lawyers to frame their political demands into legal issues and argue effectively in the courts. Second, since most human rights and public policy litigation is politically charged, litigants need lawyers who are committed to their causes and not afraid of offending the Chinese and Hong Kong governments.

Quantitative research on the United States and Canada has found that the relative capability of lawyers has played a significant role in influencing case outcomes (e.g., Haire et al. 1999; Szmer et al. 2007). Although there is no similar study of Hong Kong, it is reasonable to believe lawyer capability matters. Indeed, my interview data suggest that judges emphasize the importance of lawyer capability. Justice Hartmann said:

> The court is like a student. In respect of the matter to be disputed, the court needs to be educated by lawyers. In sophisticated areas of law like human rights and public law, having high quality counsel is of great assistance. They help judges better understand a difficult subject. In short, a high quality counsel is like a good professor who is able to illuminate difficult concepts to students. If a counsel is not particularly good, I will spend time researching and studying the case in my chamber.[26]

Justice Reyes also noted that:

> Judges need to be guided by counsel in the common-law adversarial system, especially on questions that can go either way. A counsel's arguments will be more persuasive to the judge if he presents cogent analysis and articulates effectively.[27]

Since judges in Hong Kong emphasize lawyer capability, the quality of cause lawyers is crucial to the prospect of legal mobilization. In this regard, most cause lawyers in Hong Kong possess a high level of substantive and process expertise.[28] Philip Dykes, Johannes Chan, Hectar Pun, and Mark Daly have expertise in human rights and public

[25] Chan (2009). Author's interviews with Justice Anselmo Reyes, March 4, 2008 and Justice Michael Hartmann, March 5, 2008.

[26] Author's interview with Justice Michael Hartmann, March 5, 2008.

[27] Author's interview with Justice Anselmo Reyes, March 4, 2008.

[28] Kritzer (1998, pp. 14–16) proposes two types of lawyer expertise: substantive and process. Substantive expertise is a specialization in a particular area of the

law. Dykes actively participated in drafting the Bill of Rights Ordinance in the late 1980s when he was an Assistant Solicitor-General. Chan is a public law professor and has written and practiced extensively on human rights and constitutional law. Pun and Daly studied human rights law and have practiced it since graduation from law school. The capability of cause lawyers is also manifested in their holding of the designation 'senior counsel (SC)'. Following the British legal tradition, merit is the major criterion for bestowing the SC designation in Hong Kong. Table 6.1 in Chapter 6 shows that many cause lawyers have held the SC title. In view of the strong capability and experience of cause lawyers and the lack of human rights lawyers in the government, a senior official in the Department of Justice claimed that the government is at a disadvantaged position in human rights litigation.[29]

Ability as an advocate, however, may not be the most important contribution of cause lawyers to legal mobilization. An equally important contribution concerns their willingness to take up politically charged lawsuits despite tremendous political and economic pressure. An experienced cause lawyer observed:

> Large solicitor firms in Hong Kong are generally reluctant to take up legal aid cases, especially those relating to human rights and public policy. They have the perception that this is anti-government work and is likely to affect their economic prospects.[30]

The difficulty Martin Lee experienced in finding a solicitor firm to represent him in a defamation lawsuit is an illustration. In 1993 Simon Li Fook-sean, a retired appellate court judge and pro-Beijing figure, accused Lee of encouraging the public to withdraw deposits from Chinese state-owned banks in Hong Kong in protest at Beijing's military crackdown on the 1989 democracy movement. Lee wanted to sue Li for defamation. A partner of a large international law firm originally told Lee that his case was arguable and promised to represent him. The firm later backed down, however, because other partners did not want

law; and process expertise concerns familiarity with the institutional rules and features of a particular court in which the lawyer argues.

29 Author's interview with senior official A of the Department of Justice, July 2007. Of course, the government has resources to retain experienced lawyers from the private sector. Indeed, the government has adopted such practice in most human rights and public policy litigation at the appellate courts.

30 Author's interview with a cause lawyer, November 2007.

to offend the Chinese authorities. Lee later approached more than a dozen law firms but all declined to act for him. It was only after the media exposed Lee's experience and the Law Society intervened that Lee found a British law firm for representation.[31]

Martin Lee's story is not an isolated incident. The following episode demonstrates how political and economic pressure has deterred many law firms from taking up politically charged cases. In 2007, SoCO set up a Community Law Center, which aims to bring test cases in human rights and important government policies.[32] In the process of establishing the Center, a large international law firm approached SoCO and inquired about the possibility that its lawyers could provide volunteer legal services for the Center. At a subsequent meeting between SoCO and a partner of the law firm, SoCO elaborated on the work of the Center. The firm later backed down and explained that it initially thought the Center would focus on non-political cases like family law. The law firm was reluctant to involve itself in politically sensitive cases, because it previously represented the government in some important cases and did not want to lose potential business from the government.[33]

The failure of an environmental protection group, Green Sense, to launch a lawsuit against the government's town planning policy shows how the reluctance of the legal profession to act for politically charged litigation could impede legal mobilization.[34] In 2007, Green Sense together with some district activists sought to sue the government over the designation of the use of a parcel of land near the waterfront. More broadly, Green Sense wanted to change the government's zoning policy, which has resulted in the erection of massive, wall-like buildings around the city. Green Sense, however, encountered great difficulty in finding lawyers to help them. Although a few lawyers were sympathetic to Green Sense's cause, they refused to represent the environmental protection group in the court because they feared that

[31] Author's interview with Martin Lee, February 20, 2008. For the debates arising from Lee's experience, see Wack (1994).

[32] Polly Hui, "City's first free legal advice centre set to open," *South China Morning Post*, June 5, 2006, p. A1.

[33] Author's interview with Wong Chi-yuen, December 19, 2007. Wong represented SoCO in meeting with the law firm.

[34] The discussion below is based on author's interviews with Roy Tam (Chairman of the Green Sense), December 16, 2007 and Lam Ho-yeung (Democratic Party's district councilor), January 10, 2008.

their action would offend the property developers and undermine their business prospects. Instead, these lawyers only offered basic pro bono advice behind the scenes. Without any experience of judicial review, Green Sense and district activists had to spend a week completing the notice of application for *certiorari*. On the date of submitting their application to the court, they had to frequently call lawyers for advice concerning how to handle the court procedures.

Without any legal assistance, Green Sense produced a poorly written and unclear notice of application for *certiorari*, which prompted the judge to dismiss their application. The judge, for example, pointed out that the notice failed to highlight which government decision was challenged, when it was made, and in what circumstances.[35] As an activist recalled, "The greatest obstacle in using the law to advance our cause is that we did not have the necessary legal expertise. The key to successful legal mobilization was legal support from lawyers."[36]

Legal mobilization demands litigants to frame their political claims into legal issues and present them effectively before the judges. As the process involves substantive legal expertise, active participation by cause lawyers is required. Through studying their roles in different stages of litigation, the previous discussion highlighted how cause lawyers have promoted legal mobilization in Hong Kong. My previous analysis focused on the formal and institutional roles of cause lawyers like resource mobilization. There are, however, other less visible but crucial roles that merit our attention, which include accommodating the social and psychological needs of their disadvantaged clients, and harmonizing objectives and strategies with their disadvantaged clients.

ACCOMMODATING THE SOCIAL AND PSYCHOLOGICAL NEEDS OF THE DISADVANTAGED

Most human rights litigants are disadvantaged or minority groups who have relatively low socio-economic status and/or are discriminated against by mainstream public opinion. Thus they may have substantial social and psychological distance from elitist, profit-oriented lawyers. Bindman (2002, p. 515), for example, points out that the atmosphere of the commercial law firms in Britain is forbidding to poor litigants.

35 *Ng Ngau Chai* v. *Town Planning Board and Another* [Court of First Instance 2007], paragraph 19.
36 Author's interview with Lam Ho-yeung, January 10, 2008.

Activists in Hong Kong also emphasize their social and psychological distance from elitist lawyers, as an activist said:

> In our lawsuits against public housing rental policy and the privatization of shopping and parking space in public housing estates, we did not approach commercial-oriented lawyers or those who often represented the government. Consuming a bottle of red wine that cost some ten thousand dollars was nothing to them. However, we had different life styles from these lawyers. We preferred lawyers who would be more passionate with the life of the lower class.[37]

Homosexual rights advocates also noted that typical lawyers do not understand or empathize with the concerns of sexual minorities. As Roddy Shaw commented:

> Lawyers assigned by the LAD for our gay rights cases lacked passion in equality and did not recognize the plight of sexual minorities. Some even told me that if we succeeded in overturning the government's policy on homosexual intercourse, society would become chaotic. Their lack of appreciation of our causes made it difficult for us to mobilize the law to protect our interests.[38]

In brief, the foregoing remarks by two social activists highlighted the importance of having lawyers who are sensitive and willing to accommodate the psychological and social needs of the disadvantaged.[39]

Cause lawyers in Hong Kong, through their more user-friendly practice sites and work style, have accommodated the social and psychological needs of the disadvantaged and thereby facilitated legal mobilization by the disadvantaged. Unlike large commercially oriented law firms which have luxurious offices in the heart of downtown, cause lawyers tend to practice in modest offices that are closer to the lower class neighborhood. Barnes and Daly, and Vidler and Co. operate in small and modest offices in Wanchai. Pam Baker and Co. was located in a small office above a fruit market in Mongkok. Denis Chang's Chamber, where Denis Chang, Philip Dykes,

[37] Author's interview with Wan Siu-kin, November 28, 2007.

[38] Author's interview with Roddy Shaw, December 21, 2007.

[39] In her study of the role of cause lawyering in helping a black South African village to resist forced relocation by the apartheid government from 1982 to 1985, White (1988, p. 742) also argues that lawyers' sensitivity to the unique needs of the disadvantaged was crucial to effective working relationships and successful cause lawyering.

Hectar Pun, and Jocelyn Leung practice, has a reputation for more relaxed dressing.[40] Modest and relaxed-dressing practice sites can provide a friendlier atmosphere for disadvantaged groups and improve their perception that cause lawyers are closer to their life style.

A number of cause lawyers have also moved beyond the traditional role of lawyers by providing emotional support to their marginalized clients and promoting their causes outside the courts. Michael Vidler is a case in point. A gay rights activist recalled:

> Vidler worked with me as a co-equal rather than imposing his advice on me. He brought me to meet with the barristers so that I could express my concern when they were formulating the litigation strategies. He taught me how to respond to the media in order to win their sympathy with my cause. During the court hearing, Vidler sat beside me and encouraged me whenever our side was in a disadvantaged position. Unlike other commercial lawyers who tend to be emotionally detached from their clients and cases, Vidler was emotionally committed to my case. He treated my cause as his and therefore our emotion often went in the same direction during the judicial hearing. His emotional support was critical to me. If I had not found a personally committed lawyer like Vidler, I would not have taken up the law to safeguard my rights.[41]

Apart from providing emotional support, Vidler, like many of his American counterparts, also included community action as a part of his cause lawyering work (Barclay and Marshall 2005; Trubek and Kransberger 1998). In *Leung TC William Roy* v. *Secretary for Justice*,[42] Vidler held forty press interviews in his office with a view to highlighting how the existing legal system deprives homosexuals of the right to privacy. As Vidler argued:

> Through this media campaign, I sought to change public opinion and make them more aware of the rights of sexual minorities. In addition, through interviews with international media like the BBC, I wanted to let the international community understand how Hong Kong has lagged behind in protecting sexual minorities and put pressure on the government to change the law.[43]

[40] Author's interview with Philip Dykes, November 29, 2007.
[41] Author's interview with Joseph Cho Man-kit, November 20, 2007 and March 6, 2008.
[42] *Leung TC William Roy* v. *Secretary for Justice* [Court of First Instance 2005].
[43] Author's interview with Michael Vidler, November 28, 2007.

To summarize, through their more user-friendly practice sites and work style, cause lawyers have helped advance legal mobilization in Hong Kong. Their user-friendly practice sites and participatory work style have helped to minimize the social and psychological barriers of marginalized groups to using the law. These less visible but crucial roles are beyond the scope of typical lawyers in Hong Kong.

HARMONIZING OBJECTIVES AND STRATEGIES WITH CLIENTS

Cause lawyers have also facilitated legal mobilization in Hong Kong by their willingness to harmonize their objectives and strategies with those of their disadvantaged clients. A major theme of research on cause lawyering concerns the distribution of decision-making authority between lawyers and clients. Most studies criticize cause lawyers for taking too much control in their relationships with clients (definition of clients' problems, solutions, and strategies) and for manipulating clients to pursue their own socio-political agendas.[44] In Hong Kong, human rights and public policy litigants have also sought to have their objectives and strategies taken seriously by cause lawyers. My interviews indicate that cause lawyers have generally been willing to accommodate the demands of their clients.

Unlike commercial or criminal litigants, whose ultimate goal is court victory, many social activists have taken an expressive approach to litigation. Scoring a victory is not their only or primary goal. Instead, they seek to use litigation to publicize their causes, express their values, and expose the deficiencies of the existing socio-political arrangements (McCann 1994, chapter 3; Morgan 1999, pp. 84–5). An organizer of the public housing rental litigation mentioned that, "Judicial review was a means to arouse public attention and discussion of the importance of affordable housing in Hong Kong."[45] An activist in the litigation against the functional constituency arrangement in the legislature also emphasized the expressive function of his litigation,[46] as he said:

[44] Southworth (1996, pp. 1103–6) provides an excellent review of the literature on lawyer–client decision making in civil rights and poverty practice.

[45] Author's interview with a core member of the Neighbourhood and Worker's Service Center, October 26, 2007.

[46] *Lee Miu Ling and Another* v. *The Attorney General* [Court of Appeal 1995].

> Judicial review was just part of our political campaign against the undemocratic legislative electoral system. As long as we could use judicial review to bring out the drawbacks of the functional constituency electoral system, we did not care too much about whether we could score a victory in the court.[47]

Many cause lawyers in Hong Kong are willing to accommodate the expressive needs of social activists. In doing so, cause lawyers have harmonized their own strategies and objectives with those of their clients. Two labor union activists noted:

> In bringing up labor rights cases to the courts, we not only want our lawyers to present legal arguments but also raise issues of social justice, equity and human rights. Typical lawyers, however, are often reluctant to heed to our demands. Lawyers assigned by the LAD, for example, did not want to meet with our members and discuss how to highlight the social dimensions of our cases in the courts. Accordingly, we would like to have human rights lawyers, like Hectar Pun, as our legal representation. They are more willing to communicate and discuss with us concerning the strategies to raise our demands for social reform during the court proceeding.[48]

A homosexual rights advocate also stressed the importance of having lawyers who are willing to raise the particular needs of sexual minorities in the courts. As Roddy Shaw elaborated:

> We retained human rights lawyers like Philip Dykes and Stanley Ma to represent us in litigation for two reasons. First, they have the expertise. Second and more important, gay and lesbian rights do not only involve legal issues but social and moral issues as well. We sought to raise these social and moral issues in the courts so that the public can better understand our perspectives. Human rights lawyers are more willing to accommodate our objectives and strategies. Their willingness is crucial to our effort to mobilize the law, because typical lawyers are reluctant to highlight the social and moral dimensions of gay and lesbian rights in litigation.[49]

To conclude, the foregoing comments by social activists suggest a less visible but significant role cause lawyers have played in promoting legal mobilization in Hong Kong.

[47] Author's interview with Law Yuk-kai, February 15, 2008.
[48] Author's interview with Walker Fung Kai-yuen and Huang Ngai-fung of the Hong Kong Confederation of Trade Unions, December 21, 2007.
[49] Author's interview with Roddy Shaw, December 21, 2007.

CONCLUSION: ECONOMIC MODERNIZATION AND DEMOCRATIZATION

In this and the previous chapters, I have discussed the rise of cause lawyering in Hong Kong as the city completed a transition from British to Communist Chinese rule in July 1997, and how cause lawyers have taken up the shifting political opportunities associated with the process of the sovereignty transition and actively advanced legal mobilization in Hong Kong. My study of Hong Kong cause lawyers informs the literature on economic modernization and democratization, especially the role of the middle class. Students of democratization, such as Lipset (1959), Moore (1966), Cheng (1989), and Diamond (1992) claim that economic modernization is an important requisite for democratic development. A crucial reason is that economic modernization is likely to create a middle class, which can stand up against an authoritarian state. The case of Hong Kong cause lawyers (an important group of the middle class), however, highlights that economic modernization can simultaneously facilitate and work against the efforts of the middle class to promote democratic changes. Economic modernization can hinder the efforts of the middle class to pursue democracy when large corporations side with an authoritarian regime to exert economic pressure on them.

On the one hand, economic modernization facilitates democratic changes in Hong Kong. A group of legal professionals who worked within the Hong Kong economy ended up using their skills, networks, and legalist ideology to promote political change. For example, before the opening of new legal opportunities in the 1990s, Ho Chun-yan practiced banking, trust, inheritance, and family law. With the passage of the HKBORO and the Basic Law, Ho founded his own law firm in 1995 and focused on human rights law (see Chapter 6).

On the other hand, the strength of capitalism seems to work against more democratic politics. Very few lawyers in Hong Kong are willing to sacrifice lucrative commercial and conveyancing practices and volunteer their services to the disadvantaged in human rights and public policy litigation. Michael Vidler, for example, has encountered difficulty in recruiting lawyers to join his law firm, because of its emphasis on pro bono services. More critically, Beijing and its business allies in Hong Kong have used economic pressure to deter the legal profession (particularly cause lawyers) from pursuing democratic changes. The Chinese government has imposed economic pressure on Ho Chun-yan's law firm because of his active support for the pro-democracy movement in China and his cause lawyering activities. Martin Lee, cause lawyers B and Z, and Ronny Tong have also encountered economic pressure from large business corporations in Hong Kong, because of their cause lawyering work and pro-democracy endeavors (see Chapter 6).

The case of Hong Kong cause lawyers presents a mixed picture of the relationship between economic modernization and democratization. Economic modernization can simultaneously facilitate and work against the efforts of the middle class (cause lawyers) to promote democratic changes.

8

RIGHTS ADVOCACY GROUPS AS TRANSFORMATIVE AGENTS

INTRODUCTION

The opening up of new legal opportunities does not translate automatically into legal mobilization. Rights advocacy groups are other important transformative agents who acted on the new legal opportunities and brought about legal mobilization. Column 2 in Appendices 1 and 2 illustrates that rights advocacy groups initiated, organized, and implemented many landmark human rights and public policy lawsuits in the post-colonial era. This chapter examines how rights advocacy groups have fostered legal mobilization in post-colonial Hong Kong.[1] First, I study the relationships between the broader legal-political environment and the growing trend of group-initiated litigation. Specifically, a shift in political opportunities from the legislature to the judicial branch has motivated rights advocacy groups to increasingly turn to the courts to pursue their goals. Second, drawing from Marc Galanter's framework (1974), I distinguish two types of rights advocacy groups in Hong Kong, namely one-shotters and repeat players. I argue that repeat player groups have performed a more critical role in using the law to promote progressive socio-political and legal reforms. The third part

[1] In this book, rights advocacy groups refer to voluntary organizations that are formed to promote a particular cause (e.g., environmental protection) or civil and human rights. Excluded from the book are groups that are formed and sponsored by the government (e.g., Equal Opportunities Commission) and commercial enterprises.

of this chapter examines two repeat player rights advocacy groups – the Society for Community Organization and Civil Rights for Sexual Diversities (CRSD). As will be documented below, these two groups have actively and strategically mobilized the law to advance long-range and systemic reforms.

SHIFTING POLITICAL OPPORTUNITIES AND GROUP-INITIATED LITIGATION

Column 2 in Appendices 1 and 2 shows that rights advocacy groups in Hong Kong have increasingly used litigation to advance their causes since the opening of legal opportunities in the early 1990s. Throughout the 1970s and 1980s, rights advocacy groups rarely used litigation to promote their interests. Instead, they tended to rely on protests, petitions, or mass mobilization as the major strategies to furthering their goals (Chiu and Lui 2000; Ho 2000). The establishment of new legal opportunities, however, dramatically changed this situation. In 1995, the United Ants, for example, used the Hong Kong Bill of Rights Ordinance (HKBORO) to challenge the legality of the functional constituency elections of the legislature (see column 2 in Appendix 2).[2]

As political opportunities shifted from the legislature to the judicial branch after July 1997, group-initiated legal mobilization intensified. Rights advocacy groups devoted an increasing share of their efforts to legal mobilization. The director of the Society for Community Organization (SoCO), Ho Hei-wah, mentioned that after July 1997 they found it more difficult to advance their causes in the political arena. The legislature was weakened and failed to effectively check and balance the government. Legislators, for example, could not initiate private member's bills without the consent of the Chief Executive. The executive branch usually held on to its policies when facing lobbying by SoCO. By contrast, the opening of new legal opportunities and a rights-receptive judiciary made litigation a more promising and indeed inevitable choice for SoCO.[3]

Ho's remarks were echoed by all the rights advocates that I interviewed. In short, a shift in political opportunities to the judicial branch made legal mobilization a more promising avenue for rights advocacy groups to advance their causes. Some groups like SoCO and

[2] *Lee Miu Ling and Another* v. *The Attorney General* [Court of Appeal 1995].

[3] Author's interview with Ho Hei-wah, September 16, 2008.

Civil Rights for Sexual Diversities (CRSD) have adjusted their behavior and adopted litigation as a central and long-term strategy. In the words of Marc Galanter (1974), these two groups have become repeat players in litigation. To gain a better understanding of how the two repeat player groups contributed to legal mobilization in Hong Kong, I first review the concept of repeat players.

ONE-SHOT AND REPEAT PLAYER RIGHTS ADVOCACY GROUPS

In his study of how the basic features of a legal system affect the potential of using the law to advance progressive reforms, Galanter (1974) identifies two kinds of litigating parties – one-shotters and repeat players – and argues that repeat players tend to come out ahead in litigation. One-shotters are claimants who only use the courts occasionally. They generally possess fewer resources and have higher stakes in the tangible result of the case (e.g., auto-injury claimants). Repeat players frequently use the courts to promote their interests and therefore have acquired substantial litigation experience. They possess better resources to pursue their long-term objectives through the courts and have lower stakes in the result of any single case (e.g., insurance companies).

Galanter (1974, pp. 101–3) contends that repeat players are more successful than one-shotters in litigation and often dominate the rule-making development for the following two reasons. First, repeat players possess better resources and litigation expertise in certain policy areas, which enable them to devise a more comprehensive litigation strategy like hiring expert witnesses and engaging in forum shopping. Second, repeat players have longer time horizons than one-shotters. Because one-shotters usually focus on maximizing the immediate and tangible outcome of a case, they are more willing to trade off the prospect of advancing long-term and systemic reforms for tangible gains. By contrast, repeat players have longer time horizons and therefore they are more concerned with the rule component of a case. To avoid adverse precedents that may affect the outcomes of future cases, repeat players are inclined to reach settlements on unpromising cases and to pursue promising ones. Socio-legal scholars have applied Galanter's framework to diverse contexts and generally confirm his arguments (Kritzer and Silbey 2003).

In discussing the contribution of rights advocacy groups to legal mobilization in post-colonial Hong Kong, I make a distinction between one-shotters and repeat players. Drawing from Galanter's insights, I argue that repeat player groups have performed a more productive role than one-shotters in using the law to achieve long-range and progressive reforms in Hong Kong. First, as highlighted by Epp (1998, pp. 18–9), successful rights revolution requires widespread and sustained litigation to clarify and enforce landmark decisions. Repeat player groups perform a crucial role in that regard, as they stress long-term and strategic litigation. Second, repeat player groups tend to emphasize long-range socio-legal development rather than immediate tangible gains. Third, these groups have developed their organizational structure in a way that integrates litigation with their overall organization's strategies. In the next section, I will elaborate my arguments through case studies of two repeat player groups – the Society for Community Organization (SoCO) and Civil Rights for Sexual Diversities (CRSD).

SOCIETY FOR COMMUNITY ORGANIZATION

Founded by foreign Christian churches in 1972, SoCO is a pro-democracy grassroots advocacy group.[4] From its inception to the early 1980s, SoCO emphasized using social actions and community work to further grassroots interests and social justice. During that period of time, law played a minor role in SoCO's endeavors. The process of the sovereignty transition between the 1980s and July 1997 dramatically transformed the goals and strategies of SoCO in two critical ways. First, concerned about the prospect of freedoms and rights in post-colonial Hong Kong, SoCO has set the protection of human rights as a major organizational goal since the early 1980s. Second, recognizing that post-colonial Hong Kong would have a new constitution, SoCO has started to put more emphasis on law in its effort to promote human rights and, more broadly, the cause of the disadvantaged since the early 1980s. It began actively to remold its organizational structure so that it could mobilize the law more effectively in the post-colonial period. For example, SoCO sought a number of cause lawyers like Ho Chun-yan and Johannes Chan to be its pro bono legal advisors. With the assistance of these cause lawyers and other human rights activists, in

[4] The discussion in this section is primarily based on author's interviews with Ho Hei-wah, Fung Ho-lup, and Wong Chi-yuen.

1983 SoCO set up a Civil Rights Education Center to enhance public consciousness of the importance of civil rights and liberties.

The implementation of the Basic Law in July 1997 established a new legal opportunity structure. The constitutional entrenchment of fundamental rights and liberties and the setting up of the Court of Final Appeal (CFA) opened numerous legal opportunities for SoCO (and civil society) to mobilize the law to pursue its goals. The impact of the new legal opportunities on SoCO's choice of strategies is illustrated in the different strategies undertaken by the right-of-abode movements before and after July 1997.

New legal opportunities and shift in organizational strategy

Since the mid 1970s SoCO has actively helped mainland Chinese who have married or were born of Hong Kong permanent residents to obtain the right of abode in Hong Kong. During the 1970s and 1980s, litigation was not a viable option to SoCO, given that the colonial law did not confer residency rights to mainland Chinese. Accordingly, SoCO could only rely on sit-ins, demonstrations, and petitions in the right-of-abode movement.[5]

The implementation of the Basic Law in July 1997 caused a substantial shift in SoCO's strategies in the post-colonial right-of-abode movement. Litigation became the dominant strategy because article 24 of the new constitution grants residency rights to mainland-born children of Hong Kong permanent residents. Indeed shortly after the enactment of the Basic Law in 1990, SoCO and its pro bono legal advisors found that the new constitution provided them with the legal basis to further the right-of-abode movement through litigation. Thus, SoCO actively took up the law to help thousands of mainland-born children of Hong Kong permanent residents to obtain the residency right.

On the one hand, SoCO started to organize litigation on behalf of mainland-born children. SoCO aimed to use test-case strategies to bring long-term and broad changes in the government's immigration policy toward mainland Chinese who have married or were born of Hong Kong permanent residents. It carefully selected promising cases and arguments in order to maximize the chance of achieving legal victory and to avoid setting unfavorable precedents. On the other hand, SoCO used the threat of litigation to negotiate with the then designate

[5] Author's interview with Ho Hei-wah, September 16, 2008.

Tung Chee-hwa administration. The rights group presented legal opinions of pro bono legal advisors and sought to use the threat of litigation as a bargaining chip to pressure the Tung administration to confer the right of abode to mainland-born children of Hong Kong permanent residents (Mnookin and Kornhauser 1979). The Tung administration, however, did not back down. It raised a different interpretation of article 24 of the Basic Law and contended that article 24 did not automatically confer the right of abode to mainland-born children.

As the threat of litigation failed to pressurize the Tung administration to back down, SoCO filed lawsuits on behalf of thousands of families with mainland-born children shortly after the sovereignty handover. In 1999, SoCO won the lawsuits in the CFA.

The legal victory in the right-of-abode litigation is significant to SoCO in the sense that it helped the rights advocacy group to establish litigation as a central strategy in pursuing its causes in the future. The CFA's ruling boosted SoCO's confidence in the impartiality and competence of the judiciary, especially the highest court, though the Standing Committee of the National People's Congress (NPCSC) overturned the CFA ruling. Additionally, the right-of-abode litigation enabled SoCO to accumulate valuable experience in using the law and the courts. The rights advocacy group not only learned how to work productively with cause lawyers and legal aid officers, but also how to use litigation to draw media attention to its causes.[6]

Briefly stated, the opening of new legal opportunities in July 1997 prompted SoCO to shift its strategies and put a greater weight on litigation. A victory in the right-of-abode litigation in 1999 boosted SoCO's confidence in the judiciary and reinforced its determination to use law and courts to advance social reforms. To become a competent repeat player group in legal mobilization, however, requires the group to possess the structure (e.g., legal expertise) and resources to broaden and develop cases (Milner 1987, p. 461). The next part will discuss how SoCO has organizationally equipped itself to act as a competent repeat player group.

Organizational competency and legal mobilization

Litigation is a costly and complex task. A rights advocacy group, which wants to proactively and persistently use litigation as a

[6] Author's interview with Ho Hei-wah, September 16, 2008.

significant source of leverage for political and social changes, has to possess the structure and resources to broaden and develop cases.[7] An organization must have substantial legal expertise, extensive social networks, and longer time horizons in order to successfully broaden and develop cases. Legal expertise and longer time horizons help an organization to define a case in terms of broader and/or constitutional principles so that the case can have wider socio-political implications. Extensive social networks enable an organization to gain access to potential sources of cases. Locating suitable cases for legal mobilization is particularly difficult when the mobilization involves the participation of marginalized and isolated groups.[8]

SoCO is organizationally equipped to mobilize the law because it has the following three qualities: legal expertise, a comprehensive network of field workers, and longer time horizons. I first discuss legal expertise. As mentioned in the previous section, since the mid 1980s, SoCO had started to invite cause lawyers to serve as the group's pro bono legal advisors. By 2007, SoCO had about twenty pro bono legal advisors, including Philip Dykes, Audrey Eu, Mark Daly, and Stanley Ma.[9] This legal team has provided crucial legal expertise for SoCO's legal mobilization efforts, such as advising on the prospects of potential cases, writing legal opinions supporting legal aid applications, and representing clients in courts. A constant and experienced legal team is significant to SoCO, which has adopted legal mobilization as a central, long-term strategy.[10]

[7] Case broadening refers to efforts to: (1) make a case comprehensive enough to apply to all the relevant members of a group or a class; (2) raise important or constitutional issues in the litigation. Case development refers to how actively an organization develops cases. An organization actively develops cases when it goes out and searches for problems, instead of waiting for issues to come to its door (Milner 1987: 448, 462).

[8] In his study of legal mobilization by mental patients for the right to refuse treatment, for example, Milner (1987) documents the difficulty of public advocate's offices in finding suitable mental patients to participate in the lawsuits. A gay rights advocate in Hong Kong also told me that he has great difficulty in finding suitable homosexual couples who are willing to litigate for same-sex marriage, because many homosexual couples want to maintain their privacy. Author's interview with Roddy Shaw, December 21, 2007.

[9] Author's interview with Wong Chi-yuen, December 19, 2007.

[10] The importance of having a constant and experienced legal team for the establishment of legal mobilization as a central organizational strategy is illustrated by the failure of Green Sense to mobilize the law. As discussed in the previous chapter, in 2007 Green Sense sought to use judicial review to influence the government's

Recently SoCO has taken measures to strengthen its organizational capacity to use the law. Using the American Civil Liberties Union as a model, SoCO set up a Community Law Center in 2007.[11] Managed by activist lawyer Richard Tsoi, the Center handles all litigation-related activities and aims at bringing test cases in human rights and important government policies. The twenty pro bono legal advisors provide legal expertise for all cases handled by the Center. Unlike the government Legal Aid Department (LAD), which passively waits for cases to come their way, the Center has actively found cases since its establishment. Each Friday the Center holds a legal consultation session in a town hall and provides legal advice for asylum seekers.[12]

Second, SoCO has also established a comprehensive network of field workers, who have actively searched for promising issues and cases for litigation. Since its inception in the 1970s, SoCO has adopted community action as a central strategy; and a comprehensive network of community organizers has been formed over the years. These community organizers divide their work by the following issues: child and elderly welfare; housing and social security; patient rights; community re-development; new immigrants; asylum seekers; and prisoner rehabilitation. Through the regular visit schemes, community organizers have developed systematic access to disadvantaged groups and heard their complaints firsthand. In the process, SoCO has located crucial issues and cases suitable for litigation. The two recent lawsuits discussed below show the importance of community networks in finding suitable cases for legal mobilization.

In the first case, the government-sponsored prisoners' rehabilitation program enabled SoCO's community organizers to gain access to prisoners and hear their complaints about deprivation of voting rights in the legislative elections. In response, SoCO helped a prisoner to file

zoning policy. Its efforts failed because the environmental protection group could not find pro bono legal representation. This failure discouraged Green Sense from using the courts to promote their cause in the future. Author's interview with Roy Tam, December 16, 2007.

11 In 1995, Ho Hei-wah, the Director of SoCO, went to the United States and Canada and visited legal clinics there. Ho was particularly impressed by the prominent role the American Civil Liberties Union (ACLU) plays in litigating for progressive and systemic social reforms. ACLU served as a model for SoCO when it decided to set up a community law center. Author's interview with Ho Hei-wah, September 16, 2008.

12 Author's interview with Wong Chi-yuen, December 19, 2007.

a lawsuit challenging the ban on prisoners' voting in the legislative elections.[13] In the second case, through its regular visit schemes, SoCO's community organizers discovered that many elderly and deaf-mutes failed to seek medical services, because the Hospital Authority required all public hospital patients to make appointments on the phone. In the end, SoCO filed litigation on behalf of two elderly people, challenging the Hospital Authority's policy (see Table 8.1).[14] In short, the existence of an extensive network of community organizers has enabled SoCO to integrate legal mobilization with its overall organizational structure.

SoCO's longer time horizon is the final factor which has facilitated its legal mobilization efforts. SoCO is committed to using the law to achieve long-term social changes. This commitment is not only demonstrated by its organizational features described above but also by the nature of the litigation. Table 8.1 displays the important lawsuits brought by SoCO. Most of them raised broader and/or constitutional principles with widespread socio-political implications. As a repeat player group, SoCO tends to focus on cases with reasonable prospects for creating favorable precedents and it avoids those which may set adverse precedents for the subsequent litigation.[15] In addition, SoCO generally does not support litigation that seeks short-term material benefits at the expense of broader societal reforms. As a repeat player, SoCO primarily seeks to use strategic litigation to advance progressive social reforms rather than pursuing short-term, ad hoc material gains.[16]

[13] *Chan Kin Sum* v. *Secretary for Justice and Another* [Court of First Instance 2008].

[14] It should be noted that community organizers do not account for all the litigation handled by SoCO. Given SoCO's track record in defending the interests of marginalized groups, some clients took the initiative in seeking SoCO's assistance. The right-of-abode litigation was a case in point.

[15] In 2005, SoCO had considered suing the government's new housing application and allocation system for discriminating against young single adults. The new system replaced the first-come-first-served arrangement and gave priority to older applicants. In the end, SoCO gave up the litigation plan, because its legal advisors highlighted the poor prospect of winning the case and the possibility of setting an adverse precedent for future anti-age discrimination litigation. Author's interview with Sze Lai-shan, December 19, 2007.

[16] In 2007, for example, SoCO helped some citizens to sue the Independent Police Complaints Council (IPCC) for negligently leaking their personal data on the Internet. In the end, most of them withdrew their litigation because their major concern (monetary compensation) was incompatible with that of SoCO

TABLE 8.1: Important litigation brought by SoCO (1997–2010)

Case	Summary of the case	Outcome	Date
Chan Kam Nga v. *Director of Immigration*	Right of abode of mainland-born children of Hong Kong permanent residents	Government lost	29/1/1999
Ng Ka Ling and Another v. *The Director of Immigration*	Right of abode of mainland-born children of Hong Kong permanent residents	Government lost	29/1/1999
The Director of Immigration v. *Cheung Lai Wah*	Right of abode of mainland-born children of Hong Kong permanent resident	Government lost	29/1/1999
Tsui Kuen Nang v. *The Director of Immigration*	Right of abode of mainland-born children of Hong Kong permanent residents	Government lost	29/1/1999
Lau Kong Yung and Others v. *The Director of Immigration*	Right of abode of mainland-born children of Hong Kong permanent residents	Government won	3/12/1999
Tam Nga Yin and Others v. *The Director of Immigration*	Right of abode of Hong Kong permanent residents' adopted children in China	Government won	20/7/2001
Xie Xiaoyi v. *The Director of Immigration*	Right of abode of Hong Kong permanent residents' adopted children in China	Government won	20/7/2001
The Director of Immigration v. *Chong Fung-yuen*	Right of abode of children born in Hong Kong to Chinese parents who are not Hong Kong residents but who are mainlanders visiting Hong Kong temporarily or illegally staying	Government lost	20/7/2001
Au Kwok Hung v. *Appeal Tribunal*	The power of Housing Authority to terminate tenancy	Government won	8/12/2000
Victim A v. *Independent Police Complaints Council*	Better protection of the privacy of citizens who have complained about the police	Out of court settlement	2007

TABLE 8.1: (*cont.*)

Case	Summary of the case	Outcome	Date
Wong Sam, Shum Hang-choi v. *Hospital Authority*	Disability right to use government medical services	Out of court settlement	2008
Chan Kin Sum v. *Secretary for Justice and Another*	Prisoners' voting right	Government lost	8/12/2008
Kong Yunming v. *The Director of Social Welfare*	Right of Hong Kong residents who have not stayed in Hong Kong for seven years to receive social security assistance	Government won	23/6/2009
Yao Man Fai George v. *The Director of Social Welfare*	Right of Hong Kong residents to apply for social security assistance, not subject to the requirement that they must have resided in Hong Kong continuously for at least one year immediately before the date of application	Government lost	21/6/2010

Sources: Author's interviews with Ho Hei-wah and Wong Chi-yuen.

In this section, I examined how SoCO, a longtime rights advocacy group, seized the new legal opportunities associated with the sovereignty transition and transformed itself into a repeat player group. As a repeat player, SoCO has brought various lawsuits with far-reaching socio-political implications. As a pioneer in using law to advance long-term social reforms, SoCO has inspired some younger rights groups to take on the path of legal mobilization. In the next section, I will study one of them – Civil Rights for Sexual Diversities.

(establishing a better system to protect the privacy of those citizens who have complained about the police). Author's interview with Wong Chi-yuen, September 16, 2008. See also Agnes Lam, "29 victims of police data leaks seek damages," *South China Morning Post*, July 12, 2007, p. A3.

CIVIL RIGHTS FOR SEXUAL DIVERSITIES

Founded by a group of gay rights activists in 1999, CRSD is a non-governmental organization seeking to advance the rights of lesbian, gay, bisexual, and transgender (LGBT) people who face discrimination or harassment because of their sexual orientation and gender identity. Roddy Shaw, a veteran gay rights activist, is the organization's chairperson.[17]

Since its establishment, CRSD has decided to use law as a key long-term strategy in pursuing its causes. The shift in political opportunities from the legislature to the judiciary in the post-colonial era is a major factor in this decision. Shaw explained that it is difficult to promote the causes of sexual minorities through the legislative path, given that the Basic Law has weakened legislative power. Initiation of private member's bills, for example, requires the consent of the Chief Executive. In addition, pro-government parties have dominated the legislature and defended the government's conservative policies toward sexual minorities.[18] While the legislative path has been restricted, the judicial arena has become more open. The implementation of the HKBORO and the Basic Law provides the legal basis for sexual minorities to pursue their claims in courts. For instance, article 25 of the Basic Law guarantees equality before the law for everyone. Indeed, SoCO's victory in *Ng Ka Ling and Another* v. *The Director of Immigration* in 1999 boosted CRSD's confidence in using the law.[19] Summing up, the shift in political opportunities in the post-1997 period prompted CRSD to choose litigation as a significant, long-term strategy in advancing its causes.

Organizational competence and proactive legal mobilization

As discussed above, to become a successful repeat player, a rights advocacy group has to develop its organizational structure in a way

[17] Unless specified otherwise, the discussion in this section is based on author's interview with Roddy Shaw, December 21, 2007.

[18] In spite of repeated lobbying by gay and lesbian groups, the post-colonial government and legislature refused to amend the law on the age of consent for homosexual intercourse. The law, setting the age of consent for homosexual intercourse at 21, was criticized for discriminating against young gay men. Roddy Shaw openly criticized the legislature for lacking compassion for sexual minorities. See Ravina Shamdasani, "Gay activists to take equality fight to LegCo," *South China Morning Post*, June 23, 2004, p. A3.

[19] *Ng Ka Ling and Another* v. *The Director of Immigration* [Court of Final Appeal 1999].

that integrates litigation with its overall organization's goal. CRSD has the legal expertise and longer time horizon to act as a repeat player. CRSD has operated a legal advice center. As of 2007, there are four pro bono lawyers and ten case workers (with basic legal training) working for the center. Roddy Shaw has a Master's degree in Human Rights Law. This pool of legal expertise has enabled CRSD to provide legal advice and representation to about twenty cases each year. About two-thirds of these cases were heard and settled at tribunals like the Equal Opportunities Commission and the Privacy Commission.[20]

Unlike SoCO, which has cultivated an extensive network of community organizers, CRSD does not have such a network. The lack of community organizers, however, has not hindered CRSD from getting potential cases for litigation. Given that Hong Kong is a small city and the LGBT community is narrow, Shaw and CRSD are familiar with the prominent issues the LGBT community is facing. Moreover, Shaw's longtime activism has made him and CRSD a popular and trustworthy LGBT rights defender. Many LGBT people who need professional legal assistance have turned to CRSD for help. In 2004, Timothy Lee Ting-yu (a gay rights activist), for example, approached CRSD for legal advice when he decided to litigate against the legislation that set different ages of sexual consent for homosexuals and heterosexuals.[21]

Longer time horizon, legal arguments, and proactive legal mobilization

In their study of litigation by organized interest groups on abortion and capital punishment in post-war America, Epstein and Kobylka (1992) argued that the kinds of legal arguments made by organized interest groups before the Supreme Court have been a central factor explaining the legal change that happened in both areas of law. Groups capable of strategically presenting and adjusting legal arguments that are adaptable to the political environment (e.g., the composition of

[20] In 2003–04, for example, CRSD represented a transsexual woman before the Equal Opportunities Commission and helped her to win the right to have her identity changed on her academic certificates. See Ravina Shamdasani, "Victory for woman in sex bias dispute," *South China Morning Post*, October 14, 2004, p. A4.

[21] Author's interview with Timothy Lee Ting-yu, December 3, 2007. Lee is a member of Rainbow Action (a gay rights group).

the Supreme Court and the party that controlled the White House) tended to achieve greater success in generating legal change. In short, Epstein and Kobylka remind us that the kinds of legal arguments tendered before courts can crucially promote or retard legal mobilization.

Since its establishment, CRSD has set legal mobilization as a long-term strategy in pursuing its causes. The longer time horizon has significantly influenced the kinds of legal arguments CRSD presents to courts and subsequent legal change. As CRSD stresses using litigation to promote progressive socio-legal development, it seeks to frame its legal arguments in civil rights and/or constitutional terms when it sees a favorable political environment. CRSD's strategic framing of legal arguments and its impact on promoting legal mobilization is illustrated in *Secretary for Justice* v. *Yau Yuk Lung Zigo and Another*.[22]

In *Yau*, two gay men were caught and prosecuted for engaging in sodomy in a car beside a public road in April 2004. The law used to prosecute the two men was section 118F(1) of the Crimes Ordinance. At first they pleaded not guilty and defended themselves on technical grounds (i.e., the lighting on the road was so dim that the police could not prove beyond doubt that the two men had engaged in sodomy). The two gay men later approached CRSD for legal assistance. Instead of arguing the case on technical grounds, CRSD suggested that the case should be fought on human rights and constitutional grounds. According to CRSD, section 118F(1) violated the constitutional right to equality by criminalizing homosexual buggery committed in public places. By contrast, there was no equivalent law criminalizing heterosexual buggery or sexual intercourse between lesbians committed in public places. The two gay men accepted CRSD's suggestion, which was based on its long-range commitment to use litigation to eliminate discrimination against the LGBT community. In addition, CRSD also believed that the judiciary would be receptive to its constitutional argument, given the track record of the judiciary in defending the right to equality in prominent cases including *Secretary for Justice and Others* v. *Chan Wah and Others*, and *Equal Opportunities Commission* v. *Director of Education*.[23]

[22] *Secretary for Justice* v. *Yau Yuk Lung Zigo and Another* [Court of Final Appeal 2007].

[23] In *Secretary for Justice and Others* v. *Chan Wah and Others*, the Court of First Instance, the Court of Appeal, and the CFA ruled that the village representative electoral system was unconstitutional because the system deprived non-indigenous

The constitutional argument put forward by CRSD scored victories in the District Court, the Court of Appeal, and the CFA, as the courts ruled that section 118F(1) violated the constitutional right to equality. Gay community members described the ruling as an important progressive step towards ending the discriminatory sex offence laws in Hong Kong.[24]

Yau exemplifies the significant role of a repeat player group in advancing legal mobilization in Hong Kong. Had CRSD adopted technical grounds in defending Yau and Lee, *Yau* would only have been an ordinary criminal case. As a repeat player group, however, CRSD sought to use the law to pursue long-range progressive social changes like elimination of discriminatory laws. Thus, it alerted the two gay men to their constitutional rights and suggested that they could present their legal arguments in human rights and constitutional terms. In the end, an ordinary criminal case was developed into a landmark gay rights case, which may set a favorable precedent for gay marriage litigation.

CONCLUSION

In this chapter, I presented two case studies of how rights advocacy groups seized the new legal opportunities to promote legal mobilization in post-colonial Hong Kong. First, I examined how SoCO, a longtime rights advocacy group, seized the new legal opportunities associated with the process of the sovereignty transition and transformed itself into a repeat player group. Second, I studied a relatively new rights advocacy organization – CRSD. My discussion highlighted the importance of both structure and agency in the rise of legal mobilization in post-1997 Hong Kong. The opening of new legal opportunities does not translate automatically into litigation success. The new legal opportunities provide opportunities for action, not the

villagers of the right to participate in public affairs through freely chosen representatives. In *Equal Opportunities Commission* v. *Director of Education*, the Court of First Instance [2001] held that a decade-old government policy of allocating secondary school places to primary school students was unconstitutional, because it was discriminatory against female students. See Chapter 4 of this book.

24 Chandra Wong, "Court throws out discriminatory sex charge," *South China Morning Post*, December 17, 2005, p. A1.

action itself. The capability of rights advocates to recognize and respond to the opportunities is crucial to successful legal mobilization. SoCO and CRSD have developed their organizational structures, like the setting up of a legal advice center and an extensive network of community workers, so that they can proactively use litigation to pursue their causes.

PART IV

9

THE IMPACT OF THE JUDICIALIZATION OF POLITICS

INTRODUCTION

The preceding chapters analyzed why and how the courts in post-colonial Hong Kong have increasingly been involved in making important public policies that had previously been dominated by the executive or legislative branches. Moreover, the courts have also been increasingly called to regulate the conduct of political activities, such as election regulation,[1] organization of political parties,[2] and the procedures for the legislature.[3] In other words, there is a growing trend of the judicialization of politics in post-colonial Hong Kong.[4] In this chapter, I will study the impact of the judicialization of politics. Specifically, my discussion will focus on the following three aspects: first, the growing

1 In 2008, for example, SoCO helped a prisoner to file a lawsuit challenging the ban on prisoners' voting in the legislative elections.

2 In 2007, the Democratic Party litigated against section 98 of the Companies Ordinance, which required political parties to disclose their membership lists to anyone who wanted to see them. Political parties in Hong Kong are typically incorporated as companies. Nick Gentle, "Democrats fail in bid to keep membership secret," *South China Morning Post*, May 22, 2007, p. A2.

3 In *Leung Kwok Hung* v. *The President of the Legislative Council of the Hong Kong Special Administrative Region and Another* [Court of First Instance 2007], legislator Leung Kwok-hung challenged Rita Fan for blocking pro-democracy legislators' amendments to a covert surveillance bill.

4 Judicialization of politics is defined as the process by which courts and judges come to make or increasingly to dominate the formulation of public policies that had previously been made by other government agencies, especially legislatures and executives. See Tate (1995, p. 28).

importance of legal and/or constitutional considerations and rhetoric in the policy-making process; second, the politicization of courts; and third, the politicization of government-funded legal aid.

GROWING IMPORTANCE OF LEGAL AND/OR CONSTITUTIONAL CONSIDERATIONS AND RHETORIC

As courts have more frequently participated in the policy-making processes, courts and their likely responses to controversies over public policies have become a crucial factor in the calculation of political actors. Political actors have put a greater emphasis on the legal and/or constitutional ramifications of their actions.

The Hong Kong government has taken greater efforts to preempt the judiciary from striking down or interpreting its policies in unfavorable ways. Cheung and Wong (2006, p. 132), for example, report that after the Link REIT case,[5] the government decided that important policy proposals have to undergo a judicial review test so that they are not easily opposed by judicial review. In 2005, the government took another preemptive measure in the political struggle over the term of office of the new Chief Executive (following the resignation of Tung Chee-hwa). Anticipating that pro-democracy politicians would apply for a judicial review in the struggle, the interim government (under Donald Tsang) initiated a request for the Chinese legislature to interpret the relevant provisions of the Basic Law. In the end, the Chinese legislature issued its interpretation. And the judicial review against the government had to be withdrawn.

The judicialization of politics has influenced Beijing as well. In formulating its strategies of governing Hong Kong, Beijing has become more mindful of their constitutional implications, particularly the possibility of being challenged by litigation. The promulgation of the consultation paper "On the Political Development in Hong Kong" (the Paper) in 2007 was a case in point.[6] The Hong Kong government released the Paper with a view to seeking public opinion on the further democratization of the political system. A major focal point in the debate over the Paper concerned the method of selecting the Chief Executive, specifically the requirement of adopting "democratic

5 *Lo Siu Lan* v. *Hong Kong Housing Authority* [Court of Final Appeal 2005].

6 The discussion below is based on Li Xianzhi, "The puzzle of the silence on discussing the democratic procedures," *Ming Pao*, July 16, 2007, p. A4 (in Chinese).

procedures," which was stipulated in article 45 of the Basic Law.[7] It was reported that Beijing sought to use the requirement of "democratic procedures" as a screening mechanism to ensure that only its favored candidates could stand in the Chief Executive elections. Put simply, the democratic procedures served as a form of primary elections. Throughout the debate, however, the Hong Kong government and the pro-Beijing circle were surprisingly mute on the issue of "democratic procedures." For example, they were reluctant to openly discuss their position on what constituted democratic procedures.

According to a pro-Beijing figure, their silence was a tactic to minimize the risk of being challenged by pro-democracy parties in courts. The logic ran as follows. Article 45 of the Basic Law merely stipulates the democratic procedures requirement without elaborating its definitions or contents, let alone defining it as a mechanism to oust certain types of candidates from running in the Chief Executive elections. Thus, any proposals for using the democratic procedures as a screening mechanism were likely to be opposed by pro-democracy politicians in courts.

Constitutional rhetoric has also assumed new importance in the policy deliberation process. Pro-democracy politicians and cause lawyers have increasingly raised the possibility of "judicial review" and the subsequent constitutional implications in deliberating crucial public policies. In doing so, they sought to use the law to enhance their bargaining power with the administration. The following case, which concerned the Donald Tsang administration's[8] proposed billion-dollar donations to the reconstruction projects in Sichuan province after the devastating earthquake in May 2008, can illustrate the growing trend of constitutional rhetoric in the policy deliberation process.[9]

[7] Article 45 of the Basic Law governs the selection of the Chief Executive. The article stipulates that the ultimate aim is the selection of the Chief Executive by universal suffrage upon nomination by a broadly representative nominating committee in accordance with *democratic procedures* (emphasis added).

[8] Donald Tsang, a senior civil servant and cabinet member of the Tung Chee-hwa administration, succeeded Tung as the second Chief Executive of the Hong Kong Special Administrative Region in June 2005, after Beijing forced Tung to resign in March 2005.

[9] The following discussion is based on Nick Gentle, Klaudia Lee, and Albert Wong, "Legal doubts over Hong Kong quake donation: Basic Law challenge to Sichuan gift possible," *Sunday Morning Post*, July 6, 2008, p. A1.

The Donald Tsang administration initially tried to force through the proposed donation without consulting the legislature about how the funding would be spent and monitored. Moreover, the administration suggested that the amount of its donations might be tied to those contributed by mainland provinces.[10] The administration's actions, however, aroused opposition from pro-democracy politicians and some cause lawyers, who used constitutional rhetoric to express their concern. Ronny Tong, a Civic Party legislator, remarked that linking the level of the donations to those contributed by mainland provinces might give the impression that there was some kind of levy. This contravened article 106 of the Basic Law, which prohibited Beijing from levying any tax on Hong Kong. Tong warned that if the administration insisted on rushing its proposed donation through the legislature, any dissatisfied taxpayer could challenge the proposal by a judicial review. Cause lawyer, Mark Daly, also said that the administration should adequately explain its donation decision to the legislature. This was because article 106 of the Basic Law stated that Hong Kong shall use its fiscal revenues exclusively for its own purposes and they shall not be handed to the central government.

Summing up, the aforementioned discussion demonstrated the growing importance of constitutional considerations and rhetoric in the policy-making and deliberation processes in post-colonial Hong Kong. As courts have increasingly become involved in making politically and economically consequential decisions, political actors from different partisanships have paid closer scrutiny to courts. Specifically, they have sought to influence court decisions, judicial appointments, and other legal institutions. Thus, the judicialization of politics has produced an emerging trend of the politicization of courts. In the next section, I will examine this emerging trend.

POLITICIZATION OF COURTS

The politicization of courts, defined as the efforts by political actors to influence court decisions and judicial appointments, has emerged in post-colonial Hong Kong. Court rulings and judicial appointments

[10] After the Sichuan earthquake, Beijing ordered nineteen provinces and cities to contribute 1 percent of their tax revenue to Sichuan between 2009 and 2011. See Gentle et al., "Legal doubts over Hong Kong quake donation."

have been under closer scrutiny by Beijing and its allies in Hong Kong, pro-democracy parties, and civil society.

Beijing has shown growing concerns that the judicialization of politics in the post-colonial era might undermine the executive-led political system and its control over Hong Kong. Apart from overturning the Court of Final Appeal (CFA) judgment in *Ng Ka Ling and Another* v. *The Director of Immigration* in June 1999, Beijing and its allies in Hong Kong have sought to play a more proactive and aggressive role in the interpretation of the Basic Law. In the words of a mainland scholar, Beijing sought to demonstrate that the judiciary in Hong Kong did not have a monopoly on interpretation.[11] It is reported that Beijing strengthened the roles and functions of the Basic Law Committee (BLC)[12] in the mid 2000s by upgrading the Committee's bureaucratic ranking to that of a ministry, and transferring a leading Hong Kong law expert from the State Council to the BLC.[13] The BLC was transformed from a passive into a more proactive consultative body. Instead of waiting to be consulted, the BLC has taken the initiative in studying and advising the central leadership on important issues arising from the implementation of the Basic Law. Additionally, BLC members have been more active in expressing Beijing's viewpoint on significant constitutional issues.[14] By explicitly stating its concerns and preferences, Beijing seeks to influence future

[11] Unless specified otherwise, the discussion in this paragraph is based on Li Xianzhi, "Summarizing the experience of the first decade since the sovereignty handover, the central government sought to be more proactive in using the Basic Law," *Ming Pao*, June 7, 2007, p. A6 (in Chinese).

[12] The Basic Law Committee (BLC), composed of an equal number of mainland and Hong Kong members, was established under the Standing Committee of the National People's Congress (NPCSC) in 1990. The NPCSC must consult the BLC before making an interpretation of the Basic Law. Moreover, the BLC has to be consulted when the NPCSC invalidates a Hong Kong law, a mainland law (except an emergency law) is applied to Hong Kong, and an amendment to the Basic Law is introduced. See Ghai (2007a, pp. 130, 141).

[13] The official was Zhang Rongshun, who was a former director of the Law Office of the State Council's Hong Kong and Macau Office.

[14] In 2008, Tam Wai-chu (a Hong Kong member of the BLC) openly criticized the CFA for violating the original legislative intent of article 24 of the Basic Law in *The Director of Immigration v. Chong Fung Yuen* [Court of Final Appeal 2001]. See "Tam Wai-chu argued that children born in Hong Kong to Chinese parents who were not Hong Kong residents would not enjoy the right of abode, if the NPCSC interpreted the Basic Law," *Hong Kong Economic Journal*, October 24, 2008, p. 11 (in Chinese). In *Chong Fung Yuen*, the CFA ruled that children born in Hong Kong

court rulings on critical cases. Indeed, apart from the BLC, other Chinese government agencies have started to keep closer scrutiny of Hong Kong courts as well. In 2006, for example, the State Council's Hong Kong and Macau Research Institute conducted a comprehensive study of how courts have decided constitutional cases since the handover.[15]

Aside from trying to influence court rulings, Beijing has also shown a keen interest in judicial appointments. Unlike the processes of American judicial appointments which are permeated with intensive partisan fighting (e.g., Maltese 1989; Tomasi and Velona 1987), the processes in Hong Kong are relatively insulated. Judges are appointed by the Chief Executive with the advice of the Judicial Officers Recommendation Commission (JORC). JORC's decisions are based on the candidates' proven competence, integrity, and professional qualities (Wesley-Smith 2001, p. 109). The composition of the JORC has enabled it to be relatively insulated from partisan control.[16] That said, the judicialization of politics in the post-colonial period has led political actors from diverse partisanships to pay increasing attention to the judicial appointments and in some cases even to seek to influence the appointments.

Shiu Sin–por, a high-profile pro-Beijing figure, has openly complained that post-colonial Hong Kong has witnessed the appointments of judges whose political values and rulings have occasionally conflicted with mainstream public opinion.[17] Shiu argued that the existing criteria for judicial appointments have failed to consider whether the political and ideological preferences of the candidates are consistent with the public. And the CFA's controversial judgments in the right-of-abode cases illustrated the failure. This neglect of judges' political preferences has profound socio-political

to Chinese parents who were not Hong Kong residents but who were visiting Hong Kong temporarily or illegally staying in Hong Kong had the right of abode.

15 Quinton Chan and Ravina Shamdasani, "Beijing seeking Basic Law answers," *South China Morning Post*, June 12, 2006, p. A1.

16 The Commission consists of nine members: the Chief Justice and two local judges, the Secretary for Justice, representatives from the two legal professional bodies (Bar Association and Law Society), and eminent figures from the other sectors. All members are appointed by the Chief Executive.

17 Shiu was a deputy secretary of the Basic Law Consultative Committee in the 1980s and a former director of the pro-Beijing think tank One Country Two Systems Research Institute.

implications, given that courts have become influential political institutions since July 1997. To ensure that judges would not deviate from public opinion in deciding important cases, Shiu suggested that Hong Kong could follow the American practice of incorporating judges' political and ideological preferences in judicial appointments.[18]

Pro-democracy parties and civil society have also been more concerned with judicial appointments, because courts have become alternative forums for them to pursue their causes. Ho Hei-wah, director of SoCO, expressed concern that the increasing judicialization of politics might prompt Beijing or the SAR administration to appoint more conservative judges to the judiciary in the future. Ho was worried that the court packaging might strengthen the administration's control over the judiciary and therefore undermine the feasibility of civil society using the courts to advance their causes.[19]

THE POLITICIZATION OF GOVERNMENT-FUNDED LEGAL AID

Finally, apart from seeking to affect judicial appointments and judicial decisions, political actors have also directed more efforts to influence other semi-legal institutions, notably the government-funded legal aid scheme. In Chapter 3, I discussed the centrality of the scheme in financing most human rights and public policy lawsuits that the courts heard. Due to its centrality to legal mobilization, political actors have struggled to shape the development of the scheme in ways that would best promote their interests. The recent efforts by the Donald Tsang administration to tighten control over the Legal Aid Department (LAD) and the subsequent controversy illustrated the increasing politicization of government-funded legal aid.

After winning re-election in 2007, Donald Tsang reshuffled the government bureaus. One of his measures was to transfer the LAD from the Chief Secretary to the Home Affairs Bureau. The LAD had never been put under any government bureaus since its establishment in the early 1970s. Rights advocacy groups and pro-democracy politicians strongly opposed the measure, arguing that the administration was seeking to tighten its rein on the LAD in light of the growing litigation against the government. Margaret Ng and Audrey Eu, two

[18] Shiu Sin-por, "Between law and politics," *Hong Kong Economic Journal*, May 15, 2007, p. 13 (in Chinese).

[19] Author's interview with Ho Hei-wah, September 16, 2008.

legislators-cum-cause lawyers criticized the move as enabling the administration to more easily ban politically sensitive legal challenges.[20] The Bar Association and the Human Rights Monitor also questioned that the move might undermine LAD's impartiality in deciding sensitive applications. In the end, the pro-democracy legislators voted against the administration's proposal to reshuffle the government bureaus, even though the proposal was passed with the support from the pro-government legislators.

The opposition by pro-democracy parties and civil society to the administration's efforts to tighten its rein on the LAD was no surprise, given that legal aid has been critical to their endeavors to use the law. Meanwhile, pro-Beijing figures have intensified political pressure on the LAD in politically consequential legal aid applications, with a view to weakening the growing trend of legal mobilization. The pro-Beijing community, for instance, was mobilized to publicly criticize the LAD for using government money to help right-of-abode seekers to litigate against the Tung Chee-hwa administration's deportation order.[21] To defend the LAD (and to safeguard the funding for legal mobilization), pro-democracy parties openly rebuked the pro-Beijing community.[22]

To summarize, the rise of legal mobilization has profoundly influenced politics in post-colonial Hong Kong. First, legal and/or constitutional considerations and rhetoric have played a more important role in the policy-making and deliberation processes. Second, the politicization of courts has occurred. Political actors from diverse groups have sought to influence court decisions and judicial appointments. Finally, the government-funded legal aid system, an important component of the legal complex, has also been politicized.

[20] Margaret Ng, "Safeguarding the equality of legal aid," *South China Morning Post*, June 14, 2007, p. A14; Audrey Eu, "Rule of law is more important than face saving," *Ming Pao*, June 5, 2007, p. A28 (in Chinese).

[21] Chan Wan-sang (of the DAB), "Legal aid must be properly used," *Hong Kong Commercial News*, August 12, 2000, p. A5 (in Chinese); Sze Cheung-pang (of the Chinese People's Political Consultative Conference), "Shouldn't we re-examine the legal aid system?" *Hong Kong Commercial News*, August 7, 2000, p. A5 (in Chinese); Special Issue, "The Legal Aid Department spent more than ten million dollars on the right-of-abode litigation," *Wen Hui Pao*, August 3, 2000, p. A3 (in Chinese).

[22] Margaret Ng, "Misunderstanding about abuse of the legal aid by 'illegal immigrants'," *Ming Pao*, November 24, 1999, p. A25 (in Chinese).

CONCLUSION

In this chapter, I analyzed the impact of the judicialization of politics in post-colonial Hong Kong and demonstrated that courts and their likely responses to controversies over public policies have become a crucial factor in the calculation of political actors. The final chapter will discuss the theoretical and comparative contributions of this study.

10

CONCLUSION: THEORETICAL AND COMPARATIVE CONTRIBUTIONS

Using post-colonial Hong Kong as a case study, this book examines how legal mobilization can arise in authoritarian regimes. My argument combines elements of "structure" and "agency." The key structural elements are the long-term institutionalization of the legal complex in Hong Kong, and the intervention of a critical juncture in the form of Beijing's military crackdown on the 1989 Tiananmen democratic movement and the process of the sovereignty transition. The key agentic elements are the growing strategic use of litigation in pursuit of human rights and more progressive public policies by Hong Kong's rights support structure (consisting of cause lawyers and rights advocacy organizations).

This book makes four contributions to the literature on comparative courts and rights mobilization. First, it engages and contributes to the emerging literature on judicial politics under authoritarianism by arguing that historical legacies play an important role in the rise of legal mobilization and that legal mobilization in authoritarian regimes by no means unfolds as political authorities would wish. Second, the Hong Kong case demonstrates that legal mobilization under authoritarianism requires *both* the legal complex and the rights support structure. Third, my book highlights the impact of different forms of authoritarianism on the modes of opposition mobilization. Finally, through studying how cause lawyers in Hong Kong have used their expertise and networks to actively promote democratic changes and the difficulty they have encountered, this book informs the literature on the relationships between economic modernization and democratization, especially the role of the middle class. The following sections will elaborate the aforementioned arguments.

PATHS TO LEGAL MOBILIZATION UNDER AUTHORITARIANISM

Students of comparative law and courts have long focused on democratic and/or democratizing polities. The edited volume, *Global Expansion of Judicial Power* (Tate and Vallinder 1995), for example, concentrates on established or new democracies. Ginsburg (2003) and Hirschl (2004) also argue that fear of electoral defeat in the near future motivated political elites in democratic and/or democratizing polities to empower the judiciary to preserve their policy preferences. More recently, a growing stream of studies, like Moustafa (2007) and Ginsburg and Moustafa (2008), have shown that judicial politics can happen in authoritarian settings as well. Through studying post-colonial Hong Kong, this book has also found that authoritarian regimes can experience legal mobilization.

While largely concurring with Moustafa (2007) and Ginsburg and Moustafa (2008) that judicial politics can arise in authoritarian regimes, however, my book argues that these studies have two major weaknesses. First, they are too *ahistorical*, paying insufficient attention to the role of history in affecting the outcome of legal mobilization. Ginsburg and Moustafa have fourteen chapters discussing (the failure of) legal mobilization in authoritarian regimes around the globe. Among these chapters, however, only Widner[1] emphasizes the role of historical legacies.[2]

Contrary to the foregoing studies which pay relatively scant attention to the role of historical legacies, the case of Hong Kong demonstrates the importance of historical legacies (an independent and efficient legal complex established by the British colonial rule) to

[1] Widner (2008, pp. 252, 258–9) highlights the role of historical legacies, specifically the proportion of the senior members of the judiciary who share important background traits with those in governments, in affecting the degree of authoritarian infringement of judicial independence (or authoritarian responses to legal mobilization) in Uganda and Zimbabwe.

[2] Pereira (2008, p. 29) also adopts a historical argument. However, his study does not focus on whether or not legal mobilization can arise. Instead, he examines how different histories of military-judicial collaboration before and during the establishment of the military regimes determined the wide variation in the use of security courts (or the legal strategies) by the military regimes for political repression in Argentina, Brazil, and Chile.

sustained legal mobilization. In Chapter 3, I compared the progress of legal mobilization in Shanghai and Hong Kong. I found that although Shanghai leads China in judicial and economic reforms, the lack of an efficient and independent legal complex has diverted many aggrieved individuals away from the courts. By contrast, a well-functioning legal complex left by the British colonial administration has facilitated social actors to seize the expanded legal opportunities and to actively use the courts to promote their interests in post-colonial Hong Kong.

Second, Moustafa (2007) and Moustafa and Ginsburg (2008) demonstrate that authoritarian leaders empower the judiciary for strategic reasons, including: social control, legitimation, controlling administrative agents and maintaining elite cohesion, and enhancing credible commitments in the economic sphere. This study, however, presents a quite different story. Legal mobilization in Hong Kong has by no means unfolded as political authorities would wish. Beijing, for example, inherited an independent and well-established legal complex from British colonial rule and decided that it is politically easier to live with the status quo than to overturn it.[3] Beijing's military crackdown on the Tiananmen democratic movement in June 1989 also unintentionally opened up a new legal opportunity in Hong Kong – the promulgation of the Hong Kong Bill of Rights Ordinance (HKBORO) in 1991.

KEY ROLE OF THE LEGAL COMPLEX AND RIGHTS SUPPORT STRUCTURE

This book finds that the legal complex and the rights support structure have played a key role in the rise of legal mobilization in post-colonial Hong Kong. More broadly, the case of Hong Kong highlights that

[3] Beijing finds it politically costly to overturn the legal complex in Hong Kong, especially an independent judiciary, for two reasons. First, Beijing has been bound by an international treaty – the Sino-British Joint Declaration. In 1984 Beijing and London signed the Sino-British Joint Declaration, which stipulated that the Chinese government would adopt the policy of "one country, two systems" after the sovereignty transition in July 1997. Under the policy of "one country, two systems," China will maintain the existing political, economic, and legal systems in Hong Kong for fifty years after July 1997. Second, the ultimate audience of the policy of "one country, two systems" is Taiwan. Beijing sought to use the experience of Hong Kong (i.e., a high degree of autonomy) to persuade Taiwan to accept reunification. If Beijing acts too aggressively toward the judiciary, it will undermine Taiwan's willingness to accept reunification.

legal mobilization under authoritarianism requires *both* the legal complex and the rights support structure. Thus, in their research on legal mobilization, Halliday, Karpik, and Feeley (2007a) underestimate the contribution of the rights support structure, and Epp (1998) underestimates the contribution of the legal complex as an institutional actor.

Halliday, Karpik, and Feeley (2007a) focus on how the legal complex (encompassing lawyers and judges, collectively organized by the organized bar) fights for political liberalism. But they overlook the important roles played by rights advocacy groups and government-funded legal aid in mobilizing the law. My study shows that government-funded legal aid is crucial to citizens' endeavors to use the law to promote social change, given that most litigants are economically disadvantaged (see Chapters 7 and 8).

Epp (1998) studies how the rights support structure facilitates legal mobilization. But he underestimates the significant contribution made by an independent and competent judiciary and an organized bar. The case of Hong Kong shows that an independent and efficient judiciary, which is receptive to human rights arguments, plays a crucial role in facilitating legal mobilization. Judges must be receptive to human rights arguments and actively use the new legal tools (the HKBORO and the Basic Law) in response to cases brought by cause lawyers and rights advocacy groups. Otherwise, cause lawyers and rights advocacy groups are likely to face considerable difficulties in promoting their causes in the courts. Chapter 4 discussed the relatively impressive record of the CFA and the lower courts in safeguarding human rights in Hong Kong. During the period 1998–2010, for example, citizens had about a 50 percent chance of defeating the government in human rights litigation before the Court of Final Appeal (CFA). The impressive record of the judiciary in turn encouraged many social activists to mobilize the law to pursue their interests.

FORMS OF AUTHORITARIANISM AND MODES OF OPPOSITION MOBILIZATION

Through studying the diverse causes, processes, and outcomes of legal mobilization in different authoritarian regimes, this book highlights the impact of different forms of authoritarianism on the modes of opposition mobilization. The contrasting experience of Taiwan and Hong Kong is a case in point. During the 1970s and 1980s, the authoritarian Kuomintang government seriously undermined the autonomy of the legal profession. Encountering tremendous problems in exercising their influence in the legal arena and a partial opening of electoral competition, many liberal lawyers turned to oppositional politics (i.e., forming an opposition political party) to promote political liberalization. By contrast, the presence of a well-established and autonomous bar association and the tightening up of political opportunities in the post-colonial legislature prompted many liberal lawyers in Hong Kong to use the law to pursue democratic changes.

In other words, authoritarianism wrought electoral mobilization in Taiwan but legal mobilization in Hong Kong. Here I discuss some tentative implications of this Taiwan–Hong Kong divergence for the likely modes of opposition mobilization in future China, including legal mobilization, electoral politics, and contentious politics. The contrasting experiences of Taiwan and Hong Kong demonstrate the importance of an autonomous and vibrant legal complex if social actors want to mobilize the law to pursue their interests. When the authoritarian leaders repress the legal complex and thereby hinder legal mobilization, social actors will turn to other modes of mobilization.

In the past three decades, the Chinese government implemented various measures to establish the rule of law, such as rebuilding the judiciary, reopening law schools, and promoting the development of the legal profession. Citizens have been encouraged to use the law to protect their legitimate interests. A veteran scholar of Chinese law observes that China is in transition from rule by law toward a thin version of rule of law.[4] My Hong Kong-Shanghai comparison and other studies on Chinese judicial politics (see Chapter 3), however, showed that the lack of an independent and efficient legal complex has diverted many aggrieved individuals away from the courts in Shanghai and other parts of China. Jerome Cohen notes that since taking power in 2002, the Hu Jintao-Wen Jiabao administration has done little to promote judicial reforms that would enhance judicial independence and professionalism. Worse still, starting from their

[4] Peerenboom (2002, pp. 2–9). According to Peerenboom, a thin version of rule of law emphasizes the formal or instrumental aspects of rule of law – those features that any legal system must possess to function effectively as a system of laws, regardless of whether the legal system is part of a democratic or non-democratic polity, capitalist or socialist, liberal or theocratic.

second term, the administration has adopted a more authoritarian policy toward the judiciary.[5] Given the substantial political constraints on the legal complex, I argue that legal mobilization is unlikely to become the dominant mode of opposition mobilization in China, especially on politically charged issues.

If legal mobilization is unlikely to be the dominant mode of resistance, can electoral competition help aggrieved Chinese to defend their interests? Available evidence suggests that electoral competition is the least effective mode of opposition mobilization in China today and the near future. Since the early 1990s, the Chinese authorities have implemented village elections, which are supposed to let peasants choose their representatives to manage village affairs and monitor grassroots officials. Studies, however, find that the Chinese authorities undermined village elections as an effective means of advocating the peasant interests. Cheng and Lin (2008, p. 179), for example, argue that village elections have become a mechanism for the Communist Party to co-opt social elites, sap political opposition, and weaken democratic competition. Perry and Goldman (2007, p. 14) also highlight that the Communist Party has dominated both the nominations and the results of most village elections. Additionally, a ban on opposition parties and restrictions on open campaigning have rendered many village elections to perfunctory votes of confidence on the Party's approved nominees. Finally, Diamond (2008, pp. 249–53) suggests that real electoral competition at the higher levels in China remains a distant dream, because of the large size of the Chinese territory and population, and the rising global power of China.

Given that legal mobilization and in particular electoral politics has not been very effective in promoting aggrieved citizens' interests, contentious politics seems to be a relatively viable mode of resistance. Indeed, studies have shown that contentious politics has become more widespread and disruptive since the 1990s. Xi Chen (2007, pp. 256, 277), for example, argues that Chinese petitioners have increasingly employed "opportunistic trouble-making" tactics in bargaining with the government and that such tactics generally increased the likelihood of government concessions.

[5] Jerome Cohen, "Body blow for the judiciary," *South China Morning Post*, October 18, 2008, p. A13.

ECONOMIC MODERNIZATION AND DEMOCRATIZATION: ROLE OF THE MIDDLE CLASS

Finally, through studying how cause lawyers in Hong Kong have used their expertise and networks to promote democratic changes and the difficulty they have encountered, this book informs the literature on economic modernization and democratization, especially the role of the middle class. Students of political development, like Lipset (1959), Moore (1966), Cheng (1989), and Diamond (1992) claim that economic modernization is an important requisite for democratic development. A crucial reason is that economic modernization is likely to create a middle class, which can stand up against an authoritarian state. However, this argument may be too one-sided. As discussed in Chapters 6 and 7, although cause lawyers (an important component of the middle class) in Hong Kong have actively pursued gradual democratic changes through cause lawyering, the strength of capitalism (e.g., economic pressure of Beijing and large corporations in Hong Kong) has also posed substantial difficulty to their cause lawyering work. In short, the experiences of cause lawyers in Hong Kong demonstrate that economic modernization does not necessarily foster democratic development.

CONCLUSION

Hong Kong has a unique combination of legal and political systems. On the one hand, the British colonial authorities established an independent and efficient legal complex for the city. Foreign legal practitioners have actively participated in the judiciary and the legal profession. The process of the sovereignty transition empowered the judiciary through the implementation of the HKBORO and the Basic Law, and the establishment of a final appellate court situated in Hong Kong. On the other hand, Beijing and the Tung Chee-hwa administration weakened the post-colonial legislature. The contrasting development in the legal and political arenas in turn prompted citizens and social groups to increasingly use the courts to pursue their causes.

The rise of legal mobilization in post-colonial Hong Kong has increasingly judicialized politics and politicized the courts. It remains to be seen how far legal mobilization can go under the shadow of Beijing's authoritarian rule.

APPENDIX 1

HUMAN RIGHTS AND PUBLIC POLICY LITIGATION THE PRIVY COUNCIL AND THE COURT OF FINAL APPEAL DECIDED (1981–2010)

HUMAN RIGHTS LITIGATION

Case	Background of litigants	Government won or lost?	Basic Law/ Bill of Rights Ordinance (HKBORO) invoked?	Summary of the case	Date of judgment	Legal representation for non-government party	Government legal aid
Attorney General of Hong Kong v. *Ng Yuen Shiu*	Born in China and entered Hong Kong illegally from Macau in 1976	Lost	NA	An illegal immigrant's right to a fair hearing by the government before being removed	21/2/ 1983	Louis Blom-Cooper QC and Richard Drabble	Unknown
Mak Yui-Ming and Others v. *Attorney General*	Illegal immigrants from China	Won	NA	Right of abode	27/6/ 1983	Unknown	Unknown
Attorney General of Hong Kong v. *Lee Kwong-Kut*	Fisherman	Lost	Yes, Article 11 of the HKBORO	Presumption of innocence of everyone charged with criminal offence	19/5/ 1993	GJX McCoy and Keith Oderberg	The Crown paid the respondent's costs
Attorney General of Hong Kong v. *Lo Chak-man and Another*	Ordinary citizens	Won	Yes, Article 11 of the HKBORO	Presumption of innocence of everyone charged with criminal offence	19/5/ 1993	Alan Hoo QC and Keven Chan for 1st respondent; Martin Thomas QC and Philip Dykes for 2nd respondent	Yes

Case	Background of litigants	Government won or lost?	Basic Law/ Bill of Rights Ordinance (HKBORO) invoked?	Summary of the case	Date of judgment	Legal representation for non-government party	Government legal aid
Attorney General of Hong Kong v. *Charles Cheung Wai-bun*	Bank manager	Lost	Yes, Articles 10 and 11(2) of the HKBORO	Trial without undue delay	29/3/ 1993	G. Robertson QC and W. Haldane	Unknown
Chan Chi Hung v. *The Queen*	Ordinary citizen	Won	Yes, Article 12(1) of the HKBORO	Sentencing principle – right to benefit from lesser penalty	26/7/ 1995	G.J.X. McCoy and P.Y. Lo	Unknown
Nguyen Tuan Cuong and Others v. *The Director of Immigration and Others*	Vietnamese boat people	Lost	No	The right of being screened for refugee status	21/11/ 1996	Unknown	Yes
Tan Te Lam and Others v. *Superintendent of Tai A Chau Detention Centre and Another*	Vietnamese boat people	Lost	No	Free from unlawful detention	27/3/ 1996	Michael Beloff QC, G.J.X. McCoy and Pam Baker	Yes
Ming Pao Newspapers Limited and Others v. *The Attorney General of Hong Kong*	A liberal newspaper publisher	Lost	Yes, Article 16 of the HKBORO	Freedom of expression	20/5/ 1996	Lord Lester of Herne Hill, QC, Johannes Chan, and Javan Herberg	No
Fu Kin Chi v. *Secretary for Justice*	Senior police inspector	Won	No	The right not to incriminate oneself	25/3/ 1998	John Bleach and S.H. Kwok	Yes
Thang Thieu Quyen and Others v. *The Director of Immigration and Another*	Vietnamese boat people	Partial	No	Free from unlawful detention	23/7/ 1998	Gladys Li, Hectar Pun, and Pam Baker	Yes
Chan Kam Nga v. *Director of Immigration*	Mainland-born children of Hong Kong permanent residents; assisted by Society for Community Organization	Lost	Yes, Article 24 of the Basic Law	Right of abode of HK permanent residents' mainland-born children	29/1/ 1999	Gladys Li, Margaret Ng, and Pamela Baker	Yes

Case	Background of litigants	Government won or lost?	Basic Law/ Bill of Rights Ordinance (HKBORO) invoked?	Summary of the case	Date of judgment	Legal representation for non-government party	Government legal aid
Ng Ka Ling and Another v. *The Director of Immigration*	Mainland-born children of Hong Kong permanent residents; assisted by Society for Community Organization	Lost	Yes, Article 24 of the Basic Law	Right of abode of HK permanent residents' mainland-born children	29/1/ 1999	Denis Chang, Philip Dykes, and S.H. Kwok	Yes
The Director of Immigration v. *Cheung Lai Wah*	Mainland-born child of Hong Kong permanent resident; assisted by Society for Community Organization	Lost	Yes, Article 24 of the Basic Law	Right of abode of mainland-born children of Hong Kong permanent resident	29/1/ 1999	Denis Chang, Philip Dykes, and S.H. Kwok	Yes
Tsui Kuen Nang v. *The Director of Immigration*	Mainland-born child of Hong Kong permanent resident; assisted by Society for Community Organization	Lost	Yes, Article 24 of the Basic Law	Right of abode of mainland-born children of Hong Kong permanent resident	29/1/ 1999	Denis Chang, Philip Dykes, and S.H. Kwok	Yes
Lau Kong Yung and Others v. *The Director of Immigration*	Mainland-born children of Hong Kong permanent residents; assisted by Society for Community Organization	Won	Yes, Article 24 of the Basic Law	Right of abode of mainland-born children of Hong Kong permanent residents	3/12/ 1999	Denis Chang, Gladys Li, Margaret Ng, and Pamela Baker	Yes
Eastern Express Publisher Ltd and Another v. *Mo Man Ching and Another*	Newspaper publishers	Won	No	Freedom of speech and expression; the respondents complained of a government television program that contained defamatory imputations against them	3/11/ 1999	John Griffiths, Cheng Huan, and Jason Pow	No

Case	Background of litigants	Government won or lost?	Basic Law/ Bill of Rights Ordinance (HKBORO) invoked?	Summary of the case	Date of judgment	Legal representation for non-government party	Government legal aid
HKSAR v. *Ng Kung Siu and Another*	Members of the April 5th Action Group	Won	Yes, Articles 27 and 39 of the Basic Law	Freedom of expression; the respondents were convicted of desecration of the national flag and the regional flag	15/12/ 1999	Audrey Eu, P. Y. Lo, Paul Harris, Lawrence Lau, and Ho Chun-yan represented the second respondent	Yes (2nd respondent)
Yung Kwan Lee and Others v. *HKSAR*	Prisoners	Won	Yes, Articles 8, 28, and 153 of the Basic Law	Free from arbitrary or unlawful detention or imprisonment	4/10/ 1999	Philip Dykes and Hectar Pun	Yes
Secretary for Justice and Others v. *Chan Wah and Others*	Non-indigenous villagers in the countryside	Lost	Yes, Article 21 of the Basic Law; section 7(1) of the HKBORO	Right to participate in public affairs (village representative election)	22/12/ 2000	Philip Dykes and Stephen Yam	Yes
Fateh Muhammad v. *Commissioner of Registration*	Ordinary citizen	Won	Yes, Article 24 of the Basic Law	Right of abode	20/7/ 2001	Philip Dykes, Maurice Ng, and Mark Daly	Yes
Tam Nga Yin and Others v. *The Director of Immigration*	Hong Kong permanent resident's adopted children in China; assisted by Society for Community Organization	Won	Yes, Article 24 of the Basic Law; Article 19(1) of the HKBORO	Right of abode of HK permanent residents' adopted children in China	20/7/ 2001	Gladys Li, Margaret Ng and Mark Daly	Yes
Xie Xiaoyi v. The Director of Immigration	Hong Kong permanent resident's adopted child in China; assisted by Society for Community Organization	Won	Yes, Article 24 of the Basic Law; Article 19(1) of the HKBORO	Right of abode of HK permanent residents' adopted child in China	20/7/ 2001	Patrick Szeto	Yes
The Director of Immigration v. *Chong Fung Yuen*	A Hong Kong-born infant whose parents have no right of	Lost	Yes, Article 24(2)(1) of the Basic Law	Right of abode	20/7/ 2001	Gladys Li and Kwok Sui Hay	Yes

Case	Background of litigants	Government won or lost?	Basic Law/ Bill of Rights Ordinance (HKBORO) invoked?	Summary of the case	Date of judgment	Legal representation for non-government party	Government legal aid
	abode in Hong Kong; assisted by Society for Community Organization						
Chau Ching Kay, Nauthum v. *HKSAR*	Ordinary citizen	Partial	Yes, Article 11(4) of the HKBORO	Everyone convicted of a crime has the right to his conviction and sentence being reviewed by a higher tribunal	4/12/ 2002	Audrey Eu and Wong Po-wing	Yes
Gurung Kesh Bahadur v. *Director of Immigration*	A non-permanent resident of Hong Kong, a citizen of Nepal	Lost	Yes, Articles 31 and 39 of the Basic Law	The right to travel and to enter Hong Kong conferred on non-permanent residents	30/7/ 2002	Philip Dykes and Paul Harris	No
Lau Cheong and Another v. *HKSAR*	Ordinary citizens	Won	Yes, Article 28 of the Basic Law and Article 5(1) of the HKBORO	Freedom from arbitrary detention or imprisonment	16/7/ 2002	Audrey Eu, John Mullick, and P.Y. Lo for 1st appellant	Yes (1st appellant)
Li Defan and Another v. *HKSAR*	Bank manager, businessman	Won	Yes, Article 11(2) of the HKBORO	The right of the accused to remain silent	14/3/ 2002	Andrew Macrae and Maggie Wong Pui-kei	No
Li Shuk Fan v. *The Director of Immigration*	Mainland-born child of Hong Kong permanent resident	Lost	Yes, Articles 24 and 158 of the Basic Law	Right of abode of mainland-born child of Hong Kong permanent resident	10/1/ 2002	Gladys Li and S.H. Kwok	Yes
Ng Siu Tung and Others v. *The Director of Immigration*	Mainland-born children of Hong Kong permanent residents	Partial	Yes, Articles 24 and 158 of the Basic Law	Right of abode of mainland-born children of Hong Kong permanent residents	10/1/ 2002	Geoffrey Robertson, S. H. Kwok, and Pamela Baker	Yes
Ng Siu Tung and Others v. *The Director of Immigration*	Mainland-born children of Hong Kong permanent residents	Partial	Yes, Articles 22 and 24 of the Basic Law	Right of abode of mainland-born children of Hong Kong permanent residents	30/7/ 2002	Gladys Li and Pamela Baker	Yes

Case	Background of litigants	Government won or lost?	Basic Law/ Bill of Rights Ordinance (HKBORO) invoked?	Summary of the case	Date of judgment	Legal representation for non-government party	Government legal aid
Ng Siu Tung and Others v. *The Director of Immigration*	Mainland-born children of Hong Kong permanent residents	Lost	No	Right of abode of mainland-born children of Hong Kong permanent residents	25/2/ 2002	Pamela Baker	Yes
Sin Hoi Chu and Others v. *The Director of Immigration*	Mainland-born children of Hong Kong permanent residents	Won	Yes, Articles 24 and 158 of the Basic Law	Right of abode of mainland-born children of Hong Kong permanent residents	10/1/ 2002	Gladys Li, S. H. Kwok, and Mark Daly	Yes
Prem Singh v. *Director of Immigration*	An Indian, worked as a cook in Hong Kong	Lost	Article 24 of the Basic Law	The constitutional right to acquire HK permanent resident status	11/2/ 2003	Audrey Eu, Kwok Sui Hay, and Mark Daly	Yes
Ng Siu Tung and Others v. *The Director of Immigration*	Mainland-born children of Hong Kong permanent residents	Partial	No	Right of abode of mainland-born children of Hong Kong permanent residents	9/1/ 2004	Gladys Li, Kwok Sui Hay, Sean Fang, and Mark Daly	Yes
Ng Siu Tung and Others v. *The Director of Immigration*	Mainland-born children of Hong Kong permanent residents	Won	No	Right of abode of mainland-born children of Hong Kong permanent residents	26/3/ 2004	Gladys Li, Kwok Sui Hay, Sean Fang, and Mark Daly represented the appellant 3174	Yes (one appellant) No (other five)
Secretary for Security v. *Sakthevel Prabakar*	A fisherman and a member of the Tamil minority from northern Sri Lanka	Lost	No	Right not to be subject to torture	8/6/ 2004	Nicholas Blake QC, Philip Dykes, Hectar Pun, and Mark Daly	No (government paid the cost)
The Director of Immigration v. *Lau Fong*	A Chinese non-permanent resident of Hong Kong	Lost	Yes, Articles 35 and 39 of the Basic Law and Article 10 of the HKBORO	Constitutional freedom to travel	26/3/ 2004	Philip Dykes and Hectar Pun	Yes
Leung Kwok Hung and	Member of the April 5th Action	Won	Yes, Articles 27 and 39 of	Right of peaceful assembly and	8/7/ 2005	Martin Lee, Erik Shum and Ho Chun-yan	Yes (2nd, 3rd appellants)

Case	Background of litigants	Government won or lost?	Basic Law/ Bill of Rights Ordinance (HKBORO) invoked?	Summary of the case	Date of judgment	Legal representation for non-government party	Government legal aid
Others v. *HKSAR*	Group; former members of the Hong Kong Federation of Students		the Basic Law	public processions		represented the 2nd and 3rd appellants	
Yeung May Wan and Others v. *HKSAR*	Members of the Falun Gong	Lost	Yes, Article 27 of the Basic Law	Right of peaceful demonstration	5/5/ 2005	Philip Dykes, Paul Harris, Cheung Yiu-leung, and Ho Chun-yan	Yes (4th, 5th, 6th, 8th appellants); No (other 4 appellants)
HKSAR v. *Lam Kwong Wai and Another*	Ordinary citizens	Won	Yes, Article 87(2) of the Basic Law; Articles 10 and 11 of the HKBORO	Presumption of innocence and right to a fair trial	31/8/ 2006	Clive Grossman and Hylas Chung	Yes
Koo Sze Yiu and Another v. *Chief Executive of the HKSAR*	Legislator; members of the April 5th Action Group	Lost	Yes, Article 30 of the Basic Law; Article 14 of the HKBORO	Freedom and privacy of communication	12/7/ 2006	Philip Dykes and Hectar Pun	Yes (1st appellant)
HKSAR v. *Hung Chan Wa and Another*	Ordinary citizen; Japanese tourist	Lost	Yes, Article 87 of the Basic Law; Articles 10 and 11(1) of the HKBORO	Presumption of innocence and right to fair trial	31/8/ 2006	Clive Grossman and Hanif Mughal	Yes
Ng Siu Tung and Others v. *The Director of Immigration*	Mainland-born children of Hong Kong permanent residents	Partial	No	Right of abode in Hong Kong	5/1/ 2006	Gladys Li, Kwok Sui Hay, Sean Fang, and Mark Daly	Yes
Ng Siu Tung and Others v. *The Director of Immigration*	Mainland-born children of Hong Kong permanent residents	Won	No	Right of abode in Hong Kong	13/11/ 2006	Kwok Sui Hay, Sean Fang, and Mark Daly	Yes (7 appellants); No (2 appellants)
So Wai Lun v. *HKSAR*	Ordinary citizen	Won	Yes, Articles 25 and 28 of the Basic Law; Articles 5(1) and 22 of the HKBORO	Equality before the law	18/7/ 2006	Philip Dykes and Joseph Tse	Yes

Case	Background of litigants	Government won or lost?	Basic Law/ Bill of Rights Ordinance (HKBORO) invoked?	Summary of the case	Date of judgment	Legal representation for non-government party	Government legal aid
Chiu Wing Nam Dick v. *HKSAR*	Ordinary citizen	Lost	Yes	Presumption of innocence and right to a fair trial	3/7/2007	Andrew Bruce	Yes
Mo Yuk Ping v. *HKSAR*	Ordinary citizen	Won	Yes, Articles 28 and 39 of Basic Law; Articles 5(1) and 11(1) of the HKBORO	Legal certainty	25/7/2007	Clare Montgomery QC, Ronny F. H. Wong, and Po Wing Kay	No
Ng Siu Tung and Others v. *The Director of Immigration*	Mainland-born children of Hong Kong permanent residents	Won	No	Right of abode in Hong Kong	25/7/2007	Gladys Li, Kwok Sui Hay, Sean Fang, and Mark Daly	Yes
Secretary for Justice v. *Yau Yuk Lung Zigo and Another*	Student, manager; assisted by Civil Rights for Sexual Diversities	Lost	Yes, Article 25 of the Basic Law; Article 22 of the HKBORO	Gay's right to equality	17/7/2007	Philip Dykes, Wing Kay Po, and Stanley Ma	Yes, 1st respondent; No, 2nd respondent
HKSAR v. *Ng Po On and Another*	Ordinary citizens	Lost	Yes, Article 87(2) of the Basic Law; Article 11(1) of the HKBORO	Presumption of innocence	7/3/2008	Philip Wong, William Chan, William Marshall, and Kevin K.W. Wong	No
Koon Wing Yee v. *Insider Dealing Tribunal and Another*	Businessmen	Partial	Yes, Articles 10 and 11 of the HKBORO	Right to a fair and public hearing by a competent and independent tribunal; right to protection against self-incrimination	18/3/2008	Lord Lester of Herne Hill QC, Sir John Swaine, Bernard Mak, and John J.E. Swaine	No
Ng Siu Tung and Others v. *The Director of Immigration*	Mainland-born children of Hong Kong permanent residents	Won	No	Right of abode in Hong Kong	18/3/2008	Gladys Li, Kwok Sui Hay, Sean H.J. Fang, and Mark Daly	Yes (2 appellants); No (other appellants)
Yeung Chung Ming v. *Commissioner of Police*	A former police sergeant	Won	Yes, Article 87(2) of Basic Law; Article 11(1) of the HKBORO	Presumption of innocence	25/7/2008	Gerard McCoy and Margaret Ng	Yes

Case	Background of litigants	Government won or lost?	Basic Law/ Bill of Rights Ordinance (HKBORO) invoked?	Summary of the case	Date of judgment	Legal representation for non-government party	Government legal aid
Chiu Hoi Po v. *Commissioner of Police*	A former police constable	Lost	No	Right to have a fair hearing (right to have legal representation) in disciplinary hearing	24/7/ 2009	Johannes Chan	Yes
Lam Siu Po v. *Commissioner of Police*	A former police constable	Lost	Yes, Article 10 of the HKBORO	Right to have a fair hearing (right to have legal representation) in disciplinary hearing	26/3/ 2009	Johannes Chan and Margaret Ng	Yes
Mok Charles Peter v. *Tam Wai Ho and Another*	A pro-democracy politician	Lost	Yes, Article 82 of the Basic Law	Right of appeal	13/12/ 2010	Martin Lee, Hectar Pun, Lee Siu-him, and Ho Chun-yan	No

PUBLIC POLICY LITIGATION

Case	Background of litigants	Government won or lost?	Basic Law/ Bill of Rights Ordinance (HKBORO) invoked?	Summary of the case	Date of judgment	Legal representation for non-government party	Government legal aid
ira Vergara & Another v. *orney neral*	Foreign domestic helpers from the Philippines	Won	NA	Immigration policy concerning foreign domestic helpers	27/6/ 1988	Unknown	Yes
wn Planning ard v. *iety for the tection of Harbour*	Environmental protection NGO; Christine Loh (a pro-democracy activist)	Lost	No	Environmental protection – harbor reclamation	9/1/ 2004	Anthony Neoh, Johannes Chan, and Jin Pao	No
Choi Wan HKSAR	A poor elderly person; assisted by the Alliance	Won	No	Public housing rental policy	21/11/ 2005	Philip Dykes, Johannes	Yes

Case	Background of litigants	Government won or lost?	Basic Law/ Bill of Rights Ordinance (HKBORO) invoked?	Summary of the case	Date of judgment	Legal representation for non-government party	Governme legal aid
	for Defending Grassroots Right to Housing; the Neighbourhood and Worker's Service Centre (founded and led by a pro-democracy legislator Leung Yiu-chung)					Chan, and Ho Chun-yan	
Lo Siu Lan v. *Hong Kong Housing Authority*	A poor elderly, active member of the Center for Elderly Rights. Assisted by the Alliance for Defending Grassroots Right to Housing; the Neighbourhood and Worker's Service Centre; Chan Wai-yip and Albert Cheng King-hon (legislators); To Kwan-hang (district councilor)	Won	No	Privatization of shopping and parking facilities within public housing estates	20/7/ 2005	Philip Dykes, Hectar Pun, and Mark Daly	Yes
Secretary for Justice v. *Lau Kwok Fai Bernard and Michael Reid Scott*	A senior police inspector; a senior lawyer in the Department of Justice	Won	Yes, Article 100 of the Basic Law	Civil servant pay policy	13/7/ 2005	No	No
Shiu Wing Steel Limited v. *Director of Environmental Protection*	Tycoon	Lost	No	Environmental protection	17/7/ 2006	Nigel Pleming QC and Roxanne Ismail	No
Cheng Ho Kee and Others v. *Secretary for Justice*	3,250 current or former officers of the Correctional Services Dept	Won	No	Civil servant pay policy	16/11/ 2006	Gerard McCoy and Benjamin Chain	No

:ase	Background of litigants	Government won or lost?	Basic Law/ Bill of Rights Ordinance (HKBORO) invoked?	Summary of the case	Date of judgment	Legal representation for non-government party	Government legal aid
	(organized by the Correctional Services Officers' Association)						
ai Tak Shing . The ecretary for Iome Affairs nd Another	Ordinary citizen	Won	No	Electoral arrangement for village representatives	5/11/ 2007	Philip Dykes and Kenneth K.H. Lee	No
eung Ka Lau nd Others v. *'he Hospital uthority*	165 government hospital doctors	Partial	No	Civil servant pay policy	20/10/ 2009	Denis Chang, Benjamin Chain, and Tim Kwok	No

APPENDIX 2

IMPORTANT LITIGATION BROUGHT BY PRO-DEMOCRACY POLITICIANS AND SOCIAL ACTIVISTS TO THE COURT OF APPEAL (COA) AND THE COURT OF FIRST INSTANCE (CFI) (1981–2010)

HUMAN RIGHTS LITIGATION

Case	Background of litigants	Government won or lost?	Basic Law/ Bill of Rights Ordinance (HKBORO) invoked?	Summary of the case	Date of judgment	Legal representation for non-government party	Government legal aid
Lau San Ching v. *Appollonia Liu* (CoA)	A veteran social activist, member of the April 5th Action Group	Won	Yes, Article 21 of the HKBORO	Unreasonable restrictions on the right of a candidate to stand for election	9/9/ 1994	Gladys Li and Timmy C.H. Yip	Yes
Lee Miu Ling and Another v. *The Attorney General* (CoA)	United Ants; Assistant to pro-democracy legislator Emily Lau Wai-hing	Won	Yes, Article 21 of the HKBORO	Inequality of suffrage created by the electoral arrangement of the functional constituency in the legislature	24/11/ 1995	Gladys Li and Nigel Kat	Yes
Au Kwok Hung v. *Appeal Tribunal* (CoA)	Public housing tenant; assisted by Society for Community Organization	Won	Yes, Article 39 of the Basic Law	Against the Housing Authority's decision to terminate his tenancy	8/12/ 2000	S.H. Kwok	Yes

Case	Background of litigants	Government won or lost?	Basic Law/ Bill of Rights Ordinance (HKBORO) invoked?	Summary of the case	Date of judgment	Legal representation for non-government party	Government legal aid
Wong Chung Ki and Another v. *The Chief Executive and Another (Application for leave to appeal)* (CoA)	The second appellant, Chan Shu Ying, is a member of the Democratic Party and elected member of the Regional Council	Lost	Yes, Article 39 of Basic Law; Article 21 of the HKBORO	Against the government's decision to abolish the two municipal councils	20/6/ 2000	Philip Dykes, Johannes Chan and Ho Chun-yan	No
Leung TC William Roy v. *Secretary for Justice* (CoA)	Gay rights activist	Lost	Yes, Articles 25 and 29 of Basic Law; Articles 1, 14, and 22 of the HKBORO	Homosexual's right to equality	20/9/ 2006	Philip Dykes, Hectar Pun and Michael Vidler	Yes
The Democratic Party v. *The Secretary for Justice* (CFI)	The Democratic Party	Won	Article 27 of the Basic Law	Freedom of association	21/5/ 2007	Erik Shum, Linda Wong, and Ho Chun-yan	No
Cho Man Kit v. *Broadcasting Authority* (CFI)	Gay rights activist, vice-president of the Hong Kong Ten Percent Club	Lost	Article 25 of the Basic Law; Article 16 of the HKBORO	Homosexual's right to equality	8/5/ 2008	Paul Harris, Hectar Pun, Annie Leung, and Michael Vidler	Yes
Chan Kin Sum v. *Secretary for Justice and Another* (CFI)	A prisoner; assisted by Society for Community Organization	Lost	Article 26 of the Basic Law; Article 21 of the HKBORO	Prisoners' rights to vote	8/12/ 2008	Hectar Pun and Earl Deng	Yes

APPENDIX 2

PUBLIC POLICY LITIGATION

Case	Background of litigants	Government won or lost?	Basic Law/ Bill of Rights Ordinance (HKBORO) invoked?	Summary of the case	Date of judgment	Legal representation for non-government party	Government legal aid
Ng King Luen v. *Rita Fan (Application for leave)* (CFI)	Member of the Democratic Party	Won	No	Challenged the legality of the Provisional Legislature	12/6/ 1997	Martin Lee, Johannes Chan, and Ho Chun-yan	Yes
Cheung Man Wai Florence v. *Director of Social Welfare* (CoA)	Social worker, social activist for housing and elderly rights	Won	No	Against the Social Workers Registration Ordinance which requires all social workers to be registered with the government	31/5/ 2000	Philip Dykes and Hectar Pun	Yes
The Catholic Diocese of Hong Kong v. *Secretary for Justice* (CFI)	Catholic church, outspoken critic of the government	Won	Yes, Articles 136(1), 137(1), and 141(3) of the Basic Law	Against the compulsory enforcement of the policy of school-based management in government-aided Catholic schools	23/11/ 2006	Philip Dykes, Hectar Pun, and Esther Lin	No
Leung Kwok Hung v. *President of Legislative Council of HKSAR and Another* (CFI)	Political activist, legislator	Won	Yes, Article 74 of the Basic Law	Power of legislators to propose amendments to bills which will have an impact on the government expenditure	22/1/ 2007	Philip Dykes, Hectar Pun, and Jocelyn Leung	No
Chan Noi Heung and Others v. *The Chief Executive in Council* (CFI)	Bus cleaner; political activist-cum-legislator; assisted by the Confederation of Trade Unions and the Neighbourhood and Worker's Service Center	Won	Yes, Articles 48(2) and 64 of the Basic Law	Minimum wage	16/5/ 2007	Hectar Pun and Jocelyn Leung	Yes
Chu Hoi Dick and Another v.	Social activists, members of Local Action	Won	No	Against the demolition of the Queen's Pier,	10/8/ 2007	Martin Lee and Jocelyn Leung	Yes

Case	Background of litigants	Government won or lost?	Basic Law/ Bill of Rights Ordinance (HKBORO) invoked?	Summary of the case	Date of judgment	Legal representation for non-government party	Government legal aid
Secretary for Home Affairs (CFI)				struggle for democratization of the process of urban planning			
Ng Ngau Chai v. *The Town Planning Board and Another (Application for leave)* (CFI)	Social activist for the Association for Democracy and People's Livelihood; Green Sense (environmental protection NGO); Lam Ho-yeung (Democratic Party's district councilor)	Won	No	Environmental protection – against construction of wall-like buildings on waterfront	4/7/ 2007	No	No
Kong Yunming v. *The Director of Social Welfare* (CFI)	New immigrant from mainland China; assisted by Society for Community Organization	Won	Yes, Articles 25, 36, and 145 of the Basic Law; Article 22 of the HKBORO	Welfare policy – Right of Hong Kong residents who have not stayed in Hong Kong for seven years to receive social security assistance	23/6/ 2009	Hectar Pun and Mark Daly	Yes
Yao Man Fai George v. *The Director of Social Welfare* (CFI)	A Hong Kong permanent resident; assisted by Society for Community Organization	Lost	Yes, Articles 25 and 31 of the Basic Law; Articles 8(2) and 22 of the HKBORO	Welfare policy – Right of Hong Kong residents to apply for social security assistance, not subject to the requirement that they must have resided in Hong Kong continuously for at least one year immediately before the date of application	21/6/ 2010	Hectar Pun	Yes

APPENDIX 3

LIST OF INTERVIEWEES (ALPHABETICAL BY CATEGORY)

Judges
Kemal Bokhary
Michael Hartmann
Anselmo Reyes
Cause lawyers
Johannes Chan
John Clancey
Mark Daly
Philip Dykes
Audrey Eu
Ho Chun-yan
Martin Lee
Jocelyn Leung
Gladys Li
Stanley H.F. Ma
Margaret Ng
Hectar Pun
Michael Vidler
Wong Hin-lee
Cause lawyer A
Cause lawyer B
Other lawyers
Barrister A
Barrister B
Ruy Barretto
Social activists and rights advocates
Fernando Cheung Chiu-hung

Joseph Cho Man-kit
Winston Chu
Chu Kong-wai
Fung Ho-lup
Walker Fung
Ho Hei-wah
Huang Ngai-fung
Jackie Hung Ling-yu
Law Yuk-kai
Timothy Lee Ting-yu
Leung TC Roy William
Annie Lin
Szeto May
Roddy Shaw Kwok-wah
Andrew Shum
Sze Lai-shan
Roy Tam
Richard Tsoi
Wan Siu-kin
Wong Chi-yuen
Wong Chui-shan
Wong Kwok-kei
Anna Wu
A core member of the Neighbourhood and Worker's Service Center

Pro-democracy politicians
Lam Ho-yeung
Leung Kwok-hung

Legal Aid Department
Thomas E. Kwong
Patrick Burke (a former official)

Legal Aid Services Council
Victor Li

Department of Justice
Official A
Official B

BIBLIOGRAPHY

Abel, Richard. 1988. "Lawyers in the Civil Law World." In *Lawyers in Society: The Civil Law World*, eds. Richard Abel and Philip. S. C. Lewis. Berkeley, CA: The University of California Press. 1–53.

Alford, William. 2007. "Of Lawyers Lost and Found: Searching for Legal Professionalism in the People's Republic of China." In *Raising the Bar: The Emerging Legal Profession in East Asia*, ed. William Alford. Cambridge, MA: Harvard Law School. 287–310.

Andersen, Ellen Ann. 2004. *Out of the Closets and into the Courts: Legal Opportunity Structure and Gay Rights Litigation*. Ann Arbor, MI: The University of Michigan Press.

Barclay, Scott, and Anna-Maria Marshall. 2005. "Supporting a Cause, Developing a Movement, and Consolidating a Practice: Cause Lawyers and Sexual Orientation Litigation in Vermont." In *The Worlds Cause Lawyers Make: Structure and Agency in Legal Practice*, eds. Austin Sarat and Stuart Scheingold. Stanford University Press. 171–202.

Baum, Richard. 2000. "Democracy Deformed: Hong Kong's 1998 Legislative Elections – and Beyond." *China Quarterly* **162**: 439–464.

Bindman, Geoffrey. 2002. "What Made Me a Legal Aid Lawyer?" *Journal of Law and Society* **29**: 510–520.

Black, Donald. 1973. "The Mobilization of Law." *Journal of Legal Studies* **2**: 125–149.

Bokhary, Kemal. 2004. "Justice and the Law: The Evolving Role of the Lawyer." *Hong Kong Law Journal* **34**: 133–150.

2007. "The First Decade of the Basic Law: A Judicial Perspective." *Asia Pacific Law Review* **15**: 125–136.

Burstein, Paul. 1991. "Legal Mobilization as a Social Movement Tactic: The Struggle for Equal Employment Opportunity." *American Journal of Sociology* **96**: 1201–1225.

Cai, Yongshun. 2007. "Civil Resistance and Rule of Law in China: The Defense of Homeowners' Rights." In *Grassroots Political Reform in Contemporary China*, eds. Elizabeth Perry and Merle Goldman. Cambridge, MA: Harvard University Press. 174–195.

Cai, Yongshun, and Songcai Yang. 2006. "State Power and Unbalanced Legal Development in China." In *Debating Political Reform in China: Rule of*

Law vs. Democratization, ed. Suisheng Zhao. Armonk, NY: M.E. Sharpe. 164–179.

Chan, Johannes. 2009. "Administrative Law, Politics and Governance: The Hong Kong Experience." In *Administrative Law and Governance in Asia: Comparative Perspectives*, eds. Tom Ginsburg and Albert H. Y. Chen. London: Routledge. 143–174.

Chan, Johannes, and Yash Ghai. 1993. "A Comparative Perspective on the Bill of Rights." In *The Hong Kong Bill of Rights: A Comparative Approach*, eds. Johannes Chan and Yash Ghai. Hong Kong: Butterworths Asia. 1–36.

Chan, Ming K. 1997. "The Legacy of the British Administration of Hong Kong: A View from Hong Kong." *China Quarterly* **151**: 567–582.

2002. "Introduction: The Hong Kong SAR in flux." In *Crisis and Transformation in China's Hong Kong*, eds. Ming K. Chan and Alvin So. Armonk, NY: M.E. Sharpe. 3–19.

Chen, Albert H. Y. 2005. "The NPCSC's Interpretation in Spring 2005," *Hong Kong Law Journal* **35**: 255–264.

2006. "Constitutional Adjudication in Post-1997 Hong Kong." *Pacific Rim Law and Policy Journal* **15**: 627–682.

Chen, Xi. 2007. "Between Defiance and Obedience: Protest Opportunism in China." In *Grassroots Political Reform in Contemporary China*, eds. Elizabeth Perry and Merle Goldman. Cambridge, MA: Harvard University Press. 253–281.

Cheng, Tun-jen. 1989. "Democratizing the Quasi-Leninist Regime in Taiwan." *World Politics* **41**: 471–499.

Cheng, Tun-jen, and Gang Lin. 2008. "Competitive Elections." In *Political Change in China: Comparisons with Taiwan*, eds. Bruce Gilley and Larry Diamond. Boulder, CO: Lynne Rienner. 161–183.

Cheung, Anthony, and Paul Wong. 2004. "Who Advised the Hong Kong Government? The Politics of Absorption before and after 1997." *Asian Survey* **44**: 874–894.

Cheung, Anthony, and Max Wong. 2006. "Judicial Review and Policy Making in Hong Kong: Changing Interface Between the Legal and the Political." *The Asian Pacific Journal of Public Administration* **28**: 117–141.

Chiu, Stephen Wing Kai, and Tai Lok Lui. 2000. "Changing Political Opportunities and the Shaping of Collective Action: Social Movements in Hong Kong." In *The Dynamics of Social Movement in Hong Kong*, eds. Stephen Wing Kai Chiu and Tai Lok Lui. Hong Kong University Press. 1–19.

Collier, Ruth Berins, and David Collier. 1991. *Shaping the Political Arena: Critical Junctures, the Labor Movement, and Regime Dynamics in Latin America*. Princeton University Press.

Cooney, Sean. 1999. "A Community Changes: Taiwan's Council of Grand Justices and Liberal Democratic Reform." In *Law, Capitalism and Power* in *Asia: The Rule of Law and Legal Institutions*, ed. Kanishka Jayasuriya. London: Routledge. 253–280.

Corder, Hugh. 2001. "Seeking Social Justice? Judicial Independence and Responsiveness in a Changing South Africa." In *Judicial Independence in the Age of Democracy: Critical Perspectives from Around the World*, eds. Peter Russell and David O'Brien. Charlottesville, VA: University Press of Virginia. 194–206.

Cortner, Richard. 1968. "Strategies and Tactics of Litigants in Constitutional Cases." *Journal of Public Law* **17**: 287–307.

Cottrell, Jill, and Yash Ghai. 2001. "Between Two Systems of Law: The Judiciary in Hong Kong." In *Judicial Independence in the Age of Democracy: Critical Perspectives from Around the World*, eds. Peter Russell and David O'Brien. Charlottesville, VA: University Press of Virginia. 207–232.

Diamond, Larry. 1992. "Economic Development and Democracy Reconsidered." In *Reexamining Democracy: Essays in Honor of Seymour Martin Lipset*, eds. Gary Marks and Larry Diamond. Newbury Park: Sage Publications. 93–139.

2008. "Why China's Democratic Transition Will Differ from Taiwan's." In *Political Change in China: Comparisons with Taiwan*, eds. Bruce Gilley and Larry Diamond. Boulder, CO: Lynne Rienner. 243–257.

Dotan, Yoav. 2001. "The Global Language of Human Rights: Patterns of Cooperation between State and Civil Rights Lawyers in Israel." In *Cause Lawyering and the State in a Global Era*, eds. Austin Sarat and Stuart Scheingold. New York, NY: Oxford University Press. 244–263.

2005. "The Spillover Effect of Bills of Rights: A Comparative Assessment of the Impact of Bills of Rights in Canada and Israel." *American Journal of Comparative Law* **53**: 293–341.

Epp, Charles. 1998. *The Rights Revolution: Lawyers, Activists and Supreme Courts in Comparative Perspective*. University of Chicago Press.

1999. "External Pressure and the Supreme Court's Agenda." In *Supreme Court Decision-Making: New Institutionalist Approach*, eds. Cornell Clayton and Howard Gillman. University of Chicago Press. 255–279.

Epstein, Lee, and Joseph Kobylka. 1992. *The Supreme Court and Legal Change: Abortion and the Death Penalty*. Chapel Hill, CA: University of North Carolina Press.

Feeley, Malcolm, and Setsuo Miyazawa. 2007. "The State, Civil Society, and the Legal Complex in Modern Japan: Continuity and Change." In *Fighting for Political Freedom: Comparative Studies of the Legal Complex and Political Liberalism*, eds. Terence Halliday, Lucien Karpik, and Malcolm Feeley. Oxford: Hart Publishing. 151–189.

Fu, Hualing, and Richard Cullen. 2008. "Weiquan (Rights Protection) Lawyering in an Authoritarian State: Building a Culture of Public-Interest Lawyering." *China Journal* **59**: 111–127.

Fung, Ho-lup. 2004. "The Right of Abode Issue: A Test Case of 'One Country, Two Systems'." In *One Country, Two Systems in Crisis: Hong Kong's Transformation since the Handover*, ed. Wong Yiu-chung. Lanham, MD: Lexington Books. 97–112.

Galanter, Marc. 1974. "Why the 'Haves' Come Out Ahead: Speculations on the Limits of Legal Change." *Law & Society Review* **9**: 95–160.

Gaventa, John. 1980. *Power and Powerlessness: Quiescence and Rebellion in an Appalachian Valley*. Urbana, IL: University of Illinois Press.

Gechlik, Mei Ying. 2005. "Judicial Reform in China: Lessons from Shanghai." *Columbia Journal of Asian Law* **19**: 97–137.

Ghai, Yash. 1997. "Sentinels of Liberty or Sheep in Woolf's Clothing? Judicial Politics and the Hong Kong Bill of Rights." *The Modern Law Review* **60**: 459–480.

1999. *Hong Kong's New Constitutional Order: The Resumption of Chinese Sovereignty and the Basic Law* (2nd ed.). Hong Kong University Press.

2007a. "The Political Economy of Interpretation." In *Interpreting Hong Kong's Basic Law: The Struggle for Coherence*, eds. Hualing Fu, Lison Harris and Simon NM Young. New York, NY: Palgrave Macmillan. 115–142.

2007b. "The Legal Foundations of Hong Kong's Autonomy: Building on Sand." *The Asia Pacific Journal of Public Administration* **29**: 3–28

Giles, Michael, and Thomas Lancaster. 1989. "Political Transition, Social Development, and Legal Mobilization in Spain." *American Political Science Review* **83**: 817–833.

Ginsburg, Tom. 2003. *Judicial Review in New Democracies: Constitutional Courts in Asian Cases*. Cambridge University Press.

2007. "Law and the Liberal Transformation of the Northeast Asian Legal Complex in Korea and Taiwan." In *Fighting for Political Freedom: Comparative Studies of the Legal Complex and Political Liberalism*, eds. Terence Halliday, Lucien Karpik, and Malcolm Feeley. Oxford: Hart Publishing. 43–63.

2008. "Administrative Law and the Judicial Control of Agents in Authoritarian Regime." In *Rule By Law: The Politics of Courts in Authoritarian Regimes*, eds. Tom Ginsburg and Tamir Moustafa. New York, NY: Cambridge University Press. 58–72.

2010. "The Constitutional Court and Judicialization of Korean Politics." In *New Courts in Asia*, eds. Andrew Harding and Penelope Nicholson. New York, NY: Routledge. 145–157.

Ginsburg, Tom, and Tamir Moustafa. eds. 2008. *Rule by Law: The Politics of Courts in Authoritarian Regimes*. New York, NY: Cambridge University Press.

Ginsburg, Tom, and Glenn Hoetker. 2006. "The Unreluctant Litigant? An Empirical Analysis of Japan's Turn to Litigation." *Journal of Legal Studies* **1**: 31–59.

Haire, Susan Brodie, Stefanie Lindquist, and Roger Hartley. 1999. "Attorney Expertise, Litigant Success, and Judicial Decisionmaking in the U.S. Courts of Appeals." *Law & Society Review* **33**: 667–685.

Hall, Peter A., and Rosemary Taylor. 1996. "Political Science and the Three New Institutionalisms." *Political Studies* **44**: 936–957.

Halliday, Terence, and Sida Liu. 2007. "Birth of a Liberal Moment? Looking through a One-way Mirror at Lawyers' Defence of Criminal Defendants in China." In *Fighting for Political Freedom: Comparative Studies of the Legal Complex and Political Liberalism*, eds. Terence Halliday, Lucien Karpik, and Malcolm Feeley. Oxford: Hart Publishing. 65–107.

Halliday, Terence, Lucien Karpik, and Malcolm Feeley. eds. 2007a. *Fighting for Political Freedom: Comparative Studies of the Legal Complex and Political Liberalism*. Oxford: Hart Publishing.

2007b. "The Legal Complex in Struggles for Political Liberalism." In *Fighting for Political Freedom: Comparative Studies of the Legal Complex and Political Liberalism*, eds. Terence Halliday, Lucien Karpik, and Malcolm Feeley. Oxford: Hart Publishing. 1–40.

Harding, Andrew. 2010. "The Constitutional Court of Thailand, 1998–2006: A Turbulent Innovation." In *New Courts in Asia*, eds. Andrew Harding and Penelope Nicholson. New York, NY: Routledge. 121–144.

Harris, Paul. 2007. *The Rights to Demonstrate*. Hong Kong: Rights Press.

Hendrianto. 2010. "Institutional Choice and the New Indonesian Constitutional Court." In *New Courts in Asia*, eds. Andrew Harding and Penelope Nicholson. New York, NY: Routledge. 158–177.

Hilbink, Lisa. 2007. *Judges Beyond Politics in Democracy and Dictatorship: Lessons from Chile*. New York, NY: Cambridge University Press.

Hirschl, Ran. 2004. *Towards Juristocracy: The Origins and Consequences of the New Constitutionalism*. Cambridge, MA: Harvard University Press.

Ho, Denny Kwok Leung. 2000. "The Rise and Fall of Community Mobilization: The Housing Movement in Hong Kong." In *The Dynamics of Social Movement in Hong Kong*, eds. Stephen Wing Kai Chiu and Tai Lok Lui. Hong Kong University Press. 185–208.

Javeline, Debra, and Vanessa Baird. 2007. "Who Sues Government? Evidence from the Moscow Theater Hostage Case." *Comparative Political Studies* **40**: 858–885.

Jones, Carol. 2007. "'Dissolving the People': Capitalism, Law and Democracy in Hong Kong." In *Fighting for Political Freedom: Comparative Studies of the Legal Complex and Political Liberalism*, eds. Terence Halliday, Lucien Karpik, and Malcolm Feeley. Oxford: Hart Publishing. 109–150.

Jones, Lynn. 2005. "Exploring the Sources of Cause and Career Correspondence among Cause Lawyers." In *The Worlds Cause Lawyers Make: Structure and Agency in Legal Practice*, eds. Austin Sarat and Stuart Scheingold. Stanford University Press. 203–238.

Kim, Jae Won. 2007. "Legal Profession and Legal Culture during Korea's Transition to Democracy and a Market Economy." In *Raising the Bar: The Emerging Legal Profession in East Asia*, ed. William Alford. Cambridge, MA: Harvard Law School. 47–80.

Krishnan, Jayanth. 2005. "Transgressive Cause Lawyering in the Developing World: The Case of India." In *The Worlds Cause Lawyers Make: Structure and Agency in Legal Practice*, eds. Austin Sarat and Stuart Scheingold. Stanford University Press. 349–382.

Kritzer, Herbert. 1997. "Contingency Fee Lawyers as Gatekeepers in the Civil Justice System." *Judicature* **81**: 22–29.

1998. *Legal Advocacy: Lawyers and Nonlawyers at Work*. Ann Arbor, MI: University of Michigan Press.

2001. "Litigation." *International Encyclopedia of the Social & Behavioral Sciences* **13**: 8989–8995.

Kritzer, Herbert, and Susan Silbey. eds. 2003. *In Litigation: Do the "Haves" Still Come Out Ahead?*. Stanford University Press.

Lawrence, Susan. 1990. *The Poor in Court: The Legal Services Program and Supreme Court Decision Making*. Princeton University Press.

Legal Aid Services Council. 2006. *Legal Aid in Hong Kong*. Hong Kong: Legal Aid Services Council.

Lee, H. P. 2006. "Human Rights in Malaysia." In *Human Rights in Asia: A Comparative Legal Study of Twelve Asian Jurisdictions, France and the USA*, eds. Randall Peerenboom, Carole Petersen and Albert H. Y. Chen. New York, NY: Routledge. 191–223.

Lev, Daniel. 2007. "A Tale of Two Legal Professions: Lawyers and State in Malaysia and Indonesia." In *Raising the Bar: The Emerging Legal Profession in East Asia*, ed. William Alford. Cambridge, MA: Harvard Law School. 383–414.

Liebman, Benjamin. 1998. "Class Action Litigation in China." *Harvard Law Review* **111**: 1523–1541.

2007. "Lawyers, Legal Aid, and Legitimacy in China." In *Raising the Bar: The Emerging Legal Profession in East Asia*, ed. William Alford. Cambridge, MA: Harvard Law School. 311–356.

Lipset, Seymour Martin. 1959. "Some Social Requisites of Democracy: Economic Development and Political Legitimacy." *American Political Science Review* **53**: 69–105.

Liu, Sida, and Terence Halliday. 2008. *Dancing Handcuffed in the Mine Field: Survival Strategies of Defense Lawyers in China's Criminal Justice System*. Paper presented at the Joint Annual Meetings of the Law and Society Association and the Canadian Law and Society Association, Montreal, Canada, May 29 – June 1, 2008.

Lo, Shiu Hing. 2000. "The Politics of the Debate over the Court of Final Appeal in Hong Kong." *China Quarterly* **161**: 221–239.

Lo, P. Y. 2007. "Rethinking Judicial Reference: Barricades at the Gateway?" In *Interpreting Hong Kong's Basic Law: The Struggle for Coherence*, eds. Hualing Fu, Lison Harris, and Simon N. M. Young. New York, NY: Palgrave Macmillan. 157–181.

Mahoney, James, and Kathleen Thelen. 2010. "A Theory of Gradual Institutional Change." In *Explaining Institutional Change: Ambiguity, Agency, and Power*, eds. James Mahoney and Kathleen Thelen. New York, NY: Cambridge University Press. 1–37.

Maiman, Richard. 2005. "Asylum Law Practice in the United Kingdom after the Human Rights Act." In *The Worlds Cause Lawyers Make: Structure and Agency in Legal Practice*, eds. Austin Sarat and Stuart Scheingold. Stanford University Press. 410–424.

Maltese, John Anthony. 1989. "The Selling of Clement Haynsworth: Politics and the Confirmation of Supreme Court Justices." *Judicature* **72**: 338–347.

Matsui, Shigenori. 2006. "The Protection of "Fundamental Human Rights" in Japan." In *Human Rights in Asia: A Comparative Legal Study of Twelve Asian Jurisdictions, France and the USA*, eds. Randall Peerenboom, Carole Petersen and Albert H. Y. Chen. New York, NY: Routledge. 121–157.

McCann, Michael. 1994. *Rights at Work: Pay Equity Reform and the Politics of Legal Mobilization*. The University of Chicago Press.

2008. "Litigation and Legal Mobilization." In *The Oxford Handbook of Law and Politics*, eds. Keith Whittington, R. Daniel Kelemen and Gregory Caldeira. New York, NY: Oxford University Press. 522–40.

Meili, Stephen. 1998. "Cause Lawyers and Social Movements: A Comparative Perspective on Democratic Change in Argentina and Brazil." In *Cause Lawyering: Political Commitments and Professional Responsibilities*, eds. Austin Sarat and Stuart Scheingold. New York, NY: Oxford University Press. 487–522.

Menkel-Meadow, Carrie. 1998. "The Causes of Cause Lawyering: Toward an Understanding of the Motivation and Commitment of Social Justice Lawyers." In *Cause Lawyering: Political Commitments and Professional Responsibilities*, eds. Austin Sarat and Stuart Scheingold. New York, NY: Oxford University Press. 31–68.

Michelson, Ethan. 2007. "Lawyers, Political Embeddedness, and Institutional Continuity in China's Transition from Socialism." *American Journal of Sociology* **113**: 352–414.

Milner, Neal. 1987. "The Right to Refuse Treatment: Four Case Studies of Legal Mobilization." *Law & Society Review* **21**: 447–485.

Miners, Norman. 1998. *The Government and Politics of Hong Kong* (5th ed.). Hong Kong: Oxford University Press.

Mnookin, Robert, and Lewis Kornhauser. 1979. "Bargaining in the Shadow of the Law: The Case of Divorce," *Yale Law Journal* **88**: 950–97.

Moore, Barrington. 1966. *Social Origins of Dictatorship and Democracy: Lord and Peasant in the Making of the Modern World*. Boston, MA: Beacon Press.

Morgan, Phoebe. 1999. "Risking Relationships: Understanding the Litigation Choices of Sexually Harassed Women." *Law & Society Review* **33**: 67–92.

Moustafa, Tamir. 2007. *The Struggle for Constitutional Power: Law, Politics, and Economic Development in Egypt*. New York, NY: Cambridge University Press.

Moustafa, Tamir, and Tom Ginsburg. 2008. "Introduction: The Functions of Courts in Authoritarian Politics." In *Rule By Law: The Politics of Courts in Authoritarian Regimes*, eds. Tom Ginsburg and Tamir Moustafa. New York, NY: Cambridge University Press. 1–22.

Munn, Christopher. 2001. "The Rule of Law and Criminal Justice in the Nineteenth Century." In *Judicial Independence and the Rule of Law in Hong Kong*, ed. Steve Tsang. New York, NY: Palgrave. 19–47.

Nathanson, Stephen. 1999. "Preserving the System: The Educational Dimension." In *The New Legal Order in Hong Kong*, ed. Raymond Wack. Hong Kong University Press. 649–70.

O'Brien, Kevin, and Lianjiang Li. 2004. "Suing the Local State: Administrative Litigation in Rural China." *China Journal* **51**: 75–96.

Olson, Susan. 1990. "Interest-Group Litigation in Federal District Court: Beyond the Political Disadvantage Theory." *Journal of Politics* **52**: 854–82.

Peerenboom, Randall. 2002. *China's Long March toward Rule of Law*. Cambridge University Press.

Pepper, Suzanne. 2002. "Hong Kong and the Reconstruction of China's Political Order." In *Crisis and Transformation in China's Hong Kong*, eds. Ming K. Chan and Alvin So. Armonk, NY: M.E. Sharpe. 29–66.

Pereira, Anthony. 2008. "Of Judges and Generals: Security Courts under Authoritarian Regimes in Argentina, Brazil, and Chile." In *Rule by Law: The Politics of Courts in Authoritarian Regimes*, eds. Tom Ginsburg and Tamir Moustafa. New York, NY: Cambridge University Press. 23–57.

Perry, Elizabeth, and Merle Goldman. 2007. "Introduction: Historical Reflections on Grassroots Political Reform in China." In *Grassroots Political Reform in Contemporary China*, eds. Elizabeth Perry and Merle Goldman. Cambridge, MA: Harvard University Press. 1–19.

Petersen, Carole. 2007. "Embracing Universal Standards? The Role of International Human Rights Treaties in Hong Kong's Constitutional Jurisprudence." In *Interpreting Hong Kong's Basic Law: The Struggle for Coherence*, eds. Hualing Fu, Lison Harris and Simon NM Young. New York, NY: Palgrave Macmillan. 33–53.

Pierson, Paul. 1996. "The Path to European Integration: A Historical Institutionalist Analysis." *Comparative Political Studies* **29**: 123–163.

Rosenberg, Gerald. 1991. *The Hollow Hope: Can Courts Bring about Social Change?* The University of Chicago Press.

Rueschemeyer, Dietrich, and Peter B. Evans. 1985. "The State and Economic Transformation: Toward an Analysis of the Conditions Underlying Effective Intervention." In *Bringing the State Back In*, eds. Peter B. Evans, Dietrich Rueschemeyer and Theda Skocpol. Cambridge University Press. 44–77.

Russell, Peter. 2001. "Toward a General Theory of Judicial Independence." In *Judicial Independence in the Age of Democracy: Critical Perspectives from Around the World*, ed. Peter Russell and David O'Brien. Charlottesville, VA: University Press of Virginia. 1–24.

Sarat, Austin, and Stuart Scheingold. 2005. "The Dynamics of Cause Lawyering: Constraints and Opportunities." In *The Worlds Cause Lawyers Make: Structure and Agency in Legal Practice*, eds. Austin Sarat and Stuart Scheingold. Stanford University Press. 1–34.

Scott, Ian. 2000. "The Disarticulation of Hong Kong's Post-Handover Political System." *The China Journal* **43**: 29–53.

Simpson, A. W. B. 1989. "The Judges and the Vigilant State." *The Denning Law Journal* **4**: 145–167.

Sing, Ming. 2004. *Hong Kong's Tortuous Democratization: A Comparative Analysis*. London: RoutledgeCurzon.

Skocpol, Theda. 1985. "Bringing the State Back In: Strategies of Analysis in Current Research." In *Bringing the State Back In*, eds. Peter B. Evans, Dietrich Rueschemeyer and Theda Skocpol. Cambridge University Press. 3–37.

Slater, Dan, and Erica Simmons. 2010. "Informative Regress: Critical Antecedents in Comparative Politics." *Comparative Political Studies* **43**: 886–917.

Southworth, Ann. 1996. "Lawyer-Client Decisionmaking in Civil Rights and Poverty Practice: An Empirical Study of Lawyers' Norms." *Georgetown Journal of Legal Ethics*. **9**: 1101–1155.

Szmer, John, Susan Johnson, and Tammy Sarver. 2007. "Does the Lawyer Matter? Influencing Outcomes on the Supreme Court of Canada." *Law & Society Review* **41**: 279–303.

Tai, Benny Y. T. 2002. "Chapter 1 of the Hong Kong's New Constitution: Constitutional Positioning and Repositioning." In *Crisis and Transformation in China's Hong Kong*, eds., Ming K. Chan and Alvin So. Armonk, NY: M.E. Sharpe. 189–219.

Tam, Waikeung. 2010. "Political Transition and the Rise of Cause Lawyering: The Case of Hong Kong." *Law & Social Inquiry*. **35**: 663–687.

Tarrow, Sidney. 1998. *Power in Movement: Social Movements and Contentious Politics*. Cambridge University Press.

Tate, C. Neal. 1995. "Why the Expansion of Judicial Power?" In *The Global Expansion of Judicial Power*, eds., C. Neal Tate and Torbjorn Vallinder. New York University Press. 27–37.

Tate, C. Neal and Torbjorn Vallinder. eds. 1995. *The Global Expansion of Judicial Power*. New York University Press.

Thelen, Kathleen. 1999. "Historical Institutionalism in Comparative Politics." *Annual Review of Political Science* **2**: 369–404.

Thelen, Kathleen and Sven Steinmo. 1992. "Historical Institutionalism in Comparative Politics." In *Structuring Politics: Historical Institutionalism in Comparative Politics*, eds. Sven Steinmo, Kathleen Thelen and F. Longstreth. Cambridge University Press. 1–32.

Thio, Li-ann. 2006. "Taking Rights Seriously? Human Rights Law in Singapore." In *Human Rights in Asia: A Comparative Legal Study of Twelve Asian Jurisdictions, France and the USA*, eds. Randall Peerenboom, Carole Petersen and Albert H. Y. Chen. New York, NY: Routledge. 158–190.

Tomasi, Timothy and Jess Velona. 1987. "All the President's Men? A Study of Ronald Reagan's Appointments to the U.S. Courts of Appeals." *Columbia Law Review* **87**: 766–793.

Trubek, Louise and Elizabeth Kransberger. 1998. "Critical Lawyers: Social Justice and the Structures of Private Practice." In *Cause Lawyering: Political Commitments and Professional Responsibilities*, eds. Austin Sarat and Stuart Scheingold. New York, NY: Oxford University Press. 201–226.

Wack, Raymond. 1994. *The Right to Representation: Problems and Prospects*. Faculty of Law, the University of Hong Kong.

Wasby, Stephen. 1995. *Race Relations Litigation in an Age of Complexity*. Charlottesville, VA: University Press of Virginia.

Wesley-Smith, Peter. 1998. *An Introduction to the Hong Kong Legal System*. (3rd ed) Hong Kong: Oxford University Press.

2001. "Individual and Institutional Independence of the Judiciary." In *Judicial Independence and the Rule of Law in Hong Kong*, ed. Steve Tsang. New York, NY: Palgrave. 99–131.

White, Lucie. 1988. "To Learn and Teach: Lessons from Driefontein on Lawyering and Power." *Wisconsin Law Review* 699–769.

2001. "Two Worlds of Ghanaian Cause Lawyers." In *Cause Lawyering and the State in a Global Era*, eds. Austin Sarat and Stuart Scheingold. New York, NY: Oxford University Press. 35–67.

Widner, Jennifer. 2008. "Building Judicial Independence in Semi-Democracies: Uganda and Zimbabwe." In *Rule by Law: The Politics of Courts in Authoritarian Regimes*, eds. Tom Ginsburg and Tamir Moustafa. New York, NY: Cambridge University Press. 235–260.

Wilson, Bruce, and Juan Carlos Rodriguez Cordero. 2006. "Legal Opportunity Structures and Social Movements: The Effects of Institutional Change on Costa Rican Politics." *Comparative Political Studies* **39**: 325–351.

Winn, Jane Kaufaan, and Tang-chi Yeh. 1995. "Advocating Democracy: The Role of Lawyers in Taiwan's Political Transformation." *Law and Social Inquiry* **20**: 561–599.

Wong, Timothy Ka-ying, and Shirley Po-san Wan. 2007. "Citizens' Evaluations of Legitimacy in Post-colonial Hong Kong: Results of a Longitudinal Study." In *The Hong Kong Special Administrative Region in Its First Decade*, ed. Joseph Y. S. Cheng. City University of Hong Kong Press. 75–107.

Xu, Jiatun. 1993. *Xu Jiatun Xianggang Huiyilu (Xu Jiatun's Hong Kong Memoir)*. Taipei: Lianhebao.

Yap, Po-Jen. 2007. "10 years of the Basic Law: The Rise, Retreat and Resurgence of Judicial Power in Hong Kong." *Common Law World Review* **36**: 166–191.

Zemans, Frances Kahn. 1983. "Legal Mobilization: The Neglected Role of the Law in the Political System." *American Political Science Review* **77**: 690–703.

INDEX

www.ingramcontent.com/pod-product-compliance
Lightning Source LLC
LaVergne TN
LVHW011522200926
848484LV00001B/106

* 9 7 8 1 1 0 7 0 3 1 9 9 9 *